IMPROVING SCHOOL DISCIPLINE

IMPROVING SCHOOL DISCIPLINE

Edited by

LESLIE J. CHAMBERLIN

Bowling Green State University
Bowling Green, Ohio

and

JOSEPH B. CARNOT

State University of New York
Cortland, New York

CHARLES C THOMAS · PUBLISHER
Springfield · Illinois · U.S.A.

Published and Distributed Throughout the World by
CHARLES C THOMAS · PUBLISHER
301-327 East Lawrence Avenue, Springfield, Illinois, U.S.A.

©*1974, by* CHARLES C THOMAS · PUBLISHER
ISBN 0-398-02812-5
Library of Congress Catalog Card Number: 73-198

*With THOMAS BOOKS careful attention is given to all details of
manufacturing and design. It is the Publisher's desire to present books that
are satisfactory as to their physical qualities and artistic possibilities and
appropriate for their particular use. THOMAS BOOKS will be true to those
laws of quality that assure a good name and good will.*

Printed in the United States of America
I-1

Library of Congress Cataloging in Publication Data
Chamberlin, Leslie J   comp.
  Improving school discipline.

  1. School discipline. I. Carnot, Joseph B., joint
comp. II. Title.
LB3013.C46   371.5   73-198
ISBN 0-398-02812-5

Contributors

Ruth Agnew, former instructor at North Central High School, Indianapolis, Indiana. (Deceased)

American Civil Liberties Union, New York.

Delmer H. Battrick, Principal, Theodore Roosevelt High School, Des Moines, Iowa.

Warren William Bell, Ph.D., Principal, Jennings Junior High, St. Louis County, Missouri.

Sister Helena Brand, Marylhurst College, Marylhurst, Oregon.

Richard Berndt, member of discipline subcommittee of Charlotte High School policy committee, Rochester, New York.

Edward A. Brainard, President, C.F.K. Ltd, Engelwood, Colorado.

Robert Chamberlain, Superintendent, Lansing, Michigan. (Deceased)

Stella Chess, M.D., Professor of Child Psychiatry, New York University Medical Center, New York.

Glenn H. Darling, Principal, Ellis Junior High School, Austin, Minnesota.

Gerald DeWitt, Principal, East High School, Aurora, Illinois.

Carlos de Zafra, Jr., member of discipline subcommittee of Charlotte High School policy committee, Rochester, New York.

Frank Dick, Superintendent, Toledo Public Schools, Toledo, Ohio; executive Board American Association of School Administrators, Washington, D.C.

Emelie Ruth Dodge, Instructor, Scarsdale Senior High School, Scarsdale, New York.

R. Drinkhouse, Instructor, Grandview Heights High School, Grandview, Ohio.

Dale Findley, Associate Professor of Education, Indiana State University, Terre Haute, Indiana.

Robert Fox, University of Michigan, Ann Arbor.

S. L. Halleck, M.D., Professor of Psychiatry, University of Wisconsin, Madison.

L. C. Hickman, Editor, Nation's Schools, Chicago.

Frances Holliday, former elementary school principal; former head, Department of Elementary Education, University of Omaha; Professor of Education at American University, Washington, D.C.

Jo Holt, Assistant Dean of Students and Assistant Professor of Education, Longwood College, Farmville, Virginia.

Alvin W. Howard, Associate Professor, College of Education, University of New Mexico, Albuquerque; taught on elementary and junior high levels and has been a junior high counselor and principal.

Martha W. Hunt, Head Counselor, Mount Vernon High School, Mount Vernon, New York.

David Iwamoto, Research Assistant, NEA Research Division, National Education Association, Washington, D.C.

Walter M. Jackson, Principal, Brooklyn Park Junior-Senior High School, Anne Arundel County, Maryland.

Ronald E. Jacobs, Superintendent Maplewood Local Schools, Cortland, Ohio.

J. B. Johnson, former Superintendent of Schools, District 11, Alton, Illinois.

Laura G. Johnson, Instructor, Carver School, Milledgeville, Georgia.

Walter F. Johnson, Professor of Education, Michigan State University; former public school teacher, administrator and counselor; past president of the American Personnel and Guidance Association.

Ronald R. Kyllonen, M.D., Wagzata, Minnesota.

Peggy Lippitt, University of Michigan, Ann Arbor.

Ronald Lippitt, University of Michigan, Ann Arbor.

R. B. Lynn, President of Board of Education, District 11, Alton, Illinois.

Thomas J. Matczynski, Instructor in Dayton, Ohio schools for four years and currently with Education Department of Ohio University of Athens, Ohio.

Elizabeth Mitchell, member of discipline subcommittee of Charlotte High School policy committee, Rochester, New York.

Clark E. Moustakas, Coordinator Enhancing Human Potentials Project, Merrill-Palmer Institute, Detroit.

National Association of Secondary School Principals, 1201 16th St., N.W., Washington, D.C.

Daniel C. Neale, Dean, College of Education, and Professor; University of Delaware, Newark, Delaware.

James L. Niday, Department of Education, Bowling Green State University, Bowling Green, Ohio.

Ohio Education Association, 225 East Broad Street, Columbus, Ohio.

Eric Olsen, Los Angeles attorney who served as deputy county counsel, Schools Division, Los Angeles County in 1968 and 1969.

Henry M. O'Reilly, Dean of Students, Bishop McNamara High School, Kankakee, Illinois.

J. M. Patterson, M.A. Director of Public Relations, Amoco Oil Company, Chicago; member of Rich Township High School Board; Park Forest, Illinois; former member of Executive Committee and Vice-President of Tri-County Division, IASB. Member Board of Regents, Illinois Colleges & Universities.

Carl H. Peterson, Assistant Principal, Easton High School, Easton, Pennsylvania.

William Ratigan, Senior Extension Lecturer, Michigan State University, Guidance Director Charlevoix, Michigan; co-author Theories of Counseling and author of eleven books on Americana.

Joseph Resnick, Psychological consultant, Indianapolis Public Schools, Indianapolis, Indiana.

Marjorie Carr Smith, Principal, West High School, Ithaca, New York.

John Stinespring, Chairman, Social Studies Department, Elkhart High School, Elkhart, Indiana.

Ruth Strang, National Congress of Parents and Teachers Associations, Chicago, Illinois.

Alexander Thomas, M.D., University Medical Center, Professor of Psychiatry, New York.

Kay Tift, Professor in Training and Curriculum Development, National Drug Abuse Training Center, Washington, D.C.

Stephen J. Voelz, Department of Education, Loras College, Dubuque, Iowa.

Carolyn Elizabeth Ward, Instructor, Washington School, Sault Ste. Marie, Michigan.

Morris Weinberger, Professor of Educational Administration and Supervision, Bowling Green State University, Bowling Green, Ohio.

Foster F. Wilkinson, Head, Elementary Education Department and Professor of Education, Delta State College, Cleveland, Mississippi.

PREFACE

Many educators will agree that developing effective instruction while maintaining positive student behavior is one of the most urgent and recurring problems found in the teaching profession. Due to the fact that teachers have not learned to handle disciplinary problems in the university classes—many good teachers withdraw from the teaching profession. This is also true when successful teachers move from one school to another where disciplinary situations are quite different. The teacher who learns to avoid, prevent, or control classroom situations that lead to disorder, discourtesy, or inactivity not only improves his effectiveness as a teacher but improves his job security and chances for progress.

Management of student behavior is a definite aspect of effective teaching. *Improving School Discipline* provides concrete references to achieve results in instruction developed by teachers with advice in administrating the daily educational program. Our book gives the reader a frame of reference which increases his ability to understand problem behavior and deal effectively with it. It offers a positive action approach to teaching. This material should be of interest not only to new teachers and college students preparing to enter the teaching profession, but to parents, school administrators, and experienced teachers as well.

Many will agree that the best way to prevent discipline problems from occurring and to correct others is to rely on the advice of experienced educators. The authors have collected many articles from experienced educators in the area of positive student behavior in discipline for the information of the reader. The authors are indebted to all of the students who have been in their classes and to the teachers who have taught in the several schools they have administered. Because they shared their feelings, thoughts and experiences, this book was possible.

LJC/JBC

CONTENTS

ix

Part III

UNDERSTANDING THE TECHNIQUE

IMPROVING SCHOOL DISCIPLINE

PART I

UNDERSTANDING THE SITUATION

CHAPTER I

CONCEPTS OF DISCIPLINE AND INSTRUCTION

INTRODUCTION

EFFECTIVE INSTRUCTION REQUIRES a realistic concept regarding student control and the rules, and regulations which establish order. Active concerns of students about school questions and public issues have led to disorder and a challenging of certain disciplinary procedures. The New Left and Students for a Democratic Society in the late 1960's and early 1970's have had a tremendous impact on the schools. Instruction has not been a top priority in some school buildings due to the time and energies which were directed to establishing or resolving disciplinary situations.

The materials in Chapter I present points of view which focus attention on the current concepts of discipline, instruction, and student control.

The New Look in Discipline*
by Jo Holt
Longwood College, Virginia

Anthropologists tell us that there has never been a civilization that did not exercise punishment and establish rules in the training of children.

A close look at the types of discipline used down through the years, however, reveals that a transformation has taken place.

The early years of our puritan existence brought crude, dictatorial authority by parents and schoolmasters who believed they must "break the child's will" if he was to grow up with a righteous adult conscience. We saw the husband and father who informed the world that he was the master in his own house and that his word was law.

From this rigid, authoritarian viewpoint, with the advent and popularity of psychoanalysis and psychology, the pendulum began to swing in the opposite direction. We saw the beginning of the "just let them be happy" school of thought. (We actually haven't outgrown this way of thinking yet!) The society was endoctrinated with the fear that any form of discipline would and could cause serious damage to the child. This brought about an era where children became the autocrats and the dictators.

Today, we are beginning to see the pendulum swing back to a "middle of the

*Reprinted from *Ohio Schools*, Oct. 1968. Used by permission.

5

road" view where common sense coupled with scientific knowledge is rendering a sensible solution to the problems of child discipline.

What caused this rather severe shift in thinking?

For three centuries, the people of America were rooted in self sufficient, isolated communities characterized by neighborliness and intimacy of association. To be sure, there were petty differences in each community, and even distrust among some of the members, but the people were emersed in the same point of view and saw eye to eye as to aspirations, standards of right and wrong, and ways of doing things.

During the last 75 years, however, this way of life has been rapidly disappearing, so that American society is no longer characterized by the old-fashioned community but by urban communities and metropolitan areas. This change has been brought about by the advancement of science and technology. If these twin forces of modern society have unlocked fabulous resources, conquered space, and made poverty unnecessary for the first time in history, they have also created new problems of cultural adjustment.

It is perhaps not too much to say that every significant discipline problem of today is rooted in one way or another in increasing advancement of science and technology.

It would be ridiculous to assume that the small isolated communities of a century ago were populated by angels and therefore any change from this type of community will bring a malignancy to our children. They were constituted of men and women afflicted with ignorance, prejudices, and narrow points of view which prevailed in the old fashioned village.

But whatever their shortcomings and differences, these people were basically in agreement as to the meaning of life and the rights and responsibilities of the individual.

The individual shaped his conduct, and indeed his whole life span, by the demands of local opinion and sentiment. His ideas of right and wrong, good and bad, correct and incorrect were induced by the customs and traditions of the community. In short, his whole personality was shaped to the pattern of community life.

Whatever might have been the merits of the old-fashioned community, it is rapidly declining as a force in American society and short of the destruction of modern civilization, it is doubtful that this form of social existence will be restored.

With the growth of urbanism, which has put more than half of our people in metropolitan districts of 100,000 people or more, has come a break-down of primary group relationships. Social concensus, one of the primary sources of personal stability, has deteriorated to the point where the individual is more or less socially isolated.

While science and technology have brought people closer together geographically and mechanically, specialization of labor has divided people with respect to their mental outlook. Thus, each individual carries around in his head a specialized picture of society which represents but a fragment of the total social pattern.

These same forces that have brought a decline in the local community and its role in the development of individuals have also brought a decline in the influence of the family.

The pattern of family life is always shaped by the total cultural pattern. The place of woman in the family, the way the children are disciplined, and a hundred other characteristics of family life in a particular time and place go back to the spirit, ideals, and behavior patterns of the culture. Because of the dependence of the family upon cultural circumstances, it is to be expected that as a society is modified, the family will sooner or later come in for its share of change.

The urban family presents a very different picture from the rural household. Here the work is no longer done in common. Here no longer do brother and cousin live within walking distance and group together as a family unit. The family loses its producing function and becomes mostly, if not entirely, a consuming unit. The work of the father is done away from home and that of the mother confined largely to keeping house and preparing meals. (Unless a sitter is hired to do these things, and mother too becomes a breadwinner for the family.) The children have few, if any, responsibilities except for helping mother in her work; and with modern quick frozen food, modern appliances, and labor saving devices this responsibility is reduced in many families almost to the vanishing point.

The activities of the family are thus specialized. Since each member of the urban family is related differently to the means by which the family maintains its existence, the differentiation of interests among the members increases. Their activities become more diverse and hence their experiences and points of view become more and more heterogeneous. The city family has fewer common values, common experiences, and common points of view, so that its chief cementing force tends to be economic pressure and a few emotional ties.

Another result of these changes in the pattern of family life is the almost complete isolation of children from the world of adults. Perhaps no other people in recorded history has forced its children and youth to live in a culture of their own making so completely as we have. The rise of all of the youth organizations (good and bad) certainly stands as testimony to this fact.

Another factor which relates to our change in outlook toward discipline in children is the cult of informality. This informality and its advance have been going on for so long that you might expect a reaction in opposition; but for every step taken in the direction of formality, two steps are taken in the direction of an easier code of manner and behavior.

There can be little doubt that our culture today has gone through and is undergoing some rather remarkable changes. How these will affect our way of life, the socialization of our children, and our place in the world remains to be seen. But what is important is that we realize these changes are with us and do something actively to see that they lead us toward progress rather than destruction.

The literature for the last few years has been giving a great deal of stress to the problem of child-rearing, child-behavior, child-discipline, etc. Our culture is rapidly becoming aware of the importance of these items in our survival as a major world power. Some very good thinking along the area of discipline has been reaching more and more people through the mass communication media. The members of our society are being made acutely aware that we have a problem in this area and must do something about it. Now the doing something about it can be done by a number of different agencies and people. The parents, first of all, must be considered the most important in establishing values and behavior patterns that are in agreement with the rest of the society. Next, the school plays an important part as do law enforcement agencies, the church, and the community.

Discipline in the home as a child can make life so easy in years to come. Many parents are realizing that they must take an active part in this aspect of the child's growing up if he or she is to live a fruitful and happy life.

The Easy Way

What are we doing and why? First of all, we are beginning to see that children (like the rest of us) take the easiest way in life unless they are guided by some "have-to's." We ourselves have rules and regulations which we argue about and complain about, but certainly would not do without. Since there are no set rules for good discipline, so there are no short cuts. Discipline is a training toward the long-term goal of wholesome self control, and it does not occur in a vacuum, completely detached from the life around us. Children are not born with a sense of right and wrong. It is something gradually absorbed as one grows up, until as a full fledge adult conscience, it becomes an automatic inner signal that regulates behavior. But before it becomes automatic much time, effort, and love have been applied. All children, no matter how bright they are, learn slowly and forget quickly. Good training in right and wrong should include frequent repetitions.

Dealing With Anger

No person exists without having feelings of anger. No one can grow up without anger. To make the discipline effective, our children need help in learning how to deal with their anger through the years.

We want our children to make their own decisions, but we expect these decisions to please us. We must make sure that in no situation in which we expect children to exercise self-discipline that it is beyond their capacity, and we must see that the discipline ends in success.

These are some of the ideas that current thinking on discipline have brought forward. But again I ask why? Why today are we teaching self discipline when 100 years ago the rule by the stick method was much in vogue. Our democratic society has learned that this doesn't work today. Our culture is different. We see that the discipline which sustains the dictatorship will destroy a democracy. Discipline is necessary in any society, and the discipline used in our free society must be one of self-discipline and self-control.

Twin Problem

Sociologists and mental hygienists have been working on this twin problem for some time. The fruits of their labor are now beginning to show.

And what part is the school playing in this "new look" at discipline?

A very active part. Not too many years ago (and in too many classrooms today) one could find schools in which children were expected to act like robots who surrendered full control of their every action to an all-powerful teacher. They were supposed to sit ramrod stiff in tomb-like silence ready to spring into obedient action at the command, but only at the command, of the adult who sat enthroned at the front of the class. Fortunately, very few teachers today maintain this form of discipline in their classrooms.

Children cannot develop the discipline for freedom by being held under the complete domination of the teacher day after day and month after month. Neither can it be achieved only by "taking off the lid" and allowing the children to do as they please. Organizing the classroom environment deliberately to give children experience in democratic living and removing from the classroom those practices which stand as obstacles to the achievement of discipline for freedom are highly complex and difficult tasks.

Problem Prevention

Society generally, and the community in particular, must find ways in contributing to the prevention of behavior problems. Adult education forums, parent-teacher associations, the church, and other agencies outside the school can help in this undertaking. Educational institutions must fully realize the need for their leadership and friendly helpfulness.

The close relationship existing between the work of the public schools and the future of our democratic way of life places a heavy responsibility on the teachers of America. Teachers in our society must not only do a thorough job of teaching the fundamental subjects but must do so in such a manner as to produce the kind of citizens needed in a free society.

To fulfill this obligation it is necessary that teachers understand that discipline is necessary in a free society. Without a disciplined citizenship, knowledge and material strength are to no avail. It is imperative, therefore, that the special kind of discipline which is suited to free men be clearly understood not only by the teachers but by members of the general public as well.

A Modern View of Discipline*
by Stella Chess, M.D. and Alexander Thomas, M.D.

"Tommy, come down. Come down this instant. For the last time, if I have to go up there and get you . . ."

Three-year-old Tommy, active, self-assertive, daring, insists on climbing to the top of the monkey bars and hanging there upside down. He goes too high and too fast on the swings, zooms tirelessly around the playground. Neither falls, cuts, bumps, nor his mother's mounting exasperation slows him down.

What's wrong with the way his mother is handling Tommy? Is her method of discipline faulty? Too strict, too easy, inconsistent?

Look at Joel, Tommy's friend. He likes to climb and jump, too. But he stays within the bounds set for him by his mother. He responds agreeably to her soft-spoken requests and doesn't make a fuss or ignore her when she limits his activities. Is Joel a better adjusted child than Tommy? Or could it be that he's less well-adjusted, perhaps repressed and frustrated?

In fact, neither child is better adjusted than the other, and neither mother's style of discipline is, in itself, better or more effective. The children are different in temperament, and the best discipline in either case is the one that most happily works.

Perhaps we parents have been misled into thinking that there is a single style of discipline which promotes good mental health (and one which leads to the opposite) and that this good style is "permissive" discipline. For during the last generation, child psychologists, recognizing that very harsh treatment hurts a child, veered to the other extreme of supposing that a youngster who was allowed to do just as he pleased would become happy, healthy, and magically self-disciplined. As every mother can see for herself this ex-

*Reprinted from *Parents' Magazine & Better Homemaking*, Feb., 1966. Used by permission.

treme is as absurd as the other is cruel.

Long-term studies we have made of both normal children and those with behavior problems have shown us that setting limits for children—making demands on them for courteous behavior and establishing prohibitions to safeguard them—does not crush their spirits or even displease them, as long as parents are sensitive to the individual natures of their children and don't try to impose behavior on the youngsters which doesn't suit them at all.

One mother, speaking of her pre-schooler, said, "It was never necessary to discipline him because he never did anything he wasn't supposed to." In discussing with her what she meant by this, it became clear that this youngster had been given explanations—about the dangers of running across the street, or poking into electric outlets, or getting burned on the stove—and that only a few explanations were necessary. Her child could be restricted or not permitted to have a desired object without becoming distressed.

Another child's mother said of her youngster, "He argues every point, but once he knows you mean it he will accept the rule." Then there are children who return persistently and cheerfully to a prohibited activity. Sometimes it seems to take a disaster to teach them. Other children want what they want when they want it, and respond with loud screams to all efforts to stop them from doing something.

It can be seen then that though general rules of discipline make sense, they cannot be equally successful with all youngsters. The best approach with one child may be to give explanations and to redirect activity. With another child such measures do not register. Some youngsters require an edict, with the parent riding out the storm of protest and calmly reaffirming the edict when the child has finished his screaming or door-slamming.

Tommy, who wouldn't come down from the monkey bars, has always responded with defiance to limitations. During infancy, he would show his resistance to a change in activity by violent crying. Later, as a toddler when he would climb halfway up the slide ladder, his mother's nervous approach would send him scooting up all the way to the top.

For Tommy there was no learning "once and for all" what he could and could not do. Persistent, but fairly casual repetition was needed. By the time he was three, though he still ignored many safety regulations, he was beginning to limit his activities along the lines of his mother's cautions.

As Tommy's mother began to learn (also gradually and not without setbacks), that she couldn't substantially speed up her child's capacity for self-discipline, she began to treat him in a more relaxed way. This brought its own benefits. As she nagged him less, he began to pay more attention to her suggestions. For like most children, Tommy wanted to please his mother and wanted to be acceptably self-sufficient.

His friend Joel was quite a different kind of child. Once a program was set up Joel followed it contentedly, so that his mother was not particularly conscious of disciplining him. When he was still a baby and the Christmas tree was put up with its fragile ornaments and fascinating lights, his mother told one-year-old Joel, "You must not touch, no, no." She was confident that she could then turn her back without worrying about the child's handling of the tree. And she was right. But Joel was not timid. Even then, he enjoyed being swung high on the baby swings and wasn't afraid of the slide or the see-saw.

What general guides can parents find

to help discipline children as different from each other as Joel and Tommy? First bear in mind that restrictions aren't, in themselves, necessarily harmful. No parent doubts the necessity for establishing clear-cut rules when it comes to ensuring a child's safety.

The infant who gets hold of the straight pins that his mother was using for sewing will have these objects summarily removed from his hands. Her first thought is for the child's safety, even though the youngster may cry over the loss of the pins. In such a case a mother would probably make two mental notes—to keep the pins out of her baby's reach in the future, and to teach him whatever she could to help keep him safe.

Such discipline, determined by safety, poses no particular problems. It takes more vigilance to maintain the rules with some children than with others, but all parents know they must keep their youngsters safe. However, it is not so clear to many parents when to impose other kinds of discipline. Some restrictions are set to suit the convenience of adults—refusing to allow the convenience of adults—refusing to allow a child to sit in a bus with his feet poking out into the aisle, keeping him quiet while Daddy naps, and so on. Parents differ from each other and change their minds from time to time about how much inconvenience an adult should tolerate and how much restriction is beyond a child's reasonable capacity to endure.

Our long-term observations show that children on whom clear demands have been made for good social behavior are not less happy than those who have been left to follow their impulses.

Actually, such discipline, which is no more than teaching a youngster to respect limits, is not a thing in itself, or a separate aspect of child rearing which starts abrupt-

ly at some point. It is a continuation of the basic care parents give their babies. There is a thin line between letting a baby cry because his mother has observed that no matter what she does, he seems to need ten or fifteen minutes to cry himself to sleep at night, or letting him cry because his mother is afraid that if she picks him up every time he cries, he'll get "spoiled."

Similarly with a child's progress in feeding, toilet training, and playing. A good part of learning in such matters consists in recognizing and accepting limits imposed by the outside world. These limits are based on the standards of the group for acceptable behavior, the convenience of others, and personal safety.

How to impose demands and successfully set disciplinary limits varies from infancy onward from child to child. Punishment rarely needs to be invoked for a child like Joel, who easily accepts prohibitions. But there are many children, like Tommy, who adapt to a new demand slowly, for whom discussion alone is ineffective.

For such children discipline sometimes needs to include some punishment. But punishment should be designed to show the child that continuing in a prohibited behavior will not bring him gain but loss. Each time that Tommy refused to heed a prohibition against crossing the street by himself his mother should have immediately restricted his outside play for a specified time.

Punishment which fits the crime is more effective than having one standard punishment, say restriction of television or loss of allowance. Punishments that merely reflect a parent's rage are least useful. The parent who hits the child while shouting "Didn't I tell you not to hit?" is likely to teach his child only that it is safe to hit someone else if you're the strongest one around. The parent who always punishes one child whenever there is a fight between brothers and sisters is teaching the children to be bullies and competitors, rather than to have consideration for each other.

Punishments should also be proportionate in severity to the misbehavior. A young child is not capable of distinguishing between a minor and major offense, or a minor and major danger. He learns to make such distinctions in response to the signals he is given by adults. A parent who flares up because a child has disobeyed him, without regard to the gravity of the disobedience, does not help the youngster make appropriate judgments. A child becomes confused if a misdemeanor is treated severely on one occasion and permitted on another, or if an activity is sometimes forbidden and sometimes allowed. A parent may be lenient on some occasions merely because he is too weary to say "no" again. To a child this may mean that the parent's previous restrictions were not to be taken seriously. Indeed, the parent may be training the child to persist more tenaciously if these tactics seem to succeed.

The parents of a defiant child like Tommy may need to make a mental list of issues in order of their importance. At the top of the list would be safety rules and other matters essential for the child to obey. At the bottom of the list would be minor goals. For example, it is desirable, but relatively unimportant, for a three-year-old always to say please and thank you, or willingly share his toys. It would be nice if he did, but it's not worth a big clash.

In the middle of the list would be issues of some importance but not of first priority —that a child should sit down to eat lunch when he's called instead of continuing to play. Such goals are important but a parent may go easy in her moves toward establishing desirable behavior so that it won't seem

to the child that his every move evokes her displeasure.

A different kind of disciplinary problem is likely to be posed by a very mild and adaptable child. Such a youngster may agree to all prohibitions so easily that his parents may impose many more restrictions on him than they would on a protesting youngster. Parents of such children should learn to give special attention to the child's desires, even though he expresses them quietly and without fussing.

A mild-mannered child is the very opposite of a youngster like Tommy, who expresses himself loudly and leaves no doubt in his parent's mind about how he feels. A mild child, on the other hand, may show both pleasure and displeasure gently. This does not mean that the intense child feels things more deeply than the mild child. There are better clues than intensity to a child's depth of feeling. For example, how long does a youngster stick to an activity? A noisy and intense child may raise a storm at being switched from one pursuit to another. Yet he may not, given the chance, bother to pick up the first activity again. Another child may permit himself to be easily led away from something yet return to it as soon as he can.

Children vary in all aspects of growing and mastering the physical and social world. They differ in the way and in the rate in which they learn to dress and feed themselves, to talk, read, write, and obey the rules of different games. Some children learn quickly after the first contact with a given activity. For others, learning requires many repeated instructions from mother or teacher. Neither type of child is necessarily better adjusted than the other. And neither is more or less likely to become psychologically disturbed, as long as the parent's discipline is reasonably sensitive. If a child does develop problems in learning or behavior, these are likely to have been precipitated by attempts to make him learn in a manner wholly unsuitable to him, or by being subject to demands so inconsistent, or unreasonable that no one could meet them.

Reasonable demands for compliance don't hurt children; in fact, they are a civilizing experience, bringing self-satisfaction and a sense of achievement.

Discipline Is . . .*
Sister Marian Frances, SNJM

Formulas for maintaining classroom discipline are many and varied, and what works for one teacher fails for another. Chances are, nonetheless, that any formula that proves effective is more preventive than remedial and contains the following ingredients:

Discipline is preparation—long-range and short-range. Long-range preparation is the necessary daily routine of planning, preparing material, and correcting papers.

Short-range preparation is the activity just before a class begins that results in students' entering an orderly room. The teacher has all the necessary materials ready for distribution. He has written key words on the board to guide students in following his instructions and to make oral spelling unnecessary. He adjusts windows, arranges his books, checks his seat plan, and prepares his attendance slip. The classroom is ready, and the teacher is in control. Class begins promptly without that little lull in which attention is often lost before it is even captured.

Discipline is dignity. In the classroom, the teacher lives his dignity by avoiding casual sitting positions, casual vocabulary, casual joking, familiar give-and-take — except when they are deliberately used as tools of emphasis.

Dignity expects the courtesy of a greeting when pupils come into the classroom. The teacher will not receive acknowledg-

ment from every student, but his attitude will encourage many greetings.

Since the teacher expects the class to consider education a serious business, he approaches his class in a businesslike, professional way. He is courteous, considerate, pleasant, understanding, consistent, and, in the sum, dignified.

Discipline is moving deliberately and purposefully with the apparent self-confidence of a captain on top-deck. The disciplined teacher shows that he knows exactly what he wants to do. By acting serene, he creates an atmosphere of serenity. Students assume the matter-of-fact, reasonable, practical tones and attitudes of their teachers. Generally, a student is as tense or relaxed as his teacher.

Discipline is speaking distinctly with a pleasant, friendly voice. Students will listen more attentively and ask questions more spontaneously if the "sound effects" are pleasant and harmonious. Tape recording a few periods and playing them back can reveal to the teacher poor speech habits, such as lack of tone variation or overly numerous "uh's," that detract from presentations.

The teacher who does not speak simply or slowly enough for his students to understand easily may find that students release their feeling of frustration and inadequacy by finding compensating entertainment. When a student stops doing what the teacher wants him to do he begins to do what he is tempted to do.

*Reprint from *NEA Journal,* September 1965. Used with permission.

Discipline is teaching a subject in terms of the interest level of the class. The vocabulary challenges at times, but it is within the understanding of the class. Good current allusions, based on newspaper or magazine articles, are attention-getters which act as springboards to new lessons.

Discipline is questions and answers from the students. A discussion sparked by a student's questions is usually lively because interest is tapped and channeled. The best answer is the student answer. The teacher whose students not only raise questions but reason their way to the right answers practices a special kind of personal discipline. He controls his very human tendency to save time by "just telling" the class the answers. The right answer formulated by the students does more for their development than the most dynamically articulated answer the teacher could produce.

Discipline is utilizing the natural tentencies of the students. Carefully planned group discussions and buzz sessions, or occasions when students plan and take responsibility for their own activity, give the students the chance to express their desires and clarify their purposes. They also allow the young people to experience the success of influencing their group and to grow in personal security. Such sessions give students a legitimate reason for speaking as opposed to reciting during a class period, and for moving to another part of the room.

Discipline is perceiving and understanding causes of misbehavior. The perceptive teacher notices the student who comes to class burning with resentment and rebellion. Aware that he may have had trouble at home that morning or in his previous class, the teacher avoids any conflict which will aggravate the student's sense of injury

and result in sullenness, insolence, or even violence.

The teacher realizes that many, if not all, of his students suffer from feelings of inferiority or inadequacy. Particularly affected are those who may feel out of the "in-group" because they are of a different race or religion, because they lack money, or because they cannot keep up mentally or physically.

The wise teacher knows that publicly demeaning a student or in any way implying rejection or ridicule is inviting misbehavior, which is often a defense mechanism.

Discipline is realizing that students are human beings. Students leave books and pencils at home (teachers forget things, too). To punish a student's forgetfulness by keeping him idle is retaliatory rather than remedial. The youngster feels conspicuous, frustrated; above all, he feels a sense of injury. The better course is for the teacher to provide the missing article and thus have a busy rather than a humiliated student. The "little talk" for chronic amnesia victims can come at the end of the period when he returns the article the teacher has loaned him.

Being human, students appreciate recognition. They are happy to be in charge of something. They are proud to be sent on errands, glad to be noticed in the hall.

When papers are returned, a comment by the teacher praising a mark, remarking on the completeness of a particular answer, or noting the neat attractive format or script, not only excites ambition but also promotes a pleasant teacher-pupil relationship. The morning after a play, a recital, or a game, the student who is complimented on his outstanding participation is an appreciative, cooperative person.

Discipline is knowing when to tighten,

when to loosen, and when to hold firm. A class changes its mood with the weather, with the exciting rally students screamed through during the noon hour, with the warm library period they have just sat out, with the way things went in the last class, with the pictures that appeared in the morning's issue of the school paper. Students come into the classroom with an attitude toward the teacher engendered, perhaps, by their success or nonsuccess with the assignment.

Sometimes students come in quietly, sometimes in a stampede, sometimes laughing, sometimes bitterly arguing. The bell momentarily cuts off their stream of interest, and into this small space the teacher drives the line of action he expects the class to follow through the period. He directs their vitality. By clear, simply spoken instructions he puts them to work.

If directions offer personal advantages to the students as individuals, the class as a whole will settle down. An effective means to calm a class is to have written recitation during the first ten or fifteen minutes. The teacher remarks that the lesson is of more than usual importance. He wants to credit every individual who has done the assignment with a successful recitation. Since it takes too long for each student to recite, each may earn a recitation credit by choosing two of the four questions to write on. Even if they do not finish writing in the allotted time, the work they have completed will indicate the quality of their preparation and the papers will be scored with that in mind.

Another time, he may have the student decide on the question or topic he found most interesting and then write on it for ten minutes. Students set to work with an optimistic spirit, glad to put their best answers forward. Just before they begin writing, the teacher directs their attention to the next day's assignment on the chalkboard. He suggests that if they finish the class exercise before the time is up, they look over the new material. He will answer any questions on the new assignment after the writing session is terminated. He indicates that the rest of the class period will be a build-up for the assigned work. Looking to their personal advantage, the students generally cooperate.

Sometimes a class needs waking up instead of calming down. On Monday, perhaps, when students are recuperating from a busy weekend (or giving the impression that they had the kind of weekend that requires recuperation), a buzz session can be profitable. It gives students an opportunity to compare notes, improve their homework papers, argue, and wake up.

Discipline is anticipating difficulties. The misbehaving individual makes a problem for the teacher, and also for the class. During the first month of school the teacher checks without exception infringements of class or school regulations. One individual who "gets away with it" breeds others who will try. Planning for emergencies and anticipating problems develops and maintains teacher control, strengthens students' confidence in the teacher's authority, and establishes a receptive classroom atmosphere.

Finally, discipline is having effective attitudes. Effective attitudes stimulate pupils to action. Creative thinking develops in the classroom of a teacher who shows that he appreciates a student's point of view. An instructor who is really thrilled with his subject effectively presents it as an intellectual adventure, a colorful discovery that induces similar excitement in his students. An instructor who shows interest in student affairs, who not only listens to student problems but contributes to their solutions, is an effective teacher in the classroom, in the conference room, in the give-and-take of a lunch-room situation.

Teachers' discipline is essentially self-discipline. The young teacher who is hopeful yet fearful, ambitious yet humble, idealistic yet practical, with everything to give, with everything to lose, will find his success in proportion to his ability to know himself and to use that knowledge in personal and professional growth.

Those Students Who Behave Also Have Some Rights*
R. Drinkhouse

One of the greatest causes of teacher frustration is the interruption, embarrassment, unpleasantness, and time-consumption of discipline problems.

It is unrealistic to conceive of the teacher doing what he is supposed to do under some conditions of pupil behavior. In seeking to improve instruction, then, it would seem profitable to direct our attention toward lessening or eliminating discipline problems with a view toward benefiting those who want to learn and to teach.

The first object of disciplinary action would be to protect other students and the teacher from recurrences. We are unduly solicitous of the student who presents a discipline problem. Teachers and administrators do have a responsibility to this student. But they have a much greater responsibility to the others.

The first basis for the disposal of the case of a problem student should be the consideration of the rights and privileges of those whom he has deprived rather than the effect on his own development. The ideas in a recent *Readers' Digest* article, "How About Some Justice for Non-Criminals, Too?" are applicable in the case of students who want to learn and teachers who want to teach.

A teacher who loves to teach can become quite disenchanted because of disciplinary problems. It is just as illogical to expect the teacher to accept interference from someone whom he is trying to help as it is in any other profession. The teacher is already harassed from all directions with responsibilities that are unrelated to his real job. He should have the authority and freedom to accomplish his objectives.

The President's Commission on Crime and Law Enforcement has assigned a large share of the responsibility for dropouts to the schools. The inference is clear that schools and teachers should devote more time and effort to the potential dropout. Potential dropouts who indicate by their attitude, effort, and behavior that they want to learn, deserve special attention from the school. In the majority of cases, however, the suggestion of the Commission amounts to an urge to cater to those students who delight in depriving sincere students of their opportunities and hampering teachers who are trying to fulfill their responsibilities.

Our present laws compelling children to attend school under given age and employment conditions are unfair—not only to the vast majority of students whose motives are sincere and who are cooperative in the desire to learn, but also to those who have little or no interest in school. These laws are unfair, also, to all teachers who want to teach. Margaret Mead has suggested that a student who wants to quit school should be allowed to do so with the under-

*Reprinted from *Ohio Schools,* March 1968. Used with permission.

standing that he will have to complete his education sometime, so let him come back when he is 25 or whenever he desires.

Practical aspects of discipline are not found in educational theory. The "keep them interested and there will be no problem" principle does not hold true for every student. It is not necessarily the fault of the teacher if a student is not interested.

The student who deliberately interferes with the objectives of the educational program should be counseled by those who specialize in behavior problems. The counselor is such a specialist who can direct his skills toward rehabilitation of the individual. The teacher is a specialist who should be free to direct his skills toward teaching the individual. If the proper response is lacking in the offending student, then in the best interest of everyone concerned, the use of isolation, suspension, and parental responsibility are not out of order.

The treatment should protect the offended, not the offender. It is becoming increasingly apparent in our schools and in our society that leniency and acquittal on technicalities breeds contempt for law and order. We do injustice to the offender by neglecting this opportunity to help him grow in his respect for law and order.

The foregoing may be construed as being inconsiderate of those who perhaps have not learned to appreciate the opportunities in our schools. They do deserve, and should have, help. But that help should not result in depriving sincere students and conscientious teachers of their rights, privileges, and duties.

Let's Not Forget Discipline When We Talk of Freedom*

Ronald E. Jacobs

There is a trend throughout the United States for each individual to actively stand for his personal rights and to show his stand by defying any and all authority. This is being doubly demonstrated in our public schools and institutions of higher education.

In California, it has taken the form of picketing by students speaking against the University administration: in Oberlin, Ohio, by boycotting, picketing, and embarrassing U.S. Air Force Recruiters; throughout the nation by burning draft cards, ridiculing all opposition, and by student sit-ins, riots, and misconduct.

A story in a February issue of the Cleveland *Plain Dealer* cited a group of high school students that have formed the Fifth Reich, have a Furher (Chancellor), wear

Swastikas in school, and deal in narcotics.

These are only a few, but not isolated cases. It would be too difficult to give an itemized research, city by city, state by state, all-inclusive list. These merely point up that in each instance, the individuals or individual groups are exercising their "civil rights" as guaranteed by the Constitution and in each case have either been encouraged, or at least not discouraged, by those in authority—parents, school, and civil officials—because no one wants to stymie the creative thought and expression of the individual nor prohibit the right of each individual to express his feelings in any manner he dreams proper.

It is not the intent of the author to stand apart and destroy our generation, our future. It is felt that at least one "still small voice" must exercise his individual and civil rights and "speak out" on the subject.

*Reprinted from *Ohio Schools*, May, 1967. Used with permission.

Our school and public officials are hiding their heads in the sand rather than taking the leadership in developing the program that will assure us our future freedom. One cannot blame them for this, as they are all publicly employed and must, at least in their minds, submit to the public opinion that gives the youth these rights.

Ten years from now, at this pace, we will not need to worry about this because we will have been so busy defending the "rights of each individual" that we will have sacrificed our God-given "individual rights." Let us examine some of our "rights" and analyze our freedom and obligations.

First and foremost, each of us has the right to be an individual, to think, worship, speak, learn, read, and plan for himself a life pattern that will bring the greatest amount of personal success, satisfaction, and happiness, providing that in forming this life pattern, it is not one that deters from or restricts these same rights and goals from any other individual. In other words, we must never become so conscious of one person's rights that we give them to him and unconsciously restrict the rights of others.

This is what has been happening all over. A small minority of individuals, though very loud, have taken it upon themselves to demand and obtain their rights of protest and action, regardless of how many disagree or who must be hurt by their protest.

Now that a portion of the problem is stated, what is being done, why, and what can we do?

The first two questions are disgracefully easy to answer. Nothing is being done because we do not want to do anything. We must run at full speed to uphold all "modern" or "progressive" educational and psychological theories that tell us how we will damage the "id" and stymie growth.

This author is wary about care or damage of the "id" and not sure if he wants it to grow. He is honest enough to admit that he has never seen his or anyone else's "id," and if he did, he did not know it. Dewey and Freud have one advantage over us. They are dead. Therefore, they do not have to defend these theories and if they were alive today, they could not defend them for their theories have been distorted and misused beyond all recognition.

If an individual cares to read the original works of the great proponents of progressive thought he would find that our interpretation, by action, is not the same as the authors intended. He would also find that each of the philosophers discussed the theories under only ideal conditions and demonstrated the psychological patterns by citing the abnormal.

Yet we innocent lambs have taken these studies and applied them "wholesale" to the total population under the most adverse conditions.

Freedom—individual, group or national—carries with it great responsibility. It is the obligation of each individual to protect the rights of all others. Freedom of speech must guarantee that in no way the use of this freedom denies others the same nor in any way impinges upon the rights and freedom of any others.

Discipline—self or outside—must accompany and be a part of the freedom process. Total freedom is reached only when total and healthy self-discipline is exercised by every individual. Parents and other authorities, such as the school, must awaken to the fact that they have been shirking their obligations and responsibilities. By adopting the permissive outlook, the adults have not taught self-discipline. We have not been truly permissive, because the word itself means to grant permission and therefore connotes a denial of permission at times. Rather, we have been irresponsibly passive and guilty of neglect by neither granting nor denying permission; in fact, not even expecting youth to ask permission.

We are faced with the greatest of all choices: to continue on our highway of destruction of rights and freedom; or to assume our rightful roles as the authoritative figure that will teach self-discipline by exercising our authority and control of behavior until such time of maturity and indicated self-discipline that we can discharge responsibility.

The author does not advocate dictatorial control until a point in life when a miracle occurs and self-discipline is attained and then total release. The author does not even advocate unquestioned dictatorial control at any time; but rather good old-fashioned parental care and paternal authority.

As the child matures intellectually, socially, and emotionally, authority is replaced with interest and discussion, but there is always a degree of control. When this is relinquished by the parent, it goes to the school, community, and nation, but it is there. The control remains as the catalyst for chaos.

Along with control and authority must go punishment. The author does not necessarily advocate physical punishment although this is one device. But punishment must be an integral part of discipline. Self-punishment is often the cruelest and most devastating. The punishment must be meted out with great thought so that it teaches the ultimate lesson of self-discipline. Even more important, it should be done immediately so that the child knows for what he is being punished.

Control and Punishment

The most important lesson that the child receives is that throughout life there must be control and when this is violated, there will be punishment. As maturity develops, a sense of obligation and responsibility grows and self-control and discipline evolve.

In the final analysis, we will have to reexamine our present outlook and teach a new respect for authority. Parents and community will have to cooperate and demand that schools return to the position of respect and authority and that children learn that the school has an obligation to teach discipline and a right to punish disrespect and defiance of authority. The schools also deserve the assurance and support of the parents and the entire community that they will be sustained and encouraged in the teaching of discipline and the carrying out of any punishment, if necessary.

When a return to the principles mentioned in this article take place, we will read headlines of student demonstrations to the Air Force by having mass groups supporting and enlisting to meet the obligation of the defense of this country and the continuation of freedom.

Discipline Is Caring*

Alvin W. Howard

Ask any teacher, beginning or experienced, what his biggest difficulty with

*Reprinted from *Today's Education*, March 1972. Used with permission.

children is and he will almost certainly answer. "Discipline and classroom control." As the second major difficulty, he will probably cite student achievement or lack of it in school, a problem closely related to discipline.

Good discipline is important because no group of people can work together successfully without establishing standards of behavior, mutual respect, and a desirable system of values that leads each person in the group to develop self-control and self-direction.

Good discipline does *not* result if a teacher adopts an inflexible punitive approach or if he is too permissive, pretending that annoying behavior does not exist. In *Schools Without Failure,* William Glass points out that those who would completely eliminate or substantially relax rules in their eagerness to please children don't realize that firm and fair policies of discipline indicate that adults care about young people and that children may interpret the reverse as symptom of lack of interest in them.

In their relations with pupils, teachers should be firm, fair, and friendly. A teacher needs to take firm positions on many things, but before he does he must determine what he is standing for or against and what his stand implies. Firmness does not imply rigid domination of children nor does it require snarling and growling at them to cow them into submission. Authoritarianism breeds resentment; taking a "Do it or else" position can be exactly the wrong thing for a teacher to do. (For example, a beginning teacher asks Dick, a large eighth grader, to take his seat or go to the office. He did neither, and she could not physically compel him to obey her. So, she sent for the principal who, after a quick appraisal of the situation said, "Come, Dick, you and I need to talk about this someplace else.")

Most children have a keen sense of fair play. If the pupil does something wrong, he expects to bear the consequences, but he also expects anyone else who commits the same offense to receive the same treatment. A teacher should not play favorites or punish the entire class for the sins of a few (e.g. mass detention). A better method is to have a private conference with the erring child as soon as possible about the problem. At best, detention, whether for one student or for many, is of dubious value.

A teacher should be scrupulously fair and courteous—especially if he expects similar treatment. The teacher who makes wisecracks or is flip or arrogant can expect the same from his students and is not justified in resenting their attitude. (Each day, Mr. Johnson, a first year teacher, sent a large number of students to the office for "smarting off." Yet, when the counselor pointed out to him that virtually every youngster complained that Mr. Johnson talked that way to them, the teacher was indignant.)

A teacher should demonstrate friendliness by being understanding, tolerant, and sincere with students. Efforts by a teacher to be one of the gang are seldom, if ever, successful and often prevent development of an atmosphere of mutual respect that is conducive to learning. The teacher who adopts the slang, customs, and behavior of his students will discover that they may be amused or offended by his actions or contemptuous of them. (A group of girls in one home economics class requested a different teacher because theirs was so "cutesy" that they couldn't stand her.)

Some discipline problems, hopefully minor ones, come up in every classroom. But minor problems aren't likely to become major ones if a teacher remembers the following guidelines:

1. Work at being the kind of person children like and trust, and remember that everyone needs success—particularly those

with a record of failure. Maintain the respect of the class without being condescending. (Gary, a large sixth grader who had been sent to the office for his "noncooperative" attitude, told the principal he wouldn't respond to his teacher's questions as long as he had to tell his answers to her clown hand puppet.)

2. Maintain a cheerful and attractive classroom rather than a disorderly one which might encourage unruly behavior. Also, remember that a pleasant voice, a neat appearance, and a positive attitude are contagious.

3. Get to know the students. The teacher who knows his students soon develops almost a sixth sense for anticipating trouble before it begins. Virtually every good teacher reports that some of his students say he seems to have eyes in the back of his head.

4. Be enthusiastic and courteous and keep your sense of humor. The teacher who really believes that children and learning are important tends to be enthusiastic, and that enthusiasm is contagious. Be as courteous to your class as you wish them to be with you. Also, don't "see" everything that happens; learn to ignore some things and laugh at others.

5. Make education interesting and relevant to children's lives. The teacher who believes he can get by without planning may get away with it temporarily, but before long his lack of organization and imagination will produce dreary lessons, student restiveness, increasing discontent, and ultimate chaos. My guess is that the largest number of classroom offenses occur because the curriculum is dull and the teacher has planned poorly.

6. Don't use schoolwork as punishment. (Linda told her mother that she hated both school and her fifth grade teacher. "Every time we forget to act like prisoners in a reform school," she said, "we have more written work.") Give reasonable assignments, and don't be vague and ambiguous when giving directions.

7. Never use threats in an effort to enforce discipline. What will you do if a child takes up the challenge—as someone ultimately will? A threat that is not carried out only makes the teacher look foolish. (For example, if the teacher threatens to read aloud any notes he confiscates, he may find himself in a confrontation with a militant who refuses to part with a note or the teacher may find himself looking silly after reading aloud a note that proves to be a deliberate plant.)

8. Never humiliate a child. Publicly scolding or ridiculing a student will make him bitter and will probably turn the rest of the class against the teacher. (A ninth grade teacher sharpened the fine-honed edge of his tongue against a borderline dropout. When the boy did drop out of school, the class was extremely antagonistic to the teacher for the remainder of the year.)

9. Don't strong-arm students. (A high school physical education instructor abruptly seized a tenth grade boy by the left arm, demanding, "Where do you think you're going?" The boy spun with the pull and landed a looping right hook between the teacher's eyes, breaking his nose and knocking him out.)

10. Avoid arguing with your pupils. Discussions about classwork are invaluable, but arguments that become emotional encounters with pupil freedom fighters create ill will on both sides, sometimes with rather surprising side effects. (The group of seventh graders who requested that they be transferred to another class because all they ever did was argue with their teacher knew the difference between discussion and argument.)

11. Don't act as though you expect trouble or you will almost certainly encounter some. (Mr. Potter consistently reported Bennie as a troublemaker, although no other teacher did. Bennie reported, "No matter what I do for Mr. Potter, it's wrong." Mr. Potter explained, "I had Bennie's brother two years ago, and he was a troublemaker. I told Bennie the first day of school that I wouldn't put up with any nonsense from him.")

12. Let students know you care. Caring means determining, preferably jointly with the class, what is acceptable and what is not, both in terms of behavior and achievement, continually keeping in mind that all children differ and that what is reasonable and acceptable with one group may not be with another.

13. Establish as few rules as possible and keep them as simple as possible. Examine them carefully from time to time and eliminate those that are unnecessary. (For years, one school enforced a rule that no club could meet on Thursday afternoons. When a new teacher asked why this was so, no one could give a reason. Eventually someone remembered that a long-extinct service organization had conducted activities for children in a nearby building on Thursday afternoons.)

14. Expect to handle the normal kinds of misbehavior yourself, but seek assistance for those problems that need the skills of a specialist.

Chapter I

Discussionette

1. Discuss how common sense coupled with scientific knowledge can provide a sensible solution to most discipline problems.

2. Do teachers react more often by emotion or intuition rather than by common sense?

3. Discuss how the setting of reasonable limits for children improve student control.

4. Are most teachers really sensitive to the individual needs of the child?

5. Define good behavior.

6. Do you accept the positive concept of student control?

7. Which of the definitions of discipline presented in this chapter do you believe to be the best in terms of child development.

8. Which definition do you plan on using?

9. Why do strong disciplinarians rarely make use of the so called strong disciplinary measures?

10. Why do poor disciplinarians make use of so many disciplinary measures ineffectively?

11. Does the statement, "Keep them interested and there will be no discipline problem," hold true for most students?

12. Have teachers really worked as hard on developing interest as on handling discipline problems?

13. Does freedom imply that our children must learn self-control and self-direction?

14. Are there different degrees of control and violation, which would require different forms of punishment?

Discussionette Words and Concepts

success	punishment	discipline
well-adjusted	objectives	behaved
self fulfilling	students' rights	dignity
freedom	privileges	normal

Try to use these words.

Try to explain these words.

Try to relate these words and their concepts to current or emerging educational patterns of discipline and instruction.

CHAPTER II

❦ DISCIPLINE IN THE PUBLIC SCHOOL ❦

INTRODUCTION

DISCIPLINE, SATISFACTORY OR UNSATISFACTORY, has a direct effect on the teacher's instructional success, the student's academic achievement, and the school's reputation: in general, the entire educational enterprise.

There is a relationship between school discipline and the social, economic and legal pressures and restrictions which effect students. Schools are agents of society and bring to bear pressure which influence student behavior.

In our large metropolitan cities, many students come from areas which are defined as disadvantaged, only to be placed in the traditional school with its middle class value system and told to adjust. Consequently, the child has problems adjusting to this new value systems for the six-hour school day for he must eventually return to the value system of the ghetto. Is there any doubt that this child will have problems adjusting to discipline in the public school? What can be done?

This chapter presents information that clarifies the relationship of "discipline problems" to the traditional school and suggests teacher behaviors that are appropriate for today's educational systems.

Discipline and the Public School*
Leslie J. Chamberlin

Discipline, satisfactory or unsatisfactory, has a direct effect on the teacher's instructional success, the student's academic achievement, and the school's reputation; in general, the entire educational enterprise. When a problem develops, investigation often goes only as far as the teacher and the child. More often what is needed is an understanding of the total situation; the community, the school, its pupils, and society's hopes and desires for them. Most of us would agree with this axiomatic statement, but seldom is much thought given to analyzing what is involved in maintaining satisfactory discipline in our public schools. This article is an attempt to examine the relationship between school discipline and certain social, economic and legal pressures and/or restrictions.

The Problem

The public school is a unique organiza-

*Reprinted from *Education,* January 1967. Used with permission.

tion. To survive, most organizations must continually recruit members as well as financial support. This is not true of the public schools. They are financed by society, protected by the laws of society, and their students are recruited by society. Because the public schools occupy this special place in our society, great demands are placed upon them. They are expected to realize and fulfill the educational needs of the local community, and of the nation. This country's system of public schools is a distinguishing characteristic of our democratic society and is considered our best hope for the social and economic well-being of the people.

Most students accept the educational objectives selected by society for its public schools systems and readily adapt to the educational approach of the public schools. Their acceptance might be thought of as a long continuum beginning with complete acceptance and ending with complete rejection.

Acceptance on the part of the student creates no problem for the school at least; however, those students who do not completely accept the goals and programs of the study must adapt to the situation in some manner.

A common type of student adaptation is the *"good"* student approach. This person is often looked upon by the teacher as a good citizen, for he does not cause any disciplinary trouble. Nevertheless, he does not always do well academically. Coming down the continuum we next find the *"playful"* student who directs his energies toward his own goals and objectives, disregarding, whenever possible, the goals and programs established for him. At the other end of the continuum is the *"dropout,"* the student who completely rejects the school and all it stands for. He attempts to leave school and enter the labor market,

the military service, or some other substitute activity.

With this in mind, it is possible to understand why classroom teachers and school administrators must be prepared to deal with not only the willing and anxious students but also all of those students on the behavioral continuum down to the dropout who have completely rejected society's goals and the school's efforts to reach them.

The noble goals this country has set for its schools have been repeatedly stated at various times and in various forms since the writings of Herbert Spencer in 1860. Such reports as the *"Cardinal Principles of Secondary Education," the Educational Policies Commission's "The Purposes of Education in American Democracy,"* the 1955 White House Conference on Education and President Eisenhower's 1960 Commission on Education have identified the work to be accomplished. However, while the schools attempt to fulfill these great expectations, a number of restrictions are imposed upon them which limit the action possible on the part of teachers and administrators.

Legal Restrictions

It is commonly believed in this country that certain educational objectives which are basic to our way of life can be achieved only through a free public school system. This fact is demonstrated by the school laws enacted by the several states. It is hoped that the schools will provide the education necessary for effective citizenship in our democratic society. It is frequently stated that the development of individuals to enable them to live intelligently and happily in a free democratic society should condition both the nature of the programs of education and the way they are conducted.

Although it should be assumed that all

educational legislation is well meant and that most of it is necessary to establish minimum educational standards within the various states, some school laws impose unnecessary restrictions on the operational practices of the schools. Actually some legislation represents a nuisance in the day-by-day operation of the schools. Laws pertaining to compulsory school attendance, the financial affairs of the public schools, teacher certification, classification, accreditation and approval of public schools are obviously necessary. However, laws directing what may not or may be taught and setting aside special days for the biographical study of certain minor historical figures have very doubtful value.

In most cases where individuals participate in the activities of an organization they have the right to participate or not to participate. In the case of the public schools, however, society makes the decision for the individual and creates by compulsory attendance laws a situation where the individual is required to attend school. The schools are expected to serve all of the children of all of the people. All who seek admittance must be considered and very little selection on the part of the school is tolerated. The bright and the dull, the interested and the disinterested, the emotionally stable and the emotionally unstable, the mature and the immature, the physically fit and the physically handicapped, the culturally efficient and the culturally deprived, the economically sound and economically destitute—all must be accepted and cared for.

Most of the laws regarding the public schools, including the compulsory school attendance laws that have been enacted by the several states, are in the best interest of the national welfare; few could disagree with this statement. However, when attempting to understand the many factors that have an effect on the children's behavior in the public schools, we must recognize this legal framework in which the public schools operate from day to day as one of these factors.

Economic and Social Pressures

The public schools of this nation are directly affected by the social and economic needs of our society. The main area of emphasis in the curriculum can often be traced directly to the current needs of the nation. In fact, every phase of this country's educational effort seems to be shifting and changing in an attempt to better fulfill this country's educational goals.

We have just emerged from an era when *"social studies"* commanded a large block of school time and teacher interest. Presently, great interest is being directed to the area of mathematics and science. This switch is obviously the result of a change in public thinking regarding the main task of the schools. Rather than placing our emphasis on providing the education necessary for effective citizenship in our democratic society, the schools are now attempting to provide the technical skills required by our automated, industrialized society and the current national scientific efforts.

The kinship between education and the abilities involved in running a factory, an industry, or a government, or in building bombs or flying space ships is too clear to most citizens to require much explanation. Some values are so universally accepted that subject matter pertaining to them finds its way into the school's curriculum by unanimous but silent consent. Other areas of seemingly doubtful value must compete for that precious commodity, school time. Causing a law to be enacted regarding instruction in a particular area is one method of assuring that the subject will be dealt with by the schools. This method is used fairly frequently, but not necessarily wisely.

There is a tendency to relate education to economic functions as the country becomes more aware of the handicaps of economically depressed areas and/or subpopulations. The present interest in expanding vocational education is an example of this tendency. Other programs that have been expanded because of social and economic pressure are those programs designed to serve the common and special needs of exceptional children and youth; programs to provide continued opportunities for the education of youth and adults not in regular attendance at school; and those programs primarily designed to help the individual achieve occupational confidence.

At times more than one pressure is involved in bringing about a greater emphasis upon a particular subject matter area or some other change in the school's general operating procedure. At the present time the nation is observing a revamping of its compulsory school attendance laws. This nation's belief in the value of education is certainly one of the factors behind the raising of the legal compulsory school attendance age.

However, economics also play a major role in bringing about such a change. Ever since the Industrial Revolution, the importance of the young child on the labor market has been diminishing. Now with the recent impact of automation on the industry of this nation, it has become absolutely imperative to keep the young worker off the labor market until he has been prepared to render a salable service. Generally speaking, the nation does not want a period of time between the maximum compulsory school attendance age and that time when a young person can be constructively occupied, for which youth will be unaccountable. Here we see economic and social pressure bringing changes in the school's program with minimum compliance being guaranteed by law.

Administrators have been saying for some time that the schools should attempt to meet the needs of the community, indeed of the nation. This is certainly true, but nevertheless under this arrangement the goals that the school organization attempts to fulfill are selected by society, not by the clients attending the school. Not all students agree with the goals that have been established for them. Conflicts naturally result from this and teachers and administrators have the resulting disciplinary situations to contend with.

Summary

This article is not an attempt to justify or to criticize what is being done or not being done in or by the public schools of this nation. It is simply an effort to show the relationship between certain social, economic, and legal pressures and the efforts of public school officials to establish and maintain satisfactory discipline. School officials become so accustomed to certain social and economic pressures and to working within the legal framework set up for the schools that they sometimes fail to recognize these same restrictions as important factors that affect the situation in their schools.

Certain educational objectives are considered so important to the welfare of this nation that public schools are maintained to guarantee that they are fulfilled. Laws are enacted and great social and economic pressure is exerted to cause the curriculum of the public schools to reflect the dominant values and needs of the current period. Because not all students agree with the goals that are set up for them as public school students, conflict results. The outward sign of this conflict is often between the student and his teacher. However, the real conflict is often between the individual student and society. He will not agree with or accept the educational objectives established for him and imposed on the public schools. It is important for teachers and administrators to take into account this important factor when attempting to deal with disciplinary situations in the public schools.

Academic Freedom in the Secondary Schools*

Students' Rights

If secondary school students are to become citizens trained in the democratic process, they must be given every opportunity to participate in the school and in the community with rights broadly analogous to those of adult citizens. In this basic sense, students are entitled to freedom of expression, of assembly, of petition, and of conscience, and to due process and equal treatment under the law. The American Civil Liberties Union has already described how such freedoms appertain to college students in its pamphlet on "*Academic Freedom and Civil Liberties for Students in Colleges and Universities.*" But the difference in the age range between secondary school and college students suggests the need for a greater degree of advice, counsel, and supervision by the faculty in the high schools than is appropriate for the colleges or universities. From the standpoint of academic freedom and civil liberties, an essential problem in the secondary schools is how best to maintain and encourage freedom of expression and assembly while simultaneously inculcating a sense of responsibility and good citizenship with awareness of the excesses into which the immaturity of the students might lead.

*Reprinted from *Academic Freedom in the Secondary Schools*, American Civil Liberties Union, 1967. Used with permission.

It is the responsibility of faculty and administration to decide when a situation requires a limit on freedom for the purpose of protecting the students and the school from harsh consequences. In exercising that responsibility, certain fundamental principles should be accepted in order to prevent the use of administrative discretion to eliminate legitimate controversy and legitimate freedom. The principles are:

(1) A recognition that freedom implies the right to make mistakes and that students must therefore sometimes be permitted to act in ways which are predictably unwise so long as the consequences of their acts are not dangerous to life and property, and do not seriously disrupt the academic process.

(2) A recognition that students in their schools should have the right to live under the principle of "*rule by law*" as opposed to "*rule by personality.*" To protect this right, rules and regulations should be in writing. Students have the right to know the extent and limits of the faculty's authority and, therefore, the powers that are reserved for the students and the responsibilities that they should accept. Their rights should not be compromised by faculty members who while ostensibly acting as consultants or counsellors are, in fact, exercising authority to censor student expression and inquiry.

(3) A recognition that deviation from the opinions and standards deemed desirable by the faculty is not *ipso facto* a danger to the educational process.

FREEDOM OF EXPRESSION AND COMMUNICATION

Primary liberties in a student's life have to do with the processes of inquiry and of learning, of acquiring and imparting knowledge, of exchanging ideas. There must be no interference in the school with his access to, or expression of, controversial points of view. No student should suffer any hurt or penalty for any idea he expresses in the course of participation in class or school activities.

The right of every student to have access to varied points of view, to confront and study controversial issues, to be treated without prejudice or penalty for what he reads or writes, and to have facilities for learning available in the school library and the classroom may not be derogated or denied.

1. Learning materials

Toward these ends policies should be adopted in writing establishing solely educational criteria for the selection and purchase of class and library materials including books, magazines, pamphlets, films, records, tapes and other media. These policies should provide principles and procedures for the selection of materials and for the handling of complaints and grievances about these materials.

The removal from the school library or the banning of material alleged to be improper imposes a grave responsibility. It should be exercised, if at all, with the utmost of circumspection and only in accordance with carefully established and publicly promulgated procedures. (Such procedures are detailed in the ACLU pamphlet, *"Combatting Undemocratic Pressures on Schools and Libraries — A Guide for Local Communities."*

2. Forums

Generally speaking, students have the right to express publicly and to hear any opinion on any subject which they believe is worthy of consideration. Assemblies and extra-curricular organizations are the more obvious, appropriate forums for the oral exchange of ideas and offer the opportunity for students to hear views on topics of relatively specialized interest. Whatever the forum, the faculty should defend the right of students to hear and participate in discussions of controversial issues. Restrictions may be tolerated only when they are employed to forestall events which would clearly endanger the health or safety of members of the school community or clearly and imminently disrupt the educational process. Education, it may be noted, should enable individuals to react to ideas, however distasteful, in rational and constructive ways.

The education of young people to participate in public presentations of opinions and to choose wisely among those that are offered suggests that they help plan assembly programs. The students should have the responsibility for planning other forums, especially those offered by extra-curricular organizations: for selecting the topics, choosing the speakers, and determining the method of presentation.

Students may choose speakers from their own ranks, from the faculty, and from outside the school. The community at large may provide speakers who have knowledge and insights that might not otherwise be available to students; it may introduce to the school persons whose presence enriches the educational experience. Controversies that are sometimes involved in inviting outside speakers should not deter faculty advisors from encouraging their presence at school.

Every student has the right to state freely his own views when he participates in a discussion program. Faculty members may advise the students on such matters as the style, appropriateness to the occasion, and the length of their presentations and on the avoidance of slander, but they must not censor the expression of ideas. To foster the free expression of opinions, students participating on panels should have wide latitude to state the differences in their views. For the same reason, questions from members of student audiences are ordinarily desirable and should be encouraged by arranging question periods of reasonable length at the end of talks.

3. Student Publications

The preparation and publication of newspapers and magazines is an exercise in freedom of the press. Generally speaking, students should be permitted and encouraged to join together to produce such publications as they wish. Faculty advisors should serve as consultants on style, grammar, format and suitability of the materials. Neither the faculty advisors nor the principal should prohibit the publication or distribution of material except when such publication or distribution would clearly endanger the health or safety of the students, or clearly and imminently threaten to disrupt the educational process, or might be of a libelous nature. Such judgment, however, should never be exercised because of disapproval or disagreement with the article in question.

The school administration and faculty should ensure that students and faculty may have their views represented in the columns of the school newspaper. Where feasible, they should permit the publication of multiple and competing periodicals. These might be produced by the student government, by various clubs, by a class or group of classes, or by individuals banded together for this specific purpose. The material and equipment for publication such as duplicating machines, paper and ink should be available to students in such quantity as budget may permit.

The freedom to express one's opinion goes hand in hand with the responsibility for the published statement. The onus of decision as to the content of a publication should be placed clearly on the student editorial board of the particular publication. The editors should be encouraged through practice, to learn to judge literary value, newsworthiness, and propriety.

The right to offer copies of their work to fellow students should be accorded equally to those who have received school aid, and to those whose publications have relied on their own resources.

The student press should be considered a learning device. Its pages should not be looked upon as an official image of the school, always required to present a polished appearance to the extramural world. Learning effectively proceeds through trial and error, and as much or more may sometimes be gained from reactions to a poor article or a tasteless publication as from the traditional pieces, groomed carefully for external inspection.

4. School communications

Guarantees of free expression should be extended also to other media of communication: the public address system, closed-circuit television, bulletin boards, handbills, personal contact. Reasonable access should be afforded to student groups for announcements and statements to the school community. This should include the provision of space, both indoor and outdoor, for meetings and rallies.

The school community, i.e., the administration, faculty and the student organization, has the right to make reasonable regulations as to manner, place and time of using these communication media.

The electronic media are monopolistic by nature, and their audiences are captive. When these are used as vehicles for the presentation of opinions, the guarantees and procedures applied to school assemblies should similarly be invoked with respect to choice of topics, balance of participants and freedom of expression.

5. Restrictions on political thought

Not only should the student be guaranteed freedom to inquire and to express his thoughts while in the school; he should also be assured that he will be free from coercion or improper disclosure which may have ill effects on his career.

a. Loyalty oaths

Loyalty oaths are, by their inherent nature, a denial of the basic premises of American democracy. Whether imposed by the school itself, or by an external political authority, oaths required as a condition for enrollment, promotion, graduation, or for financial aid, violate the basic freedoms guaranteed to every individual by the Bill of Rights.

b. Inquiries by outside agencies

The solicitation by prospective private, governmental or other outside agencies or persons of information about students is a practice in which there are inherent dangers to academic freedom. To answer questions on a student's character, reliability, conduct, and academic performance is part of the school's responsibility. But questions about a student's values and opinions may be deemed invasions of edu-

cational privacy and impingements on academic freedom. A teacher's ability to resist such invasions of privacy will be strengthened if the school proscribes the recording of student opinions and adopts policies on responding to outsiders' questions that safeguard academic freedom.

Even in schools that have adopted policies to prevent the recording and disclosure of individuals' beliefs, there will be times when the teacher has to rely on his own judgment in deciding to reply or not to reply to questions about students. Both educational and personal liberty considerations should help guide the faculty member faced with inquiries that may invite the disclosure of religious, political, social, and other opinions and beliefs. Education often calls for probing, hypothesizing, and thinking out loud. Reports to persons outside the school on students' opinions therefore threaten the learning process. Moreover, an atmosphere conducive to an understanding of freedom and of the need for an interplay of ideas in a free society will hardly prevail if teachers report to outsiders on opinions expressed by their students.

The opinions and beliefs of secondary school students, although often stated with great enthusiasm, are highly subject to change. Many youths have great eagerness, exuberance, idealism, and propensity for adventure, but limited experience. The community, its laws, its parents, and the schools themselves therefore recognize that students are not as accountable for their actions as adults. Consistent with this attitude, schools should understand this difference and refrain from answering questions about students' beliefs.

6. Freedom of religion and conscience

All students are entitled to the First Amendment guarantees of the right to practice their own religion or no religion. Under the terms of the amendment, as repeatedly interpreted by the Supreme Court, any federal, state, or local law or practice is unconstitutional if it has the effect of extending to religion the mantle of public sponsorship, either through declaration of public policy or use of public funds or facilities.

Students' rights in this area are protected by judicial decisions which have found the following practices unconstitutional:

a. The recitation of any form of prayer as a group exercise,
b. The reading of the Bible as a form of worship; mandatory Bible instruction; use of schools for Bible distribution,
c. Sectarian holiday observances,
d. The showing of religious movies in class or assembly exercises,
e. The use of public school facilities for religious instruction, either within school hours or for after-school classes, whether by church or lay groups.

The teaching of religion should be distinguished from teaching factually about religion as, for example, an aspect of world history or of social sciences. Even in teaching about religion, the younger the child, the more wary the teacher must be of indoctrination. Certainly, public schools may explain the meaning of a religious holiday, as viewed by adherents of the religion of which it is a part, but may not seek to foster a religious view in the classroom or otherwise.

Although a salute to the flag and oath of allegiance are commonly accepted practices in school assembly exercises, exemptions should be granted to a student whose religious scruples or other principled convictions lead him to refuse to participate in such exercises. The Supreme Court has held that the protection of freedom of religion under the First Amendment encompasses such exemption on grounds of religious belief. There should be no distinction in this respect between student objection based on religious conviction and that based on non-religious grounds of conscience.

FREEDOM OF ASSOCIATION

The right to individual free expression implies in a democracy the right to associate for the exchange of opinion or the statement of ideas held in common.

1. Extracurricular activities

Students should be free to organize associations within the school for political, social, athletic, and other proper and lawful purposes, provided that no such group denies membership to any student because of race, religion or nationality, or for any reasons other than those related to the purpose of the organization (i.e., a French club requirement for competence in French). The fact of affiliation with any extramural association should not in itself bar a group from recognition, but disclosure of such fact may be required. Any group which plans political action or discussion, of whatever purpose or complexion and whether or not affiliated with a particular legal party, should be allowed to organize and be recognized in any educational institution. The administration should not discriminate against a student because of membership in any such organization.

Student organizations are entitled to faculty advisors of their own selection. If no volunteer is available, a faculty member should be assigned to provide the required supervision, in order that the organization may exercise its right to function in the school.

The use of rooms and other facilities should be made available, as far as their primary use for instructional purposes permits, to recognized student organizations. Bulletin boards and access to school-wide communications systems should be provided for the use of student organizations, and they should be permitted to circulate notices and leaflets. The legitimate power of school authorities to safeguard school property should not be misused to suppress a poster or piece of literature by reason of objections to its content.

The nature and type of programs, projects and procedures of any student organization should be within the province of student decision, subject only to emergency ban by student government or principal in the event that a proposed activity clearly threatens the health and safety of the students, or clearly and immediately threatens to disrupt the educational process. Such a ban should not become permanent unless its justification is established through open hearings and argument.

A student organization should be permitted to use the name of the school as part of its own name, and to use this name in all activities consistent with its constitution. The school may adopt such regulations as will prevent any student organization from representing overtly or by inference that its views are sanctioned by the school. Restrictions may fairly be placed on the use of the school name in extramural activities (such as participation in public demonstrations or parades), but any such restrictions should be without discrimination in respect to all student organizations.

The administration and the faculty should not discriminate against any student because of his membership or participation in the activities of any extra-curricular student association.

2. Out-of-school activities

The school has no jurisdiction over its students' non-school activities, their conduct, their movements, their dress and the expression of their ideas. No disciplinary action should be taken by the school against a student for participation in such out-of-school activities as political parties and campaigns, picketing and public demonstrations, circulation of leaflets and petitions, provided the student does not claim without authorization to speak or act as a representative of the school or one of its organizations. When a student chooses to participate in out-of-school activities that result in police action, it is an infringement of his liberty for the school to punish such activity, or to enter it on school records or report it to prospective employers or other agencies, unless authorized or requested by the student. A student who violates any law risks the legal penalties prescribed by civil authorities. He should not be placed in jeopardy at school for an offense which is not concerned with the educational institution.

FREEDOM OF ASSEMBLY AND THE RIGHT TO PETITION

The right *"peaceably to assemble"* is constitutionally bracketed with the right to *"petition the government for a redress of grievances."* Accordingly, individual students and student organizations should be permitted to hold meetings in school rooms or auditoriums, or at outdoor locations on school grounds, at which they should be free to discuss, pass resolutions, and take other lawful action respecting any matter which directly or indirectly concerns or affects them, whether it relates to school or to the extramural world. Nor should such assemblages be limited to the form of audience meetings; any variety of demonstration, whether it be a picketline, a *"walk,"* or any other *peaceful* type, should be permissible. The school administration is justified in requiring that demonstrations or meetings be held at times that will not disrupt classes or other school activities and in places where there will be no hazards to persons or property; it also may require advance notice when necessary to avoid conflicts and to arrange for proper protection by faculty or policy.

The right to distribute printed material, whether produced within or outside the school, should always be recognized, subject only to limitations designed to prevent littering, except when such distribution would clearly endanger the health or safety of the students, or clearly and imminently threaten to disrupt the educational process, or might be of a libelous nature. But the administration may require that the distributor be a student enrolled in the school.

In general, subject only to reasonable restrictions of time and place, students should be free also to collect signatures on petitions concerning either school or out-of-school issues. Neither the administration nor the faculty should have the right to screen either the contents or the wording of the petitions; they should receive them when presented and give their fullest consideration to the proposals therein.

Similarly, the wearing of buttons or badges, armbands or insignia bearing slogans or admonitions of any sort should generally be permitted as another form of expression.* No teacher or administrator should attempt to interfere with this practice on the grounds that the message may be unpopular with any students or faculty, or even with the majority of either group. The exercise of one or another of these techniques of expression may, under certain circumstances, clearly and imminently constitute a danger to peace or clearly and imminently threaten to disrupt the educational process. Such a situation might require staying action by the administration, similar to a temporary injunction, and subject to revocation if and when a hearing determines that the facts no longer warrant it. Interference in this way with the exercise of student rights should seldom occur, and should be undertaken with the greatest reluctance and only when accompanied by careful explanation.

---

*In 1966, a U.S. Court of Appeals upheld the right of Mississippi high school students to wear "freedom buttons" in school "as a means of silently communicating an idea" and therefore legally protected by the First Amendment. (*Burnside* v. *Byars* 363 F.2d 744 1966).

STUDENT GOVERNMENT

The functions and powers of student government organizations, and the manner of selection of their officers, as well as the qualifications for office, are matters to be determined as the respective school communities think desirable, but certain rights should be guaranteed within the structure of any student government, if it is to fulfill its role as an educational device for living in a democracy.

1. The organization, operation and scope of the student government should be specified in a written constitution, formulated with effective student participation.

2. The government should function with scrupulous regard for all constitutional pro-

visions, which should be changed only by a prescribed process of amendment in which there should be effective student participation.

3. No constitutional provision, by-law or practice should permit decisions, including expenditures of student organization funds, to be made exclusively by the faculty or administration.

4. All students should have the right to vote and to hold office.

5. The statements, votes, decisions or actions of a student incident to his role in student government should be judged solely within the sphere of the school civic life, through the medium of electoral action by his peers, or through pre-established constitutional process. Full and free participation in student government should be encouraged by an understanding that neither marks, course credits, graduation, college recommendations, nor other aspects of scholastic life will ever be adversely affected as a consequence of a stand or action with which faculty or administration may disagree. Nor should such penalties ever be invoked for failure to make financial contribution in support of any school activity.

6. In respect to the selection of officers of the student organization:

a. All students who meet the qualifications fixed by the school constitution should be permitted to be candidates. However, disqualification for a specified period from participation in extracurricular activities, including student government, might in appropriate cases be imposed as a penalty for serious or repeated infractions of school rules.

b. Candidates should be free to speak without censorship, subject only to equally enforced rules as to the time and place of their speeches.

c. All candidates should have equal opportunity to publicize their campaigns.

d. Candidates should be permitted to group into slates or parties, if they so desire.

e. Voting and vote-counting procedures should make provision for scrutiny by representatives of all candidates.

f. The candidate chosen by vote of the students should be declared elected, with no faculty veto.

g. Any electoral rules which may be adopted should apply equally, without discrimination, to all candidates.

STUDENT DISCIPLINE

The regulations concerning appropriate student behavior in the school at large should preferably be formulated by a student-faculty committee. Regulations governing the school as a whole should be fully and clearly formulated, published, and made available to all members of the school community. They should be reasonable. Specific definitions are preferable to such general criteria as "conduct unbecoming a student" and "against the best interests of the school," which allow for a wide latitude of interpretation.

1. The right of due process

To maintain the orderly administration of the school, minor infractions of school discipline may be handled in a summary fashion. In every case a student should be informed of the nature of the infraction with which he is charged. The teacher and/or administrator should bear in mind that an accusation is not the equivalent of guilt, and he should therefore be satisfied of the guilt of the accused student prior to subjecting such student to disciplinary action.

A student's locker should not be opened without his consent except in conformity with the spirit of the Fourth Amendment which requires that a warrant first be obtained on a showing of probable cause, supported by oath or affirmation, and particularly describing the things to be seized. An exception may be made in cases involving a clear danger to health or safety.

The penalties meted out for breaches of school regulations should be commensurate with the offense. They should never take the form of corporal punishment. Punishment for infractions of the code of behavior should bear no relation to courses, credits, marks, graduation or similar academic areas, except in cases where they relate to academic dishonesty.

Those infractions which may lead to more serious penalties, such as suspension or expulsion from school, or a notation on the record, require the utilization of a comprehensive and formal procedure in order to prevent a miscarriage of justice that could have serious effects on the student and his future. Such hearings should therefore be approached not in terms of meting out punishment but rather as an attempt to find the best solution for the student's needs consistent with the maintenance of order in the school.

The procedure should include a formal hearing and the right of appeal. Regulations and proceedings governing the operation of the hearing panel and the appeal procedure should be predetermined in consultation with the students, published and disseminated or otherwise made available to the student body. Responsibility for the decision reached as a result of the hearing rests solely with the administration. It may seek the opinions and participation of teachers and students in reaching its conclusion.

Prior to the hearing, the student (and his parent or guardian) should be:

a. Advised in writing of the charges against him, including a summary of the evidence upon which the charges are based.

b. Advised that he is entitled to be represented and/or advised at all times during the course of the proceedings by a person of his choosing who may or may not be connected with the faculty or administration of the school and may include a member of the student body.

c. Advised of the procedure to be followed at the hearing.

d. Given a reasonable time to prepare his defense.

At the hearing, the student (his parent, guardian or other representative) and the administrator should have the right to examine and cross-examine witnesses and to present documentary and other evidence in support of their respective contentions. The student should be advised of his privilege to remain silent, and should not be disciplined for claiming this privilege. The administration should make available to the student such authority as it may possess to require the presence of witnesses at the hearing. A full record should be taken at the hearing and it should be made available in identical form to the hearing panel, the administration and the student. The cost thereof should be met by the school.

In those instances where the student is being exposed to a serious penalty because of an accumulation of minor infractions which had been handled in summary fashion, or any instance where evidence of prior infractions so handled is presented at the hearing by the administration, the student (his parent, guardian, or other representative) should be permitted to reopen those charges and present evidence in support of the contention that he was wrongfully accused and/or convicted of the minor infraction.

After the hearing is closed, the panel should adjudicate the matter before it with reasonable promptness and make its findings and conclusions in writing, and make copies thereof available in identical form and at the same time, to the administration and the student. The cost thereof should be met by the school. Punishments should so far as possible avoid public humiliation or embarrassment. Group punishment should be used only if every member of the group is guilty of the infraction. Cruel and unusual punishment should never be imposed.

2. The role of the police in the secondary schools

Where disciplinary problems involving breaches of law are rampant, schools cannot be considered sacrosanct against policemen and the proper function of law officers cannot be impeded in crime detection. Whenever the police are involved in the schools, their activities should not consist of harassment or intimidation. If a student is to be questioned by the police, it is the responsibility of the school administration to see that the interrogation takes place privately in the office of a school official, in the presence of the principal or his representative. Every effort should be made to give a parent the opportunity to be present. All procedural safeguards prescribed by law must be strictly observed. When the interrogation takes place in school, as elsewhere, the student is entitled to be advised of his rights, which should include the right to counsel and the right to remain silent.

PERSONAL APPEARANCE

The matter of acceptable dress and grooming is a frequent issue in schools. Education is too important to be granted or denied on the basis of standards of personal appearance. As long as a student's appearance does not, *in fact,* disrupt the educational process, or constitute a threat to safety, it should be no concern of the school.

Dress and personal adornment are forms of self-expression; the freedom of personal preference should be guaranteed along with other liberties. The reconciliation of the rights of the individual with the needs of the group was well expressed in the decision by California Superior Court Judge W. G. Watson in the case of Myers v. Arcata Union High School District. (1966)*

*Superior Court of California, Humboldt County (unreported)

FREEDOM FROM DISCRIMINATION

No student should be granted any preference nor denied any privilege or right in any aspect of school life because of race, religion, color, national origin, or any other reason not related to his individual capabilities. It is the duty of the administration to prevent discrimination and to avoid situations which may lead to discrimination or the appearance thereof, in all aspects of school life, including the classroom, the lunchroom, the assembly, honors, disciplinary systems, athletics, clubs and social activities.

THE RIGHTS OF MARRIED AND/OR PREGNANT STUDENTS

The right to an education provided for all students by law should not be abrogated for a particular student because of marriage or pregnancy unless there is compelling evidence that his or her presence in the classroom or school does, in fact, disrupt or impair the educational process for other students. This includes the right to participate in all the activities of the school. If temporary or permanent separation from the school should be warranted, the education provided elsewhere should be qualitatively and quantitatively equivalent to that of the regular school, so far as is practicable.

Teaching in the Large City*
Leslie J. Chamberlin

"He beat me up because I didn't bring him a quarter," one of the smaller boys tells the teacher as he tries to explain the near-riot on the school bus going home from school. "You got to have a wild opener to play this game," says one seventh grader to his fellow elementary school students as a schoolhouse card game gets under way. Try to extort money from a fellow student under threat of physical harm? Play cards in the corner of the school basement? Yes, and let's add purse snatching, gang fighting, car theft, breaking and entering, muggings, assaults, drinking, and dope when it is available. But what is more important, let's add that these are daily happenings throughout the negative neighborhoods of this country's metropolitan areas, where most of the inhabitants have learned to live their daily lives on the edge of sensation.

Present Problems

About 8,000,000 people in this country are living in whole or in part on some kind of relief. Most of these people live in the negative neighborhoods, where the inhabitants have grown used to living with next to nothing. An eight-room house that used to be the home of one family may now contain eight families. A short street may be inhabited by over 4,000 people. Most of the people have never had much, have nothing now, and expect little from the future except more of the same—nothing.

What happens to a youngster who grows up in such an environment? Try to explain the great American Dream of bettering yourself through education to a schoolboy who has been taught by example from his earliest years that the present is all that you can really count on. In any choice involving pleasure today versus possible betterment in the future, the people whom he knows choose the pleasure regardless of how minor the immediate reward. Try to convince him that he should "be good—work hard—stay in school" for some 12 to 16 years so that he can enjoy a better life in the distant future. Everything that he lives with and has grown up with would seem to tell him that he had better enjoy

*Reprinted from *The Clearing House*, April 1965. Used with permission.

himself today, for tomorrow will only be worse.

Every large city in the U.S. has its negative neighborhoods, illustrating an illogical truth of want amidst plenty, of the physically underdeveloped and the overfed, of the educationally deprived amidst the educationally pampered. About one-third of all of the children attending the public schools of our larger U.S. cities could be described as disadvantaged, and most of these live in such neighborhoods.

Society takes the child from the negative neighborhood, places him in the traditional school with its middle-class values system, and tells him to adjust. Is it any wonder that as this child attempts to make his way through school he has a great deal of trouble? He is discouraged by parents who often don't really care. Frequently he is intimidated by discrimination. Sometimes he is taught by teachers who are unprepared for large city teaching and are unable to cope with the situation. He is unaccepted by the larger group who wonder why he doesn't embrace their behavior standards. Very often he is pushed and kicked out of school by an institution that is only too glad to get rid of another problem. Things that to his thinking are everyday occurrences now turn out to be crimes for which he is put out of school. So he is put out by society's agent, the school, but then quickly told to get back in by society itself. Dropped out — dropped in, kicked out — kicked in, until he is finally old enough to go back to his neighborhood and take his place in the vicious cycle where the poverty stricken, poorly educated family passes down the habit of poverty and ignorance to the new generation.

What Is Being Done Educationally

The larger cities of this nation have long been concerned with the education of im-migrants. The educational problems of the newcomers to our country and to our large cities are not over. The American Dream of economic salvation through the public schools has worked before and so it is being hard pressed to help the new in-migrants to the large cities: the rural whites, the Southern Negroes, the Puerto Ricans, the Mexicans, the Cubans, and other smaller groups.

The traditional sphere of action has been to *get these kids in school*, which is no easy task in itself. But just school attendance isn't doing the job this time. The new in-migrant to our large cities is different in many ways from his predecessor, the European immigrant. The times are not the same, and the schools that are looked to for salvation are usually the oldest, most overcrowded, and poorest equipped in the local school system. Furthermore, it is in these urban areas that the greatest part of this country's population lives. The U.S. is predominantly urban at present, with the trend being toward more and larger cities. It seems evident that it will be in these large urban areas that this country will win or lose its fight for a more highly educated citizenry.

Throughout this nation, efforts are being made to find solutions to these problems. Most of the projects place their emphasis on the school dropout or the young delinquent. Michigan, Texas, Illinois, Maryland, California, and most other states have conducted such programs. The New York City school system has taken a slightly different approach to the problem in the Higher Horizons Program, in that an effort is made to overcome the cultural differences or environmental lack of the student's negative neighborhood environment by a strong exposure to culture and a heavy dose of counseling. Other approaches to the problem that are being tried are to allocate extra money for the schools in the problem areas of the city for plant improvements, extra equipment, and the like; to use bilingual teachers in the areas that are populated with the foreign born; to set up Work Experience Programs and Continuation Schools; and to establish Delinquent Centers for the worst of the culturally different.

There is such concern about the delinquency and dropout problem that volunteer programs to help combat the situation have also been organized. The Stay in School Project sponsored and conducted by a Federation of Women's Clubs of Indianapolis, Indiana, is such a program. The program attempts to encourage the individual dropout to return to school by helping him solve his personal money or home problem and by providing a one-to-one counseling situation with a volunteer counselor.

Another project that illustrates what can be done by a volunteer group is a self-improvement program organized and sponsored by a St. Louis parochial school. St. Bridget's Catholic School, in cooperation with the St. Louis Board of Education's high school equivalency examination program, using college students and nuns as volunteer teachers, has helped a number of St. Louisans obtain certificates equivalent to bona fide high school diplomas. This continuing tutorial program is providing an opportunity for many who had to quit school, and who now have responsibilities that prevent them from returning, to spend their Sundays studying mathematics and social studies and improving their reading skills.

Most of the local programs have experienced some success and have brought about some improvements, but they have hardly scratched the surface of the problem that faces this nation. No organized

overall rehabilitation program is presently in operation. This country has an alarming dropout rate, and running concurrently with this trend is the constantly increasing importance of education in this country's technical economy. While more and more students leave school, the individual's need for an education is growing and growing.

Needed Programs

One thing is clear. This country must increase its efforts in the areas where the problems are. Where the huge negative neighborhoods exist — the great cities. Where people can be born, live most of their lives, and die in abject poverty — the great cities. Where the school systems are overcrowded and are struggling under the weight of their responsibilities — the great cities. Where the school dropout and delinquency problems are the worst — the great cities. Where the in-migrants flock in large numbers seeking employment, shelter, and their future — the great cities.

It has been predicted that within the next 50 years the population of this country will reach 400,000,000 people. It is also expected that 320,000,000 people, four-fifths of the entire population, will be living in the urban centers. Since we seem to be unable to deal effectively with the more pressing problems of our present metropolitan areas, what will these tremendous cities of the future be like? Obviously, this country must find workable solutions to the present problems of our great cities and plan ways to deal with the staggering growth to come.

Special programs are needed to assist the large urban areas, similar to the $252,000,000 Appalachia Poverty Bill which will support enlarged vocational and literacy training programs in that area. The Economic Opportunity Act of 1964, with its proposals for a job corps for school dropouts and young men who fail to qualify for military service; a plan to help out-of-work youth finish high school through a work training program; a work-study program to assist college students with the financial burden of attending college; and basic education and/or work training for welfare recipients — these represent the type of assistance that will have to be provided if the great cities of this nation are to become vital productive living centers rather than vast burying grounds for the unwanted.

The large city school systems of this country are trying to provide education for the bulk of this nation's children on the basis of little more than a limited local tax. Significant additional support from both state and federal governments for the large city school systems must be provided if they are to adopt and carry through programs capable of solving the problems that are destroying our great cities. Since the local school people are well acquainted with the local problems, the programs that are to attack these problems should be controlled locally. Local school authorities know local needs and will be better able to direct such programs. Also, locally controlled programs encourage initiative and self-reliant enterprise.

One of the more publicized consequences of living in the so-called slum areas of a large city is the cultural degeneracy that can result. For the school age child this is a very serious handicap. It could be offset to a great extent by having these children begin their education at age two or three, in order to supply the preschool training that they often fail to receive in their homes. After-school study centers which could provide materials, facilities, and surroundings for proper study should also be established. Remedial and cultural enrichment education should be considered a vital part of the school life in these neighborhoods. New York's Higher Horizons Program has shown that the right type of school experience can overcome some of the effects of a negative neighborhood.

Research dealing specifically with the learning difficulties of the culturally deprived should be stepped up. Comparatively little money is being spent on educational research. U.S. industry knows from experience that research paves the way to improvement, and therefore spends almost 10 percent of its gross revenue on research. Less than one-tenth of one percent is spent on this country's educational research.

Traditionally, educational research has been very limited. Primarily it has consisted of small, easily handled projects. The controversial issues and hard-to-limit research are often avoided. Too often the "end" desired is simply the "doing" of the research. Much innovation and creative thinking is going to be demanded of the educational researchers if any real contribution is to be made.

We must realize that our war on poverty, our counterattack on the effects of automation, and our hoped-for blitz of unemployment all begin in the classroom. The long-range success of all such programs depends entirely on the very heart of good education—good teachers. Teacher training institutions must begin to offer courses that will help to prepare our teachers for teaching assignments in the large cities. Regardless of where they attend college, many will go to Chicago, St. Louis, New York, Detroit, and the other large cities to teach. These young teachers need to be given an understanding of the various large-city neighborhoods and what they can expect of their pupils in the way of behavior and academic achievement.

The large-city school systems should provide orientation programs for new teachers that go beyond a chat with the superintendent and instructions on how to order audio-visual materials. Programs that attempt to prepare the new teacher for the more serious problems that he will face are needed.

The great cities of this nation are in serious trouble, and they do not have the financial ability to solve their problems. Additional state and federal assistance to these areas is imperative. It would seem that the schools are the most suitable agency both to attack the general situation and to aid the individual person. Adequately supported, locally controlled educational programs to help these areas must be designed and carried out.

The Delinquent in the School*

Glenn H. Darling

"All writers tend to agree that the school does not have a custodial responsibility for the socially and emotionally disturbed and that the school should not become a repository for the overflow from state institutions," comment the editors of the *Encyclopedia of Educational Research*. At the same time a United States Senate Subcommittee of the Judiciary on Juvenile Delinquency describes the detention facilities for delinquents throughout the country as the "shame of the nation," while the United States Children's Bureau says that state institutions continue to be "over-crowded, understaffed, and financially neglected and that their programs are more custodial than therapeutic."

Most schoolmen would agree that the foregoing statements are essentially true, and that although the schools "should not become a repository for the overflow from state institutions," there is in fact a very definite trend in this direction. Because of the understaffed, underfinanced condition of many of our state institutions, juvenile judges are hesitant to place any but the most extreme delinquents in them. The results of this hesitation can be seen in the

public school classrooms. The management of delinquents in the schools, then, is a very real and present problem.

Before considering the role of the classroom teacher and the school administrator in connection with the delinquent, we would do well to review three facts which seem basic to any consideration of the delinquent and his school experience:

Fact One: "School and church personnel should not expect to work many 'miracles' of character reformation — and certainly not by dealing with children en masse. It is possible to salvage even severely maldeveloped children, but it takes extremely intensive, long, personalized treatment. In a real sense, an adult who hopes to improve a child with immature character can only expect to do it by taking on the security-giving functions as well as the guiding functions ordinarily performed by the parents. To do this effectively requires unusual wisdom, unusual personal maturity, and sometimes almost superhuman patience. It also requires a strong, personal *caring about* the child."[†]

This statement seems to indicate strongly that for a real delinquent to be reformed, he or she must have a close relationship with one particular individual who will

*Reprinted from *The Clearing House,* April 1963. Used with permission.

stick with the delinquent through a long period of struggle and provide the delinquent with security.

Fact Two: "In teaching character as in teaching intellectual knowledge, no one can teach what he does not know. In character education, this includes much more than intellectual knowledge, alone; it requires that the 'teacher' of character personally possess genuinely mature feelings, attitudes, and ethical behavior, or no success can be expected.†

Fact Three: "Children do as we do, not as we say. Their character tends to be an accurate reflection of the way their parents act toward them, no matter what contrary pretenses some parents try to present to society. There is no way for parents to explain away or to give away this responsibility; it is a simple, inexorable fact."‡

Thus it seems evident that the adult to whom the delinquent is attached is actually a parent substitute. This adult may be a psychologist, a police officer, a social worker, a teacher, or other individual. In all probability the delinquent would not be a delinquent if he had one parent worthy of attachment and giving of security.

The Classroom Teacher

The delinquent, then, must have some one reliable, important adult to whom he can attach himself. In some instances this might be a classroom teacher, but the usual role of the classroom teacher would be supportive rather than major. Let us explore some of the attitudes necessary on the part of the classroom teacher if he is to carry out this supportive role. None of these suggestions is particularly new. All are tremendously important as well as diffi-

†Robert F. Peck, Robert J. Havighurst *et al.*, *The Psychology of Character Development* (New York: John Wiley and Sons, Inc., 1960), p. 190.

‡*Op. cit.*, p. 189.

cult to apply. Each has been violated from time to time with consequent failure.

(1) *Draw a circle and take him (or her) in.* This is sometimes difficult. It requires personal maturity on the part of the teacher; however, the teacher cannot bring about desirable change in another person, no matter how eloquent the teacher may be, if he cannot communicate with that person. There is no communication with a child who has been isolated emotionally.

Any person who is judgmental, who wants to pin labels on people, who sees people and issues as all black or white, is in the wrong vocation if he is in teaching, as children in trouble have more need of friends and helpers than of judges. Judging, like vengeance, might well be left to the deity.

Psychologically, the adolescent youngster is almost entirely shaped by his heredity and environment. He has done little independent thinking or living as yet. Like the old revivalist who saw the drunkard in the gutter, it could well be said of the delinquent, "There but for the grace of God, am I." None of us chooses our parents or our childhood environment.

Most teachers are from stable families. Most aggressive or delinquent youngsters are from unstable families. Teachers must continually remind themselves that not all people live in stable, middle-class homes. School people dare not judge others on the basis of their own limited experiences.

Our Judeo-Christian tradition teaches that we are all made of the same stuff and that each person is of priceless value. No matter how a person appears, he is of inestimable value in the scheme of things and entitled to the same consideration as are we ourselves. There is every practical, psychological, and philosophical reason to "draw a circle and take him in"; yet as immature human beings we sometimes fail.

Emotional acceptance is the first step in helping a person who has problems. Without this step no results can ensue.

(2) *Expect the best.* Expectations as well as emotional acceptances or non-acceptances are apparent. Like the proverbial slip, expectations show when least anticipated. Children read us like books and our every personality flaw basks in an exposed light. This is teaching!

Someone has said that only an optimist should teach. Expectations, whether negative or positive, are catching. These expectations should be working for the teacher and his youngsters. The teacher's sights must be focused on the potentiality of each individual. Paul in his beautiful essay on love writes that love "hopeth all things." The good teacher "hopeth all things."

Every school person is acquainted with the teacher who borrows trouble. He listens avidly to tales of troubles some youngster has had other places and "gets ready" for the time when this student enters his class. I once knew a teacher who took a day of preschool week going through the cumulative records to find out who the "lemons" were. As could be predicted, few of his lemons ever turned sweet.

When a child with problems enters the room, teachers need remind themselves that he is under a new set of circumstances with different personalities and with a new opportunity for success. Teachers dare not doom that opportunity by fearful expectations.

(3) *Build up his self-concept.* Adolescents with problems almost uniformly have low estimates of themselves. They are at odds with their environment and basically blame themselves, protecting their inner selves with layers of rationalizations. These layers themselves are disagreeable things and are repugnant to others and cause those in authority and others to increase the feeling of failure by expressions of criticism. Thus an ever deepening cycle of self-depreciation, hostility, and withdrawal or aggression is set up.

How is such a cycle to be broken? Some techniques which have been successfully used in interrupting the cycle are:

(a) Seizing upon every favorable characteristic or action, recognizing this, and reinforcing it with praise or acceptance.

(b) Setting up opportunities for small successes and indicating approval of these successes.

(c) Paying no attention to failures in matters that are not overpoweringly important.

(d) When discipline or criticism is necessary, couching it in terms of criticism of the act — never of the person. Never characterize a person by his act. "Never condone a sin; but never condemn a sinner," says Dr. Henry Crane. The labeling of a person as "stupid," "unthinking," "selfish," or "lazy," at once isolates that person emotionally and starts again the cycle of self-depreciation and hostility. What school person has not been extremely remorseful at times after having done this very thing as a result of being sorely tried.

(4) *Establish reasonable but clearly defined limits.* "My folks don't care when I get in. They don't care enough about me even to tell me what to do," a so-called delinquent once complained. All are entitled to the security of limits. Most delinquents have not had this security at home either because the parents have not cared or because the parents lacked the will and consistency to hold limits.

Teachers can help bring some order to the delinquent by holding to reasonable limits. School people need from time to time to re-examine their established limits, asking themselves "Have we set limits on the really important things or on picayune matters?"

Indeed, youngsters with problems will step over the limits at times, but the resultant discipline should be directed at the act, not the person. A limit is a restriction. It is likewise an indication that someone cares. If the child feels emotional acceptance, the chance of his working successfully within reasonable limits is greatly enhanced.

(5) *Be a people watcher.* There is so much to learn about how people grow, what makes them tick, how personality develops, and how it may be warped, that this can be a lifelong hobby — in fact, should be a lifelong hobby for the teacher. To avoid having the same experiences over and over, teachers need to have contact with minds that are especially penetrating. All school people need to learn from those who they feel are especially successful in working with youngsters; and they need personally to observe the human animal under a variety of conditions. To do this, it is necessary to get out of the classroom and see how youngsters live at home and at play and under all conditions. Books likewise provide many valuable vicarious experiences and new understandings.

(6) *Remember that Rome was not built in a day.* The student who has serious problems has probably taken much time in acquiring them. The school can manipulate only a part of the delinquent's environment. Progress, therefore, may be slow, but the goals are extremely worthwhile. School personnel must push for progress but should also take the long view when efforts do not immediately or initially meet with large successes. Progress in personality development is usually marked by a series of small and faltering progressions.

Besides the extremely important role of support, the classroom teacher is in a position to observe early tendencies toward delinquency and to alert others to this and thus initiate preventive work when it can yet be extremely valuable.

The Administrator

The school administrator performs a key role in the matter of working with the delinquent in the school. It is he who often determines the person who will play the major role in the attempt to rehabilitate the delinquent. The administrator must act as a catalyst and bring together all agencies and all people who can contribute to rehabilitation. This might include parents, psychologists, police, welfare workers, and others. One of the important responsibilities of the school administrator in this area is working with his teachers in an effort to maintain a school atmosphere conducive to rehabilitation. Additionally, the school administrator must continually work for adequate facilities, which may include counselors, psychologists, school social workers, and other individuals as well as suitable curriculums, particularly for students of lower academic ability. Community-wise the concerned administrator will work for adequate and rehabilitative state institutions. He will always be alert to discover and develop administrative mechanisms which will enhance the role of the family and which will provide for flexibility in working with the delinquent.

The administrator who treats his teachers with respect and consideration will find his teachers treating their students this way. The administrator must be continually aware of the feelings of students and teachers. Are all students being tied down by numerous rules designed to get at a few offenders? Are students developing a slow burn because the vast majority are being scolded for the acts of a few? Are curricular materials realistic in the light of the abilities of individual students? Are rules clear cut and few in numbers? Are parents involved? Does the administrator think in terms of *our* school or *my* school?

The Community

The community, likewise, has its role to play in making it possible for the school to work effectively with delinquents. Nothing is so important to a school as teachers who are understanding and dedicated. Community conditions will, in the long run, determine the quality of teachers in the school. It is likewise the responsibility of the community to provide adequate facilities for the handling of extreme and hard-core cases of delinquency. The community must provide the school with facilities such as counseling services if the school is to do a job with delinquents. Sometimes community conditions are such that the school efforts are overwhelmed and defeated. The school does not work in a vacuum but as part of the community.

One writer has said that the good school is good for the normal youngster and is also good for the delinquent. The delinquent needs the same kind of consideration that every other student needs, except more of it.

Reflections of a Ghetto Teacher*

Thomas J. Matczynski

In the midst of this country's unparalleled abundance, there is another nation which continues to exist in grinding deprivation. This other nation is the home of the ghetto child who waits impatiently for the public school to unlock the door to a better life.

Unfortunately, these schools, which are the hope of the future for the ghetto are, themselves, sub-standard.

Having taught in the ghetto as a white person, I am convinced educators must begin anew to solve the plight of the disadvantaged.

I find myself wondering how many of us have really seen the inadequate housing facilities in the ghetto. How many of us know what it is like to make ends meet and raise five children on an income of $3,000 a year. How many of us ever think about the organic brain damage or retarded growth and learning rate that can

*Reprinted from *Ohio Schools*, November 1968. Used with permission.

result from inadequate nutrition? Are we really aware that the ghetto has an increased vulnerability to disease, to withdrawal, to apathy, to alienation, to frustration and to violence?

How many teachers have stood at the head of their class and realized that half of their class was hollowbellied or have seen the pitiful sight of a young black child whose nose is a swollen mass of hardness due to the rat bites obtained as baby in his crib?

Having lived as well as taught in the ghetto, I have seen all of this and much more.

I have seen the sickening sights of poverty which is a psychological process that destroys the young before they can live and destroys the aged before they can die. It is a pattern of hopelessness and helplessness. It is a view of the world and of oneself as static, limited, and expendable.

Pressing heavily on the ghetto school is

the gigantic task of helping in the cause of social justice, job training, and curriculum renovation.

Any attempt to solve these problems of the inner city and the disadvantaged youngster must involve educational reforms that affect the self-image of the ghetto child, the buildings, the curriculum, and the faculty.

Those who work in the ghetto constantly speak of uplifting the self-concept or self-image of the disadvantaged youngsters. This is a must in the ghetto, where from the time he is born the black child is ridiculed, scorned, downtrodden, and ignored. This is done in words and deeds, consciously and unconsciously.

The ghetto black youngster is told he is not worthwhile, incapable of bettering himself, unable to learn, and cannot associate with the better educated. This is not necessarily related to the black child verbally. In fact, most of the time this is communicated by people's actions or expressions.

This is done so frequently that when the child enters kindergarten he is starving for love, kindness, and affection. Instead of receiving this kindness in the classroom, however, he often is told he smells and must wash. Instead of affection, he is told he must get down to the standard, middle-class school work. Instead of love, he is disliked and sometimes even hated by the teacher whom he knows as all knowing and all powerful.

I believe that before a disadvantaged child is told to wash, he must feel kindness and love from his teacher. Why is it that a teacher must treat all pupils alike, beginning at the same place with every student and following the same procedure throughout the entire school year? I see nothing wrong with spending as much time as possible — even the entire school year — expressing kindness and having the child feel he is truly loved and is a worthwhile person.

This must be the first objective of teaching. How can a teacher begin teaching without knowing the child, who he is, his likes and dislikes, and his very problems of existence? As teachers, we must see that the disadvantaged child is happy, feels good, is not hungry, and is able to give love as well as receive love.

I can see nothing wrong in dismissing the entire curriculum for some students. The standard, traditional, conservative, middle-class school curriculum has absolutely no meaning in the ghetto. In some cases, it is even losing its appeal and worth for the white middle-class student who sees it as irrelevant to today's society.

The child reared in the ghetto more often than not sees and feels deprivation, unwantedness, and immortality. Yet, he opens a first grade reader and sees Dick and Jane playing and living in a nice neighborhood, talking to a friendly policeman, wearing nice clothes and receiving the love of both parents. He sees nothing from his own world — perhaps throughout his entire school life. How then can he cope with his problems?

One means the author has found to be worthwhile in helping the black child to improve his self-concept is through the black press. There are a number of Negro newspapers and magazines which can be used to emphasize the brighter side of Negro life and success. *Ebony, Sepia, Jet* and the *Negro Digest* are just a few magazines which help the black child to identify with great Negroes past and present. The *Negro Digest* is useful though it is utilized at times by black power advocates. These publications can be invaluable in providing motivation and improving the self-concept of the ghetto youngster.

Another method is to utilize adult

Negroes in the classroom. The black child as well as the white child needs to know that there are Negroes who are city commissioners, lawyers, engineers, editors, doctors, plumbers, railroad engineers, and steel workers. He needs to be able to have these people talk to him and be able to ask them questions.

What a difference this can make on a student and his study habits. An attitude of *what's the use* can sometimes be changed to a feeling of wonder and a craving for self improvement.

Still a third way of helping the ghetto child improve his self-image is through projects that develop creativity.

There are immeasurable benefits from giving a disadvantaged child the opportunity to create a painting or a piece of sculpture; to express his ideas in a theme; to be able to help stage a play; or to see his work of art recognized as worthwhile.

These are only a few of the ideas teachers can utilize in helping the child from the inner city improve his self concept.

The curriculum, itself, is often a deterrent to education for the ghetto child. We expect students to study and learn material that is outdated and unrelated to the student's real world; material that will never be used or appreciated.

The result of holding the student who is not capable of learning at the rate of his classmates in an ordinary classroom is often discipline problems, a poor self-image, and eventual departure from school.

One solution is to remove the youngster from the traditional curriculum and put him into vocational training, planned and utilized in cooperation with local industrial leaders. Most of these students enjoy using their hands. Let them go into industry, learn the necessary skills and earn a wage for their effort.

Elementary children can be introduced

to homemaking, shop work, grooming, modern dance, creative art, and basic economics in its simplest form. These youngsters need to know how to get a job, how to budget money, and how to live an adequate and happy life — not bank financing, theme writing and Shakespeare.

The enormous problem of reading deficiency must be tackled from the earliest possible moment. Remedial reading courses and parental involvement in this problem must be in constant progress.

One approach that can be beneficial to the ghetto child is the non-graded school. How much easier and pleasant it is for a student to go through school learning at his own rate without traumatic experiences. The ghetto youngster has much to gain from the informal atmosphere where he can learn by experiencing things, by investigating and discovering. The teacher is no longer a manipulator but rather an initiator. He no longer pulls the strings or is the center of attention. Instead, he poses the questions which the students can investigate.

The introduction of Negro history into inner city schools is an important curriculum change that is long overdue. Negro history or culture courses must not, however, be isolated in the curriculum.

They should not even be restricted to American history. Negro history should be woven into all phases of the curriculum: music, art, literature, science, math, and history.

Nor is there any reason to limit this subject to the ghetto. Negro history should also be taught in those schools with predominately white students. All students need to know of Benjamin Banneker, Phyllis Wheatley, Paul L. Dunbar, Nat Turner and others who were part of this forgotten and misplaced history.

There are many other aspects of the

curriculum that must be adapted to the needs of the inner city.

The typical ghetto school should be a friendly place, not a place of fear and embarrassment as it has been in the past. It should be open day and night and throughout the week and year. With so much to contribute to the community, it should never close.

Remedial work, recreational activities, home management, cooking and sewing classes, shop and construction work, modern dance, dietetics, creative arts, and human relations courses are just a few of the many classes that could be taken by both adults and children. How rewarding to see father and son or mother and daughter going to the same classes, excited over the prospect of learning something practical that will better their real existence.

Just as outdated as the curriculum are the buildings themselves. For the most part, the ghetto schools are 50 to 60 years old. They were planned and built with concepts of education and philosophies which have changed drastically in the last half century. Time and time again, study groups and teachers have related to boards of education that in most ghetto schools, the educational equipment is obsolete. Studies have shown that with the latest technological equipment, students not only learn faster but accumulate a greater storehouse of knowledge.

A further consideration is the pride instilled in the youngster who comes to a clean school, sits at a mar-free desk, is able to see the latest films, and to utilize other modern equipment. The opportunity to provide this must not casually be tossed aside with the excuse that it is too expensive.

While there are many excellent and creative teachers in the ghetto we do not find the inner city facilities on an even par with the suburban schools.

Teachers in the ghetto are usually unprepared to teach black children. When I began, I had no conception of the enormous problems encountered in the ghetto. The unfortunate result is that the unprepared teacher must learn through trial and error, and it is primarily through error.

Many other ghetto teachers are those who have been teaching for 30 or 40 years, have gone through the transitions of the neighborhood and often resent the new community and the changing standards. This is reflected in their instruction, their attitudes, and in their dedication.

Still another group of teachers in the ghetto are teachers who are not equipped to teach a particular area of the curriculum. I remember a teacher who was qualified to teach home economics but was instructing two sections of reading and three of history.

Finally, as in all types of school districts, there are those teachers who are illequipped, unprepared, or below standard in accumulated knowledge, methodology, and technique. These are the teachers who do not have certificates or have just made it through college. They are hired on a temporary basis because of teacher shortages in the ghetto schools. Usually these same teachers are hired year after year. These are the teachers who have the most disciplinary problems because they come to class ill-prepared and unorganized.

Those assigned to the ghetto schools should be the best possible teachers in the school system. They should be master teachers because the situation warrants the most creative, the most liberal, and the best trained teachers possible. The teacher in the ghetto school should be youthful, or at least have a young spirit about him.

Children can recognize this instantaneously and will get caught up with the teacher's spirit, creativity, and his outlook on life.

Teachers new to the ghetto as well as regular teachers should receive special training before they enter the ghetto school system. This is essential to the success of the teacher as well as the students. Through a workshop situation, the new teacher can become more familiar with the life, standard of living, educational difficulties, aspirations, teaching techniques, motivations and the realizations of the black community.

Another aspect that must be considered is the integration of the staff. The black community demands an integrated school faculty with Negro and white principals so that their children may be able to recognize all aspects of our total environment.

Despite talk about solutions and experimentation with these approaches, schools are slow to implement them into the educational programs of the ghetto schools. I would hope that we have the courage to stand up to boards of education with conservative policies and help turn these potentialities into actualities. Only then can true progress be accomplished in the ghetto classroom.

Chapter II

Discussionette

1. As an individual teacher, what could you do to help the urban youngster if you taught in a large city school system?

2. Could you *really* meet the needs of this urban child if you yourself had never lived in an urban area?

3. Are teachers who grew up in urban areas successful teaching in rural areas?

4. What educational objectives do you consider so important to the welfare of this nation that the laws enacted about them are completely justified?

5. How would you handle students who are in conflict with these objectives?

6. Discuss the "facts" which educators must face regarding the delinquent and his school experience.

7. What can the teacher do to help meet the needs of this student-delinquent in the school program?

8. What is the role of the teacher when faced with a delinquent in the schools?

9. Are many white people in this country *really* familiar with ghetto life?

10. What type of curriculum is best for ghetto youngsters?

11. Can a non-graded school help a ghetto child? A multi-unit school? etc.

12. Describe a situation where a situation might require a limit on freedom for the purpose of protecting the students and the school from harsh consequences.

13. Might this situation disrupt the academic process seriously?

14. Would the consequences of this situation be dangerous to life and property?

15. Could this situation be controlled within the limits of the faculty's authority?

Discussionette Words and Concepts

strong-arm	educate	growth
punishment	rights vs. responsibility	threat
economic needs	humiliate	discipline
freedom of expression	delinquent	standards

Try to use these words.

Try to explain these words.

Try to relate these words and their concepts to current or emerging educational patterns regarding discipline in the public school.

COMMON CAUSES OF DISCIPLINARY PROBLEMS

INTRODUCTION

ALTHOUGH THERE ARE DIFFERENCES of opinions concerning classroom control and methods for achieving it, all teachers will agree that a pleasant, well-disciplined classroom atmosphere results in more effective learning for all. However, some teachers do not set the stage or create an environment of a pleasant, well-disciplined classroom atmosphere. Consequently, discipline problems develop due to teacher behavior and influence.

Ambiguous rules, traditional rules, teacher attitude and behavior, etc. are a few of the common causes of disciplinary problems. Quite often teachers have actually sown the seed of their own disciplinary problems without knowledge or forethought to the repercussion of their own actions.

Too often teachers perpetuate rules without knowing why they do so, what purpose the rules serve, or what the total effect of the rule is on either the class as a whole or an individual student.

Teachers must be aware of their own actions and consequences which cause disciplinary problems to develop. Chapter III isolates and highlights the common causes for discipline problems in the public schools.

An Unguarded Moment*
Leslie J. Chamberlin

Furthermore, your child is a louse . . . L-O-U-S-E!" After carefully spelling the word, the teacher would have continued to make other statements about the child, but by then the parent had a few points to make herself. This statement, made to a parent by an irritated teacher during a parent-teacher-pupil-principal conference, led to an embarrassing situation for all concerned.

Words are usually, but not always, the materials used by teachers to build such situations. Recently, one thirteen-year-old New York girl was awarded over $40,000 by the State Supreme Court in a damage suit which resulted from a teacher's striking the girl and pushing her from her desk. Spur-of-the-moment discipline using a ruler, pointer, or whatever happens to be in the hand; what was meant to be a light push or shove to encourage a slow or obstinate student to follow directions; or a well meant, but not quite ethical, comment to the class about a particular person or situation, can often result in trouble for the teacher and everyone professionally associated with him.

Why do well educated, professional people allow serious situations, such as those described, to develop? How do they

*Reprinted from *Instructor,* February 1971©. The Instructor Publications, Inc., Dansville, N.Y.

become so deeply involved in these problems? A first impulse, especially if one is close to the situation, is to say that this teacher or that child is at fault and then to forget the problem, if possible. But I suggest that the problem is far more complicated and that many other factors need to be carefully examined.

Some Causes

"I like to be free and not have to stay in that crowded old classroom, . . . and it is so hot, and the janitor . . .," remarks one fourth-grader to another. Poor working conditions, such as over-crowded classrooms and poor heating or ventilating systems, can often be the indirect cause of disciplinary problems.

A lack of special programs, equipment, or facilities for the atypical child complicates the situation for the average teacher to such an extent that serious problems can develop. The seemingly nervous child who cannot remain at his desk or be quiet under any circumstances; the belligerent child who cannot get along with anyone, including the teacher; and the child who never finishes an assignment, even under the best situations, are special problem children who belong in programs especially designed and equipped to help them. When these programs and equipment are not available, and the atypical child is held in the regular classroom, problems result from the child's attempts to gain acceptance and to "save face."

A teacher may compensate for a poor physical setting, but he usually cannot change it very much. At times, however, the underlying cause of persistent discipline problems is the teacher. When students persistently talk back to the teacher or attempt to irritate by other means, such as refusing to follow directions or do any schoolwork at all, the cause may be the teacher's attitude toward the children or his manner of talking to them and dealing with them.

There are other factors, such as a child's home surroundings or his neighborhood environment, which contribute heavily to a disciplinary situation. The individual teacher can do little to alter these circumstances; nevertheless, he must be aware of them in order to allow for and compensate for their influence whenever possible.

Prevention

Beginning and experienced teachers who remain artless in this area often think of improving a poor disciplinary situation by moving a child to a different location in the classroom or simply telling the child that they "won't stand for that" in their classrooms. These techniques are usually satisfactory for restoring peace temporarily; however, good teachers know that maintaining a good learning climate is far more complicated.

Good classroom discipline is a climate composed of many factors, such as an understanding of the student's economic and cultural background, his religious beliefs, his home environment, and his neighborhood environment. Over and above these things there must be something about the teacher — a personality leadership — a charisma. In good disciplinary situations the whole often seems to be more than the sum of its parts. The factors, taken separately, could not bring about the climate for learning that the sum does. The proper factors must be present in the proper proportions for the right personalities. If a teacher is maintaining adequate classroom control, he is:

1. Providing a situation that is free from serious distractions.

2. Developing and supporting respect

for authority in the classroom and in the school.

3. Developing student ideals, interests, and skills which contribute to self-control and good citizenship.

4. Attempting to present a pleasing, sympathetic, and dynamic, but not dominating, teacher personality to the pupils.

In more cases than not, the initial impulse of a teacher responding to a disciplinary situation within his own classroom is one of anger, resentment, and often personal hurt. This reaction only defeats the teacher's efforts to maintain a good learning situation. In most cases there is nothing personal in the child's act, and even in the few cases where there is an attempt on the part of the child to hurt the teacher, the situation is only worsened by responding with a personal reaction.

Discipline problems should be dealt with objectively and firmly, but without rejecting the misbehaving child as a person. The teacher needs to look at the whole situation and try to locate the cause of the trouble.

To maintain a consistently good climate for learning, the teacher's attitude toward the children must be a positive one. He must attempt to understand the child's side of the situation and the factors that might be affecting his behavior. In general, the teacher must attempt to comprehend children — youthful, vigorous, joyful, potential, but also insecure, full of doubt, and wanting to please. He must have a flexible attitude and a responsive nature that reacts to the children's needs and desires. He must be unafraid, fairly uninhibited, and capable of plain talking when necessary.

The good teacher invites, encourages, and stimulates children to behave, participate, and learn. He realizes that modern discipline, which emphasizes self-control and self-direction, is one of the most diffi-

cult things a child must master. He realizes that any contribution he should make toward pupils' worthwhile development depends largely on his skill in managing pupils in a manner which conforms to a psychology of self-direction.

Control

All teachers have discipline problems, some so persistent that an individual may feel that he is sure to lose his temper or do something desperate. Techniques to safeguard these situations are needed. Every teacher needs to plan for the possibility of such a situation developing. He should have a plan of action which will give temporary but immediate relief to the situation.

For example, there are times when a pupil should be sent from the classroom without many words. A written slip should be kept ready for such occasions. A good practice is to say just a few words to the child at the door to let him know why he is being sent out. Sending an offending pupil from the room, usually to the principal's office, is one of the most frequently used methods of classroom control. To insure that the practice is not over-worked, however, a teacher should send a child from the room only when the best interest of the class demands it. Also, before sending a child from the room, the teacher should consider using various alternate disciplinary approaches.

Whenever a pupil is sent out of the room as a temporary measure, this should be made clear to all concerned at the outset. If the teacher wishes the principal to handle the problem, this should be understood by everyone, and the circumstances connected with the situation should be put in writing.

Sometimes just arranging for a child to be by himself for a time solves the immediate situation and gives the teacher time to delve deeper into the trouble. Sending the child on an errand, asking him to work on some special project, or just asking him to stand in the hall or somewhere away from the class are useful ways of arranging for him to be alone for a short time.

But just when should a teacher take action? Just when is a classroom situation considered serious? At one time or another these questions trouble most teachers, especially the beginning teacher. There seem to be three stages in the development of a serious disciplinary situation:

1. Whispering and inactivity.

2. Laughing, talking, writing notes, and horseplay.

3. Complete disorder, which often involves tripping, punching, throwing missiles, catcalls, and open disrespect for the teacher in charge.

A classroom situation that reaches the second or third stage should be considered serious, and steps to restore order should be taken immediately.

Professional teachers realize that one of the best ways to improve their teaching effectiveness and to avoid disciplinary pitfalls is to welcome classroom visitation by professional supervisors. Supervision will encourage the teacher to work for the best possible classroom control.

Supervisors may notice antagonistic or belligerent pupil attitudes that result from teaching techniques. They may notice flippant remarks or unfriendly looks of which the teacher is completely unaware. If this information is presented to the teacher in a professional way, he then can take corrective action.

Supervisors also are usually more experienced and more familiar with the community resources that are available to help with a particular problem. Superior teachers learn to seek this advice and make use of available community help. For example, where poor home surroundings or a negative neighborhood environment are contributing to a school problem, the teacher must use all of the resources available to control and improve the situation in which he is involved.

Good teachers report that thorough lesson planning, conferences with students and parents, and a careful study of the characteristics of the persons who are involved help to control pupils without punishing too frequently. Proper classroom organization saves time and energy, and helps to preserve order. Devising definite methods of seating pupils, recording attendance, directing traffic, distributing and collecting materials, arranging and caring for equipment, regulating light, heat, and ventilation, and seeing that desks and floors are kept neat, are all important factors in maintaining good classroom control. By decreasing the number of disciplinary situations that may develop, the teacher increases his teaching effectiveness.

Student Violence and Rebellion*
David Iwamoto

"What are these kids coming to?" an out-

*Reprinted from *NEA Journal*, Dec. 1965, p. 10. Used by permission. Article based in part on: National Education Association, Research Division. *Students Behavior in Secondary Schools, 1964.* Research Report 1965-R12. Washington, D.C.: the Association, August, 1965. 36 pp.

raged teacher asked his principal after being punched in the face by a student. "Can't we call the police?"

A short while before in the same school system a student riot had prompted an investigation by a committee of prominent citizens. The committee had found that violence and open disrespect toward teachers were rampant in many school buildings and that administrators were apparently either afraid to act or were unable to cope with the situation.

In another city, a newspaper reported attacks on five teachers in one day. This brought to forty-five the number of physical attacks against teachers in a three-week period, the paper said.

In Detroit, Chicago, New York, and in other large cities proposals have been made that policemen be stationed in or near some schools to curb student violence. Some teachers in these school systems are asking their administration for medical and life insurance because of increasing student attacks.

To learn the extent of student violence and rebellion, and to study the opinions of teachers on the causes, the NEA Research Division recently conducted a sample survey of the nation's public secondary school teachers. The questionnaire asked: "During this school year, has any act of physical violence against a classroom teacher or principal been committed by a student *attending your school?*" An act of physical violence was defined a "striking or attacking with fists, knife, gun, or other object that could cause physical injury."

Nearly 15 percent of the teachers replied, "yes." The percentage of affirmative answers from teachers in large school systems (25,000 or more students) was more than three times higher than that from teachers in smaller systems (50 to 2,999 students), 24.0 percent as compared with 7.4 percent.

The percentage of all teachers reporting an act of physical violence against themselves was 1.4 percent, but the figure for teachers in large systems was 2.5 percent, nearly twice as high. A projection of the

1.4 percent to the total population of public secondary school teachers in the United States suggests that as many as 10,000 classroom teachers were physically attacked by students during the first seven months of the last school year. This number includes more than twice as many men teachers as women teachers (6,800 to 3,200).

Fights among students occur occasionally in almost all secondary schools, but nearly 6 percent of the teachers, including the 11 percent of those in large systems, said that fights occurred frequently in their schools. Most fights seemed to have broken out spontaneously; gang fights were rare.

Nevertheless, weapons which the newspapers often associate with juvenile gang warfare turned up in quantity in some schools, according to the survey. In one incident a year ago, the principal of a junior high school in a large city got wind of an impending "rumble" between two juvenile gangs. With the cooperation of the police, he instituted a search of student lockers. The search yielded a small arsenal — bicycle chains, clubs, brass knuckles, ice picks, a hatchet, a butcher knife, and three homemade zip guns. In another city, a high school student was found carrying a sawed-off shotgun to school. His explanation: "I brought it for protection."

The Research Division survey found that about 8 percent, or some 53,000, of the nation's secondary school classroom teachers either confiscated or asked others to confiscate a dangerous weapon from a student in their classrooms last year. Nevertheless, fewer than 1 teacher in 100 indicated that carrying of dangerous weapons was widespread in his school.

Organized strikes or demonstrations have become a well-publicized vehicle for student protest against teachers, administrators, or school regulations. About 4 percent of the survey respondents said that they knew of one or more demonstrations in their school *during* school hours. In addition, 3.4 percent recalled such demonstrations *outside* school hours.

According to the survey, the most common type of demonstration was a boycott or partial boycott of the school cafeteria. However, not all cafeteria "sit-outs" were directed against the allegedly poor quality of the food. In one high school, seniors refused to eat in the cafeteria after accusing the administration of withholding such privileges as leaving the auditorium first or going to "senior court" — a place outside the building — during study hall periods.

In one high-income suburban community, students put out a clandestine publication urging classmates to boycott the cafeteria on a particular day. Speaking as the "only uncensored voice" in the school, the pamphleteers charged that students played no significant part in governing the school and that the cafeteria was a mess. On the designated day, more than half the students who normally purchased their noon meal in the cafeteria stayed away at lunchtime. But the cafeteria manager had seen the publication too and had scheduled a menu of hot dogs and cheese sandwiches which could be prepared as needed. As a result, little food was wasted, the manager said.

Most cafeteria demonstrations were reported to have been peaceful, but in one school students began their protest by throwing empty milk cartons on the floor and then at each other. The lunch period ended in a flurry of fist fights.

Many high school demonstrations originate with the seniors, who often look upon themselves as a privileged group. When they feel their privileges are denied, they will occasionally do something outlandish in defiance of school regulations. For instance, senior boys in one school protested by dressing up like panhandlers and going through the halls begging for privileges.

In another school, seniors organized a "stay-at-home day." In still another school, they refrained for one day from doing any work in their classes as a protest against a ruling that restricted attendance at their senior prom to seniors only.

Sometimes the cruelest kind of student group action is that directed against an individual teacher. One teacher in the survey told of a case in which "odds were announced and bets taken in school by certain students who claimed they could make a young beginning teacher cry before the semester was over."

According to the survey, the most common form of organized group action against a classroom teacher is the gathering of signatures on a petition that is to be presented to the principal or some other school authority. But in one reported instance, students walked out of a classroom during a lesson and marched in a body to the principal's office. Harassment of certain teachers by constant irritating interruptions and sarcastic responses is an old but still used technique, report the teachers.

Mass coughing and clapping and stamping in unison were commonly reported study hall disturbances. One teacher said students who felt that the required assembly programs were "insufferably boring and a waste of time," greeted the introduction of a program with loud and persistent clapping, shouting, and whistling.

Not all student demonstrations were related to seemingly trivial causes. School boycotts and demonstrations in protest of alleged racial segregation or integration were reported by teachers both in some northern and in some southern school systems. Few such demonstrations have led to violence.

Newspapers throughout the country have carried stories with such headlines as "Students Attack Teacher," "Weapons Seized in School Raid," "Gang Invades High School Prom." The number and frequency of these stories leave the impression that our schools are overrun with student violence and rebellion. How true is this impression?

Although the 1964 Research Division survey did find numerous incidents of violence, rebellion, strikes, and demonstrations in some schools, *it found the vast majority of schools to be free of such disturbances.* For example, 98.6 percent of the high school teachers said that they had *not* been attacked by students, 85.3 percent were in schools where *no* attacks had been reported against teachers, 92.4 percent had *not* found it necessary to confiscate dangerous weapons, and 96.4 percent knew of *no* student strikes or demonstrations in their schools during school hours.

Furthermore, when the Research Division asked teachers, "In your opinion, about how many of your students are real troublemakers—the type who cause trouble frequently and who cause a lot of trouble?" more than a third reported that not even one such student was in their classes. A projection based on these responses indicates that, in the opinion of teachers, only 3 students in 100 are real troublemakers.

The survey also asked teachers to rate each of their classes according to its general behavior (excellent, good, fair, or poor). They rated 78 out of 100 classes excellent or good and only 4 out of 100 poor; 18 out of 100 were rated fair.

Other surveys, such as the one reported by Eugene Gilbert in *This Week* magazine (Feb. 7, 1965), indicate that teen-agers are generally more responsible today than they were ten years ago. The statistics quoted by Gilbert show, for example, that more teen-agers work at parttime jobs now than in 1955, more stay in school and graduate, and more go on to college. In addition, a greater percentage of teen-agers perform regular chores at home than was true ten years ago, and more teen-agers are involved in volunteer community service work than ever before.

Why then do some teen-agers get into trouble? How do teachers see the causes for misbehavior and rebellion?

The Research Division survey listed seventeen factors or conditions frequently mentioned as causes of misbehavior in school and asked teachers to indicate the extent to which each is directly or indirectly responsible for whatever misbehavior exists in their schools. The four most significant factors, according to teachers, were closely related to the students' family life. These were:

- Irresponsible parents
- Unsatisfactory home conditions (low income, inadequate housing, broken families)
- Lack of training or experience of students in moral and spiritual values
- Increased availability of automobiles to teen-agers.

Various studies tend to support the teachers' opinion on the causes of misbehavior. For example, the noted sociologists, Sheldon and Eleanor Glueck, concluded that by considering five factors in the home environment of a five- or six-year-old it should be possible to predict quite accurately whether he will become a delinquent.

These factors are discipline of the boy by the father, supervision of the boy by the mother, affection of the father for the boy, affection of the mother for the boy, and the cohesion in the home. If these factors are rated low in the boy's home, regardless of whether he lives in a slum or a high-income suburb, the chances are good that he will become a delinquent.

Crumbling family structure seems to be the greatest cause of delinquent and troublemaking behavior among students who come out of slum environments, but similar problems can occur under conditions far removed from those in the slums. Although more parents are giving their children more of the "good things in life" than ever before, many parents are withholding the most needed element of all— sound parental guidance—so say the teachers in the NEA Research Division survey.

Although the teachers listed home factors as contributing most to adolescent behavior problems, they were not willing to place all the blame on the parents. They also placed high on their list such school-related factors as lack of special attention for academically retarded students; school program or curriculum unsuited to the needs of some students; overcrowded classes; lack of authority by teachers to determine and administer punishment; and failure to receive support from principals and other school authorities in dealing with behavior problems.

Where the school itself contributes to the cause of disorder, teachers urged self-examination and correction. Troublemakers, they found, were usually themselves deeply troubled by personal problems. Where teachers and administrators seek to help a student get to the root of his personal problems, they may be helping him to stay out of trouble in school.

Behavior: Disturbed or Disturbing?*

Ronald R. Kyllonen, M.D.

Because children spend such large blocks of time during their actively growing and developing phase of life under the guidance and control of the schools, teachers should consider some of the problems involved in the recognition and interpretation of disturbed childhood behavior.

These problems most often arise from a difficulty in definition. What do we mean by disturbed behavior? Too often we mean simply disturbing behavior, behavior that is annoying and intolerable to us as individuals, and our judgment is, therefore, based on our own conceptions of what is acceptable and normal behavior.

The active or disruptive child gets noticed because he is disturbing, but what about the quiet child? From the psychiatrist's point of view, the quiet, withdrawn

*Reprinted from *NEA Journal*, September 1964. Used with permission.

child is probably just as much in need of help, because he may be disturbed even though he is not disturbing others. We all view the extremely lazy child as abnormal, but what about the perfectionistic child?

Let us consider two aspects of the standards by which children such as those just mentioned are judged.

First, we must recognize that behavioral standards are in a large measure culture-bound. What we would clearly define as deviant behavior in midwestern suburbia might be completely acceptable in the jungles of the big city or darkest Africa. We define behavioral patterns in terms of our own background. Generally speaking, the teaching profession is middle-class in its values. As teachers, we must, therefore, remind ourselves that definitions, attitudes, and ideas do not apply when an attempt is made to project them into a different ethical and cultural milieu.

In the middle class, for instance, it is not considered unmanly to be intelligent or educated, and sex-role differences are not extreme. Stable, middle-class boys, therefore, generally have no hesitancy about achieving in school and are reasonably comfortable in partially identifying with women teachers.

We encounter difficulties, however, with children from backgrounds in which educational achievement or partial feminine identification are not acceptable.

An example of this is the case of a seventeen-year-old boy who was a patient of mine for two years. He was simply not able to perform scholastically until he came under the tutelage of a male English teacher with whom he could identify. He adopted many of the teacher's manners and ideas while working under his guidance. Thus, this relationship with a well-educated male adult improved the boy's poise, self-confidence, and social performance as well as his scholastic achievement.

In addition to assessing and understanding differing cultural values, teachers need to understand the difference between male and female patterns of behavior. We expect and encourage boys and girls to behave differently.

The traditional belief has been that maleness and femaleness are largely "wired into" the individual and that psychological sex identity is based on the genetic sexuality. This does not appear to be the case. According to J. L. and J. G. Hampson, "in the human psychologic sexuality is not differentiated when the child is born. Rather, psychologic sex becomes differentiated during the course of the many experiences of growing up, including those experiences dictated by his or her own bodily equipment."

The Hampsons conducted an interesting experiment in their study of children born with an ambiguous sexuality, that is, external genitalia that are not clearly male or female. All the children studied took on a sexual role compatible with the sex to which they had been assigned whether this did or did not coincide with their basic genetic sex. Their behavior was, therefore, determined by their learning experiences in active involvement with the adults and world about them.

In a systematic study reported by E. K. Beller and P. B. Neubauer, "overall differences were found in the patternings of problems for boys and for girls. Aggression, hyperactivity, and temper tantrums constituted an interrelated cluster of impulsiveness which appeared more often in boys than in girls." The study found that in girls there was also a patterning of symptoms relating to impulse control as a central difficulty, but "the interrelated problems of girls pointed toward overcontrol and indirect expression of impulses." This particular study, on a group of children of pre-school age, suggested that "boys in our culture tend to express defiance by lack of impulse control, whereas defiance by overcontrol is more common in girls."

What does this mean in terms of the assessment of problems? Since three to four times as many boys as girls are referred for treatment because of psychiatric problems, one might conclude from this that girls are stronger. This does not seem to be the case, however. It appears, rather, that the defense of passivity conforms closely with the behavior our society sanctions, condones, or at least expects of girls.

Among those children who, in the adolescent years, require such drastic measures as institutionalization, the girls are, as a group, more disturbed than the boys. In a sense, the populations of girls and boys are not really comparable, since, in most cases, we overlook the problems of girls as long as their overt behavior conforms with the cultural norms, and we become alarmed only when their self-concept becomes so disordered that the only clear avenue of expression open to them is sexual activity.

People generally recognize deviation from expected behavior more readily in boys. The effeminate child is often an object of contempt and avoidance. Maleness tends to be equated with the capacity to be outwardly and vigorously assertive and competitive. It is safe to say that the boy who is noncompetitive, nonassertive, and nonvigorous is having a problem in his basic identification.

Many schools provide remedial reading, remedial writing, and speech therapy, but to my knowledge none has yet offered a course in remedial role-playing behavior within the school situation.

Incoordination and poor physical performance is something that accumulates from year to year. The boy who can't catch well at ten avoids playing catch and ends up at sixteen being excluded from activities because he is clumsy, poorly coordinated, and "throws like a girl."

Meanwhile the physical education instructor or coach may spend his time with the already adept, well-equipped athlete and ignore the poorly coordinated, highly anxious, fearful boy.

Such youngsters are clearly having trouble and are not infrequently referred for psychiatric treatment. What might work equally well, however, would be to provide a noncoercive, protective opportunity for these children to acquire the basic physical skills away from the critical eye and scorn of their classmates. In this way they could learn to cope with the competitiveness and aggressiveness of their play situation. Incidentally, if the boy identifies with the teacher in the course of this tutelage, this could have some corrective, if not frankly preventive, worth.

Often, the boy himself will be the first to sense that he is not meeting the cultural expectations of masculinity. His reaction will be to fight back in whatever way he sees fit.

In the primary grades the pattern is frequently that of hyperactive, disturbing, disruptive behavior coupled with a poor performance in reading and arithmetic. In the elementary years, poor grades in all school subjects may seem to be the main trouble, although disruptive or deviant behavior may also cause concern. Sooner or later, boys who exhibit these symptoms in school are likely to be in trouble with the community and its laws, regulations, and rules.

To link these behaviors in a graphic fashion, we might say that each is a manifestation of the "squashed male" syndrome. This choice of a label does communicate and convey the underlying factor that his very masculinity has been squashed out of him. His deviant, protesting-too-much manner contradicts the basic fear he feels inside.

Too frequently people respond with annoyance and anger at these boys and see them as frankly nasty. Those who listen carefully to the message these boys are sending, however, can often detect a pattern of vague depression and anxiety. Their disruptive behavior is usually an attempt to reassure themselves that they are not weak or to deny failure and create the illusion of success.

I hope that this brief discussion about how cultural bias and expectations affect sexual roles may stimulate further thought.

Early referral and early treatment greatly enhance the possibility of dealing effectively with emotional problems. Therefore, teachers who see and observe numbers of children on a regular basis should consider disruptive behavior carefully for signs of underlying problems, which may then be referred to the proper professionals, rather than try to coerce the child into line without understanding the total picture.

Teachers, like therapists, must also be aware of themselves. They must take an occasional introspective look in order to understand what types of children they work best with, to note what types of children give them particular trouble, and at least to speculate on the reasons why this is so.

There are pleasing signs of a revolution in the teaching system today: Conformity is stressed to a lesser degree, individual originality is allowed, and students can be direct and open in relationship to the adults about them. In the case of either boys or girls, directness, openness, and frank expression of feelings may prevent many of the deviant and disrupted behavioral patterns that result when feelings are forced to go underground.

Student Unrest*

S. L. Halleck, M.D.

● College students can no longer be taken for granted. Though the great majority of them remain largely content, conservative, and apathetic, a determined minority of restless ones have forced us to examine and sometimes to change institutions, rules, and values that were once considered inviolate.

Restless students include those who have rejected the political and economic status quo and are making vigorous attempts to change the structure of our society. These are the student activists.

Other students reject the values of their society as well as the values of their own past and are developing a style of life that is contradictory to the Western ethic of hard work, self-denial, success, and responsibility. Such students sometimes participate in efforts to change the society, but for the most part they are withdrawn and passive. These are the alienated.

Both activists and alienated students tend to come from middle- or upper-class homes. They are sensitive, perceptive, and highly intelligent individuals.

Both activist and alienated students have

difficulty in relating to the adult generation. They are articulate, irreverent, humorless, and relentless in their contempt for what they view as adult hypocrisy. Highly peer-oriented, they turn to one another rather than to their parents when shaping their beliefs or when they are seeking emotional support.

Alienated students and, to a lesser extent, activist students find it difficult to sustain goal-directed activity. Their capacity to organize for any kind of action is limited. They often fail at work or school.

Alienated students live at the edge of despair. Although they seem at times to be enjoying life, there is always a sense of foreboding about them. Activist students are more emotionally stable but are also prone to deep feelings of hopelessness and self-pity.

No hypothesis thus far advanced can be considered a sufficient explanation of the roots of student unrest. At best, each provides a partial explanation that sheds only a small light upon a highly complex phenomenon.

Those who are critical of student activism and alienation are most likely to

*Reprinted from *Today's Education*, September 1968. Used with permission.

seek its causes in factors that they believe have created a moral weakness in our youth. They believe students are restless because they lack discipline, values, or purpose. Their deficiencies are blamed on the disturbed family; their behavior charged to unresolved conflicts within the family unit.

These hypotheses emphasize the decline in authority of the paternal figure, the confusion of sexual roles in our society, and the break with tradition that such confusion produces. But sociological studies of students and their families do not support any hypothesis of family pathology. In fact, such studies suggest that activist students, at least, come from rather stable families. The most we can say is that some aspects of student restlessness may be related to family disturbance.

Many people say student unrest results from too much permissiveness in rearing children. Proponents of this view argue that some parents, through painstaking efforts to avoid creating neuroses in their off-spring, have abdicated their responsibility to teach and discipline their children. In so doing, they have reared a generation of spoiled, greedy youth who react to the slightest frustration with an angry or infantile response.

The permissiveness hypothesis cannot be lightly dismissed. There is considerable evidence that activist and alienated students are members of well-educated families, deeply committed to liberal doctrines. In such homes, children are given unusual freedom to criticize, debate, and question. They frequently attend primary and secondary schools dedicated to the ideal of progressive education, schools that in their efforts to maximize freedom and creativity seek to minimize discipline and frustration.

The response of such students to discipline is in no sense adaptive. Arbitrary regulations enrage them. Even rational forms of discipline, such as the need to master basic concepts before moving on to more abstract ideas, bother them. Restless students also react inappropriately when their demands are not immediately met. They are apt to protest violently, to give up and withdraw, or to wrap themselves in a cloak of despair. Much of their abrasiveness and some of their ineffectiveness can be explained by their uncompromising demands for immediate gratification.

Many who are concerned about the dangers of permissiveness also believe that our culture has been "psychologized" to an extent where youth becoming unwilling to assume responsibility for their own behavior. When a behavior is totally explained, people tend to act as though they are no longer responsible for that behavior. The adolescent who participates in a riot, for example, may say, "How could I do otherwise? I am moved by forces over which I have no control."

Other critics of student unrest often blame it all on the alleged hazards of growing up in an affluent society. They argue that unearned affluence, unless accompanied by a tradition of service and commitment, creates a sense of restlessness, boredom, and meaninglessness in our youth. The child raised in an affluent society has difficulty finding useful goals, they contend. He does not learn to use work or creativity as a means of mastering some aspect of the world. He is therefore caught in a never-ending search for new diversions and new freedoms that sooner or later begin to pall.

It does seem probable that man is less likely to be troubled when he is deeply involved in some monumental task that dominates his life goals. In a relatively poor society, the very need for survival creates a structured and seemingly purposeful life; in a rich society, on the other hand, man has the time and freedom to question the meaning of his existence.

Critics of student unrest would reserve their harshest barbs for those newly wealthy parents who, being themselves so caught up in a materialistic, pleasure-seeking life, fail to meet their responsibility of teaching children the kinds of values that would lend meaning to a young person's existence.

A second group of hypotheses put the student in a more favorable light. They regard him as a victim of man-made circumstances and maintain that student unrest is a legitimate and rational effort to change these circumstances. The student is viewed as either a helpless victim of a world he never created or as a hero seeking to cleanse the world of the evils of previous generations.

This generation of students has grown up in an age when the world has been divided into two large camps that compete with each other ideologically, politically, and sometimes militarily. And since the Russians launched their first satellite, the competition has spread to education. Students today are trained in a school system that emphasizes the competitive acquisition of knowledge as a source of power and stability. By the time they leave high school, they are better educated than any previous generation but they are also more overworked.

The student arrives at college at least partially "burned out." Even if he maintains some enthusiasm for academic work through the undergraduate years, by the time he reaches graduate school he increasingly asks himself whether the intensive search for knowledge is worth it.

He gradually begins to view our never-ending competition with the communist world (and sometimes competitiveness it-self) as a form of mass paranoia, and he views the university as an agent of the government that contributes toward the perpetuation of the paranoid system. He reacts by protest or withdrawal.

Although student unrest began long before the war in Vietnam ever escalated to massive proportions, in my opinion there can be little doubt that in the past few years this conflict has been the major factor influencing the behavior of students. Much of the restless behavior of students can be directly related to their efforts to do something to stop the war or to their sense of total frustration because they are powerless to stop it.

The draft and the inequities engendered by the II-S deferment also contribute to unrest. The average male college student is plagued with fears that he will fail in school, will be drafted, and will perhaps be killed in a conflict he may not consider vital to our interests.

A second issue is guilt. The undergraduate student knows that he is spared from military service only because he is richer or smarter than someone else. While he may believe that the war is immoral, he also believes that his privileged status is immoral. When he accepts the II-S status, he suffers guilt. And I believe much of the activism on our college campuses is a means of atoning for that guilt or of denying the relevance of the society that created such guilt.

Many believe that student unrest is an appropriate response to the deterioration of the quality of life across the nation. Overpopulation, which results in crowds, traffic jams, and businesses run on the basis of mass production, has taken much of the joy out of life in our towns and cities. People begin to feel faceless and insignificant.

Students, it can be argued, are among

the first to sense the painful anonymity associated with bigness. The problem is particularly serious on overcrowded campuses where students are usually isolated from their teachers and other adults. A sense of student-faculty intimacy or a sense of scholarly community are sorely lacking on our large campuses. Students find it difficult to develop a sense of identification or loyalty toward a university that they perceive as monolithic and impersonal.

Guided by the philosophy of Herbert Marcuse, many students are convinced that constructive change within our society cannot be brought about by working through the present system. They argue that our society is so complex, our systems of checks and balances so intricate, and our interplay of pressure groups so self-equalizing that really effective change is no longer possible.

Although they have no sort of vision as to what will replace the older order, they are convinced that our society is fundamentally irrational and must be destroyed.

Finally, the civil rights movement not only increased youth's awareness of a historical injustice that made it difficult for them to be proud of this country but also served as a training ground for future radicals. Commitment to the Negro's cause has taught students the psychological meaning of oppression and has encouraged them to seek out and attack sources of oppression in the students' own lives.

So much for the critical and sympathetic explanations for unrest. Other explanations of student unrest focus upon impersonal or neutral processes. According to these hypotheses, the causes of unrest reside in changes in our highly complex society that demand new modes of psychological adaptation by students.

Postwar America has been characterized by a massive and continuous growth of technology. Moreover, the rate at which technology changes our lives is itself increasing. No one can predict what life will be like in 20 years, 10 years, or even 5 years.

Kenneth Keniston has described how some youth, exposed to an ever-increasing rate of technological growth, have come to perceive that the values of the past will be totally inappropriate for the world in which they will be adults. Moreover, they feel powerless to anticipate or direct the future. In this environment, where hope no longer sustains, it is adaptive to be cool, to learn to live in the present.

The advantages of living in the present are more or less obvious. One is more flexible and superficially, at least, more comfortable. One need not delay gratification or be tortured by the mistakes of the past or be deluded by unrealistic hopes for the future.

The disadvantages of life in the present are more subtle, yet more powerful. To live in the present one must narrow his commitments. He must travel light and be ready for anything. More intimate relationships are unlikely, since they cannot be sustained by reference to past experience or to promise of a better future. Passion and romantic longing must be avoided because they may breed pain or impair one's flexibility. In short, if carried to extremes, life in the present is a selfish life incompatible with the growth of that intimacy and passion man has always found essential to a fulfilled life.

The psychological impact of TV has been linked to the troubling behavior of students. Fredric Wertham believes that the massive degree of violence that young people see on television makes them more violent and less responsible. Vance Packard has argued that chronic exposure to the values implied in TV commercials could create a generation of unrealistic, demanding, and now-oriented youth. I would like to propose my own hypothesis of student unrest based on the manner in which TV (and other kinds of mass media) influences the character structure of youth by prematurely confronting them with the harsh truths and realities of life.

The relatively slow growth and development of man requires him to be dependent upon others for a long period of time, and he, therefore, learns to rely on others for an optimal amount of structure and order in his life.

The relatively slow growth and development of man requires him to be dependent upon others for a long period of time, and he, therefore, learns to rely on others for an optimal amount of structure and order in his life.

Each individual finds his own identity at least partly by experiencing limitations imposed by others, by respecting others, and by emulating those who are respected. Man's first taste of authority—and life—is familial.

The most well-meaning parents must on occasion deceive their children because they know that children would find many of the hard and cynical facts of life unbearable. In the past, most young people did not begin to experience the world as adults know it until after they had reached adolescence. Usually, the adolescent absorbed this new knowledge gradually and rather painlessly. Even when he did feel that his parents had deceived him, his awareness of their dishonesty came so gradually that his resentment and rebelliousness were restrained. Today it is different. The mass media communicate information to all age groups immediately and without selectivity.

Television and other media acquaint youth with the cynical facts of life at a time when such truths may be indigestible. They communicate knowledge so quickly that there is little opportunity for anyone to live comfortably with myth or self-delusion. Beliefs once accepted are vigorously scrutinized.

The effect on our youth of premature emergence of truth has been to create a deep skepticism as to the validity of authority. Neither the family, the church, the law, nor any institution commands the automatic respect it once did.

What is more, today's youth have grown up in a world that has increasingly turned to science rather than religion for many of the answers to the questions of life.

The restless student is one who has taken the message of science, rationality, and the perfectibility of man literally. He is more open to action and change than were earlier generations of students. In his conviction that there are rational solutions to any problem, he is intolerant of the irrationalities of those who prevent progress. And he is not equipped to understand or deal with the depth of that irrationality in man which resists change and leads man to seek his own destruction.

Hopefully, this review has been more than an exercise in cataloging. By emphasizing the diversity of explanations of student unrest, I have tried to show the intellectual futility of searching for simple explanations of a highly complex phenomenon. As citizens, we may wish either to support or attack the causes that restless students have dramatized. But as scholars concerned with educating and understanding and helping students, we need a more objective approach. We must recognize that there is some truth to the most critical as well as the most sympathetic hypotheses.

These hypotheses raise many questions for those entrusted with the management of our colleges. Does the emphasis on education as a means rather than an end have any meaning in an affluent society? Should youth be encouraged to remain in a passive role as students throughout the first third of their lives? Are there means of bringing young people into important roles in the power structure of our colleges and our social system before they come to the age of 25 or 30?

Is the II-S classification anything more than a bribe that weakens the moral position of dissenting students and creates havoc upon our campuses? Should it be abolished? To what extent can we continue to depersonalize and enlarge our campuses without creating a generation of alienated youth who feel no sense of identity, no sense that they have a voice in what is done to them, and no sense of commitment to anything but their own selfish interests?

I believe that the neutral hypotheses are the most intriguing and the most valid explanations of student unrest. If progress itself, in the form of technology, science, or new media, is the most severe stress in the lives of our young people, then we are faced with a seemingly impossible task: controlling progress and change rather than allowing these forces to control us.

If we do nothing else, we must at least begin to take a look at the impact of technological progress upon man's personality. Only a handful of scientists and philosophers are seriously concerned with studying man's psychological future. No university or government agency has ever created a department or institute to study this problem.

The only effective solution would require a drastic revision of many of the traditions and structures of our society. Our first need is to study and to plan, to determine what kinds of technological progress are consistent with making man a better human being and what kinds are not. The latter must ultimately be rejected. We must find a way to communicate those values that are essential to man's survival to our children in an open and questioning but noncynical manner. I doubt that man can live without intimacy, without compassion, without ideology, without faith, without autonomy, without privacy, and without beauty, and still be man. We must reexamine our time-honored reverence for affluence, power, and bigness and face the possibility that affluence bores, that power corrupts, and that big institutions diminish the stature of man.

Conflict with a Pupil*

Clarke E. Moustakas

The inevitable conflicts in the classroom —between pupil and teacher, and between pupil and pupil—can become occasions for growth, when the caring of one person gives another strength and help.

A confrontation is a meeting of persons involving an issue or dispute. The confrontation happens sometimes suddenly and unexpectedly, and almost always un-

predictably. To be effectively resolved, it requires that the individuals remain together until there is a resolution of feeling. The individuals may end the confrontation still at odds as far as the issue is concerned, but if they separate at odds with each other, the confrontation is not resolved.

In a classroom confrontation, the child must be free to maintain his own identity. He must be respected as he is, with his

*Reprinted from *NEA Journal*, January 1961. Used with permission.

own concepts and perceptions, however wrong they may appear to be.

When the teacher forces the child to accept a viewpoint or cuts the child off or pressures him into agreement, the child soon realizes that the only acceptable path is the path of conformity and acceptance of authority. Such a child may become insensitive to himself, unresponsive to his own experience, and unfeeling in his associations with others.

In contrast to the confrontation which does not get beyond the initial criticism is the confrontation in which the teacher exposes the child to his misdemeanor, but remains with him and enables him to come to terms with the wrong-doing. In this creative confrontation, the relationship between the two unfolds into more meaningful expressions of self, release of feelings, and resolution of conflicts. The relationship moves toward greater mutual insights and awareness, and toward the growth of a sense of responsibility in the child.

Such a confrontation is illustrated in "A Cluster of Grapes," an autobiographical story of Takeo Arishima, recently translated by Kazuko Yoshinaga. This is the story of the painful shame a Japanese child experienced in facing his beloved teacher with his dishonesty.

Takeo was fond of drawing pictures, but the paints he had were not very good— they would not produce the vivid colors he longed to put on paper. A classmate and friend, a Western boy named Jim, had a beautiful boxed set of imported paints. They would make vivid colors for any artist!

The Japanese boy became increasingly tempted by the box of paints. One day, while the other children were at lunch, he stayed behind and took two of the beautiful paints and shoved them into his pocket. But the other children soon found out, and at recess they yelled at him, "You have Jim's paints, don't you? Put them here."

He gave up the paints, and the children led him crying into the teacher's office. They told the story of the theft. The teacher asked Takeo if the story were true. He could not answer; he could only sob.

The teacher sent the other children away, then asked Takeo, "Did you return the paints?" When he nodded affirmatively, she asked gently, "Do you think your deed was desirable?"

The boy just cried; he was so ashamed he wanted to die. The teacher spoke again, "It's all right, if you understand well." Then she reached outside the window and cut a cluster of grapes from a vine that grew there. She gave them to Takeo and said, "Go home now, but you must come to school tomorrow, no matter how you feel."

Next morning, when Takeo arrived at school, Jim greeted him and pulled him into the teacher's office.

"You both understand," the teacher said. "Now you will become good friends." The two boys shook hands; Jim was radiant and smiling. The teacher reached outside the office and picked another cluster of grapes. She divided the bunch and gave half to each boy. Now both boys were smiling.

And to Takeo, the sight of grapes would always remind him of the confrontation and of how his teacher had met his theft with love. She had been concerned with him as a person and had recognized that he was caught in a crisis of childhood. She had let him see that she continued to love him even when he was in trouble.

The teacher had entered into the situation and remained until a positive emergence of self was realized. This is exactly what a true confrontation offers—an opportunity for the teacher to meet the child on a new and vital level.

The confrontation offers the chance for a completely new understanding and awareness because it is not a routine exchange between individuals. It is a real meeting, a coming to grips with life. It is a challenge to all of the teacher's reserve. It brings strength where there is weakness, good where there is evil, openness where there is restrictiveness, beauty where there is ugliness.

Conflict with a pupil can be the supreme test for the teacher. But the teacher must face this conflict bravely and with love; when he does, both he and the child come through the experience to a meaningful way of life, a life where confidence continues unshaken, even strengthened.

Games Teachers Play*

Leslie J. Chamberlin and Morris Weinberger

Although there are differences of opinion concerning classroom control and methods for achieving it, all teachers will agree that a pleasant, well-disciplined classroom atmosphere results in more effective learning for all. Good teachers realize that to a very large extent they themselves create the climate in their classrooms. But even a good teacher may play classroom "games" that lead to pupil boredom and disinterest, and result in behavior problems.

The game of ambiguous rules, for example, is a common cause of classroom disturbance. Teacher and pupils learn the rules and then spend hours playing the game with repeated student testing to make the rules specific. In "How wide is an aisle?" for example, the students' team "scores" whenever there is a foot in the aisle without reprimand and the teacher "scores" when he catches someone. Repeated trials by students, with a scolding each time ("get your foot out of the aisle"), result in both sides' eventually agreeing on an imaginary line that is the boundary. A foot inside or on the line is acceptable but one-quarter inch over is not. This game may take an hour to play on a day early in the fall but is played more quickly when students reopen the game out of boredom in the spring. Similar games are "But you've been to the bathroom" (a game more often won by students) and "When is a pencil dull?" (a game the teacher usually wins).

Uncritical enforcement of traditional rules is another cause of classroom misbehavior. Too often teachers perpetuate rules without knowing why they do so, what purpose the rules serve, or what the total effect of the rule is on either the class as a whole or an individual student.

Among the most common classroom "games" are the teacher's attitudes and behavior. Children behave much like the adults around them. While it is flattering to have a student imitate him, the teacher must realize that anything he does before children, for good or ill, remains with them longer than most adults realize. Though a teacher may recognize the pupil imitations of his virtues, it is much more difficult to recognize faults secondhand, and he may be using a teaching technique which has become a disciplinary pitfall and the cause of problem after problem. Flippant remarks, sarcasm, and unfriendly looks are often unconsciously used in teaching. A

*Reprinted from *Instructor*, February 1971, the Instructor Publications, Inc. Used by permission.

person who is truly objective will notice antagonistic or belligerent pupil feedback, but many teachers fail to recognize it. When one *knows* one is right, it is hard to hear or see contradictory evidence.

The art of listening is not to be taken lightly, for this is how the teacher interprets what people, especially his students, are trying to tell him. Unfortunately, most teachers feel they are listening when they are only hearing the words. Listening involves understanding from the speaker's viewpoint, a detail often missed by even good teachers. Teaching involves the interactions of human beings and a good teacher learns from what he hears as well as from what he sees.

Teachers should also realize that the life goals of children and of adults are usually different, and that children of different ages have different goals. A student's actions should be evaluated in terms of the individual or group goal being sought at the time. A student will select from his different behavioral patterns the actions he believes will help him to achieve his personal goal and then behave accordingly. Teachers who learn to adjust their thinking to what is appropriate student behavior in terms of the child's age and his goals will seldom need to apply external controls. Failure to see this viewpoint means that the teacher will be out of step with his class most of the time, and have many disciplinary situations.

Using the lecture method is a pitfall for many beginning teachers. It often fails to meet the interest, needs, and abilities of the students. Yet a lecture can be an efficient technique occasionally, if the content is at the children's level of understanding, is adapted to student needs and goals, and is brief. A teacher who comes to class poorly prepared, with a bare minimum of correct information, and no thought of its interest level, should hardly be surprised when the students fail to pay the rapt attention he would like.

Too many people believe that knowledge of subject matter is nearly all of the professional preparation required to teach. This point of view defines learning as the mere acquisition of factual knowledge. But learning affects not only factual knowledge but habits, understandings, attitudes, emotional control techniques, and social values as well. In fact, learning to like to learn may be the most important thing a teacher can help a student acquire.

Some problems develop from the way a teacher implements his teaching. Classwork that is too advanced, too verbal, or in a poorly planned sequence will create difficult situations for both the teacher and the students. Behavior standards that are too high or too low, or a classroom that has too much or too little organization, may result in boredom or fatigue.

An important factor affecting the environment of every classroom today is the increased emphasis on education. Students are expected to read more, study more, write more, and learn more. The problems posed by this pressure are creating anxiety and additional indirect disciplinary pressures within the classroom. It takes conscious effort and constant readjustment for even experienced teachers to match their teaching to student needs, abilities, interests, and time.

Many problems of discipline are actually responses to inadvertent teacher behavior. Difficult as self-assessment always is, a conscientious teacher will examine his day-to-day habits with care, to make certain that what he calls student misbehavior isn't really his, and to understand the behavior games that he and his students play.

Drug Abuse*

Frank Dick

As much as educators must constantly insist on maintaining a priority for basics, balance and proper context, we also know that we live in a volatile society where new problems can develop so rapidly that at times they demand *out*-of-context attention to bring us up to date.

On a national scale, a phenomenon of drug dependence and abuse has developed such a pattern. The growth of hard drug (heroin, etc.) addiction has progressed at a recent rate of 20 percent per year, but the variety of "all other" drug abuse categories has been escalating at a rate of 50 percent per year. Of even more concern is that the average age of initial usage has moved steadily downward at a rate of six months each year until the typical drug abuser is 14.5 years old.

It is the advice of these professionals that our various schools not be primarily conditioned by their own immediate observations or beliefs as to whether they have an immediate problem within their own school situations. Not only has drug abuse shown an ability to show us suddenly within apparently calm settings, but the prime goal of all education is to prepare their students to live in the "outside" world, not within the walls of the school.

Experience has shown that early preventive education is the most helpful in heading off a significant portion of such incidence. Especially in the lower grades, a knowledgeable teacher with clear, fact-based attitudes has been proved to be many times more effective than one-time assemblies of outside panelists. The best of all places and ways to "handle" this

subject is within the mainstream of related instruction.

DETECTION

General

Detection of drug abusers is a very difficult procedure and one that is rarely 100 percent effective. Students may display the effects of some of the dangerous drugs, but these effects may be caused by drugs which are being used legitimately. However, persistent symptoms or changes in attitude and habits are the most proper source of suspicion.

Radical personality changes are often indicative of possible drug abuse. Sudden changes in attendance, discipline and academic performance may also indicate that a drug problem exists.

Abrupt changes in a student's style of dress or health habits may be telltale signs of drug abuse. Changes in a student's social patterns, such as associations with new friends or new activities with old friends, are sometimes related to a drug problem.

Drugs and possible symptoms of their abuse:

Depressants

Symptoms of alcohol intoxication, without the odor of alcohol on the breath.
Staggering, stumbling and a general disorientation.
Lack of interest in classroom activities.
Extreme drowsiness or falling into a deep sleep while in class.
Slurred or indistinct speech.

Stimulants

Extreme hyperactivity.

*Reprinted from *Drug Abuse,* Toledo Area Program on Drug Abuse and the Family Life Education Center, 1971. Used with permission.

Highly irritable and argumentative moods.

Excessive talking on nearly any subject.

Dilation of the pupils of the eyes, even in extremely bright light.

Bad breath, with an unidentifiable odor.

Chapped, reddened, cracked or raw lips, due to incessant licking of the lips.

Going for long periods of time without eating or drinking.

Tremor and heavy perspiration.

Hard Narcotics

Cough medicine and paregoric bottles in wastebaskets.

Traces of white powder around the nostrils.

Nostrils red and raw.

Needle injection marks on arm, especially near the inner surface of the elbow.

Use of long-sleeved garments, even in hot weather.

Presence of equipment needed for injection, including bottle caps and bent spoons which are used for heating the solution, small balls of cotton, syringes, hypodermic needles and eyedroppers.

Lethargic or drowsy appearance.

Occasional symptoms of deep intoxication.

Constricted pupils which may fail to respond to light.

Glue

Odor of glue on breath or clothes.

Excessive nasal secretions.

Red, watery eyes.

Complaints of double vision, ringing ears and hallucinations.

Lack of muscular control.

Drowsiness, stupor and unconsciousness.

Discovery of paper bags or rags with dried plastic cement on them.

Frequent expectoration, nausea, loss of appetite.

Hallucinogens

User may sit or recline in a dream-like state; may be fearful and appear to be full of terror; may wish to escape from group activities.

Marijuana

Use of this drug may be hard to recognize unless the user is extremely intoxicated. Symptoms include:

Excessive animation or near hysteria.

Loud and rapid talking.

Great bursts of laughter at highly unlikely times.

Appearance of sleepiness or even stupor.

Pupils of the eyes may be dilated.

Perspiration or pallor.

Badly stained or burnt fingers from smoking marijuana cigarettes.

Odor, somewhat sweet and like burnt rope, remains on breath and clothes for hours.

Unusual appetite, especially for sweets.

Red, watery eyes.

Possession of cigarette papers.

Note To Teachers

If drug abuse is suspected, it should be handled like any other extreme behavioral problem. The specific case must be referred to the counsellor or, where a counsellor is not available, to the principal of the school. Under no circumstances should the teacher try to handle the problem himself.

TECHNICAL TERMS

Abuse — the misuse of drugs or other substances by a person who has obtained them illegally or readily and administers them himself without the advice or supervision of a qualified person.

Central Nervous System — the brain and spinal cord.

Chromosomes — threadlike bodies in a cell which carry the genes that control hereditary characteristics.

Compulsion — a compelling impulse which causes a person to act in a way that may be contrary to his good judgment or normal actions.

Convulsions — an involuntary series of contractions of the muscles.

Delirium — a condition marked by confusion, disordered speech and hallucinations.

Dependence — the need for and the reliance upon a substance. This can be both physical and psychological.

Depressant — any of several types of drugs which cause sedation by acting on the central nervous system.

Hallucination — a sensory experience which exists inside the mind of an individual and is a false perception of the actual conditions.

Hallucinogenic — causing or producing hallucinations.

Intoxication — the temporary reduction of mental and physical control because of the effects of drugs or other substances.

Narcotic — any drug that produces sleep and also relieves pain.

Paranoid — a person suffering from a mental disorder in which he has fears that others are threatening him. Delusions of grandeur are also common to a person who is paranoid.

Pharmacology — the science dealing with the production, use and effects of drugs.

Psychosis — any severe mental disorder or disease.

Sedative — any substance which calms or quiets body activity.

Stimulant — any of several types of drugs which act upon the central nervous system to produce excitation, sleeplessness and alertness.

Withdrawal — the extremely painful illness that results when a drug or other substance upon which a person has become physically or psychologically dependent is withheld from his body.

Chapter III

Discussionette

1. How would you handle the three stages of a developing behavioral problem, i.e.: (1) whispering and inactivity? (2) laughing, talking, writing notes, and horseplay? (3) complete disorder?

2. What can be concluded from the four most significant factors which cause misbehavior and rebellion in students?

3. Discuss these four factors both pro and con from your own personal experience and family life. Are there other causes?

4. If one of these incidents happened in your school, how would you approach the problem?

5. If behavior is determined by learning experiences, how might early referral and early treatment enhance the possibility of dealing effectively with emotional problems?

6. Have school administrators and teachers been more inclined to suspend students who have been disciplinary problems rather than try to understand and assist in treating emotional problems?

7. Is student unrest on the college campus related to previous methods of teacher and administration and understanding group behavior which has failed?

8. Have most colleges and universities been sensitive to the needs of the student body?

9. What character traits should a teacher have in order to meet a confrontation with a pupil bravely and with love?

10. What other behavior games might teachers and students play?

11. What do you consider as the best approach to the drug problem at the high school level? at the junior high level? at the grade school level?

12. Where can school people go for additional help in understanding and helping the student addict?

Discussionette Words and Concepts

ethics	defense mechanism	emotion
motivation	experience	stimulants
compulsory attendance	discrimination	economic needs
legal restrictions	unrest	attitude

Try to use these words.

Try to explain these words.

Try to relate these words and their concepts to current or emerging educational patterns regarding common causes of discipline problems.

PART II

UNDERSTANDING THE
PEOPLE INVOLVED

CHAPTER IV

⟅THE TEACHER'S ROLE⟆

INTRODUCTION

Aᴿᴱ ᴛᴇᴀᴄʜᴇʀs, ɪɴ ᴘᴀʀᴛ, to blame for the behavioral problems that occur in their classrooms? Just what is the teacher's role in maintaining adequate student control and classroom discipline? Most teachers are the architects of their own misery in regard to student behavioral problems. Too often teachers are overly concerned with maintaining order and control which causes an emphasis on quiet and strict conformity rather than on activity and investigation. A teacher who gets credit for a quiet classroom may be conducting a funeral service for learning. The materials presented in this chapter will help the reader to determine what kind of control techniques are likely to fit his own personal working methods.

Discipline? Follow the Yellow Brick Road*
Ruth Agnew

Too often, discipline is regarded only as stringent punishment for refractory pupils. Actually, discipline is a positive factor in life—a highly developed set of inner controls which safeguard a person by providing him with a pattern of behavior that will be acceptable to society and will contribute to his own welfare and progress.

One of a teacher's primary concerns is to develop student behavior patterns congenial to learning. To this end, he strives to work out techniques that will lead to his students' disciplining themselves. Planning enjoyable classroom activities is one such technique. If pleasant experiences seem to come naturally and casually in a class (regardless of how carefully planned

*Reprinted from *NEA Journal,* October, 1964. Used with permission.

they actually may be), the students become enthusiastic and cooperative.

A teacher can provide pleasurable classroom experiences and thereby lessen his need to worry about discipline by assuming a Pied Piper role and tantalizing his students with stimulating ideas. Through the magic act of divining pupils' interests and releasing their various talents, a teacher can lure his students to follow the most fascinating journey along if we may have selected another allegory from fiction) a "yellow brick road" like the one in the *Wonderful Wizard of Oz,* and this one leads to self-discipline.

These fictional symbols are of unorthodox educational terminology, and for the teacher actually to refer to himself as a piper or mention a yellow brick road would disgust older students and confuse younger ones. Nevertheless the teacher who infuses the spirit suggested by these symbols latches on to the imagination of the student. The philosophy behind the symbol is invested with a kind of alchemy to which humanity at large responds pleasurably. It is based on a strong human motivation—curiosity.

By small degrees the Pied Piper teacher captures his class and teases it to successive states of learning, often through a roundabout procedure or a seemingly unintentional incident.

A good teacher, aware that students thrive on success, finds ways in which they can succeed. No matter how limited his ability, every student has some contribution to make. The Pied Piper applauds any degree of success. He lets his students taste that heady wine, praise, even if only a drop of it.

One first year teacher wrote "neat" or "very neat" on papers devoid of every virtue but appearance. Whether the pupils' knowledge was increased by such comments may be questioned, but certainly their attitude toward their work improved.

The philosophy signified by following the yellow brick road is that learning isn't difficult in small steps and that each little success makes the goals more attainable. Although enticing students to follow along the yellow brick road approaches an art, it will not be a mystery to the new teacher, with his fresh viewpoint and dedicated purpose.

It is not as individual travelers but as a group of friends that pupils must take to the yellow brick road. The teacher needs to present opportunities for them to become acquainted. He may do this by providing a social period of ten or fifteen minutes a week—called the "visiting period," "making classroom friends," "living a little," or whatever designation is appropriate to the age and sophistication of the group involved—during which the students discover and share mutual interests and concerns.

Naive and simple as the idea of this getting-acquainted period may seem, it can provide a positive and effective approach to successful discipline. Young people wield a tremendous influence over each other, and class approval or criticism plays a major role in constructing or destroying desired behavior.

Getting acquainted nips hostilities in the bud and prevents possible displays of aggressiveness. When his classmates are his friends and he knows they are interested in him for himself, a pupil does not feel that he has to act up to attract attention.

For the show-off's opposite, the shy child, making friends is even more important. The opportunity for a shy, inhibited girl to visit with a gifted, popular boy might encourage her to speak out more freely and to try to accomplish more.

Naturally, when students know each other better, there may be more activity and minor disturbances, but the teacher's overall task is lightened by the increased class unity. Students vie not only for self-recognition but for opportunities to serve each other and the class. Instead of competing, they all contribute to a common cause.

The congenial atmosphere places the teacher in an advantageous position. He is the leader of an enthusiastic group, a group eager to continue methods that promise enjoyment. Because students expect further satisfying experiences, they are attentive to the teacher's suggestions or instructions.

Often, the piper finds the keynote for

his initial tune in the field of literature. Wonderful results can come from a student's identifying himself with a character in a book.

One teacher inherited a group of ninth grade English students who had become the despair of the school. They were notorious for their ingenious methods of class disruption and teacher disintegration. Their reading level was so low that they comprehended only the simplest subject matter.

One day this class encountered the word "decorum." A certain fascination accompanied its sound. What did the word mean? One boy ventured that it meant "holding your mother's coat for her." This student's acknowledgement that he had some acquaintance with manners called forth a volley of other illustrations from the class, not all of them advocated by Amy Vanderbilt.

The teacher recognized the keynote. If she could build it into a tune, she might improve class attitudes and behavior. With the help of Booth Tarkington's *Penrod,* she went to work. She read the entire book aloud, for the vocabulary was not a graded one, and many of the words would have been difficult to understand without the help of voice inflection. Penrod became the class hero. When the pupils first met him, he was a sort of juvenile ne'er-do-well. Despite his admiration for a pretty and proper little girl's "decorum," Penrod thought and behaved as they did.

The class became a captive audience, teased by promises of more *Penrod* into doing stints of planned developmental silent reading. The teacher wondered if the enchantment would hold. Would these ardent admirers resent their hero as his behavior became more proper?

They did not. Instead, by the time the last page had been read and Penrod had emerged as a proud and dignified gentleman, the students had become so proper they were almost stuffy.

The changes in the class attitude had been encouraged by frequent discussions of their own exploits and of the increasing degrees of "decorum" they were attaining as the boys emulated Penrod and the girls tried to be more like the girl whose feminine virtues Penrod admired so much.

Now they laughed with indulgence at their past misdemeanors, secure in their present knowledge of proper behavior. Boys opened doors for girls. More than once, eager students competed to help the teacher carry her books to her next class.

Class alchemy had worked its magic. No dictum handed down by any teacher could have achieved such wonder. The piper's tune had called them to satisfy a longing which they secretly wished to fulfill. Penrod supplied a means which saved face for them and which subtly carried them from distorted attitudes to acceptable behavior.

Educators agree that carefully planned learning situations are safeguards against disciplinary problems, but even so, long-range plans are not inviolable. The yellow brick road allows for occasional pleasant meanderings and unexpected detours that provide relaxation on the trip to the goal. An imaginative teacher can discard an entire unit if he sees that some other material will better serve his purpose.

In certain respects, of course, the teacher must be adamant. Rules must be followed; infractions punished. But the teacher who has caught the fancy of his class can be in command of most situations, with the students his allies when isolated cases of misbehavior occur. Consider cheating, for instance. Although it is not to be tolerated, merely handing down teacher decrees never eliminates it. However, if a class has reached the point where pride of accomplishment motivates it, the members themselves often provide the controls.

If the reader is dismayed by the involvement of such an approach to discipline, I suggest that he consult Gilbert Highet's *The Art of Teaching*. In this classic best seller, the author searches out all aspects of teaching, devoting a section to the prevention and remedy of misbehavior. One should consult a master for a sound approach. I feel that he would concur with me that the teacher who views his profession as a true art is ready to pipe the magic tune that will draw his pupils after him along the yellow brick road.

Discipline and Teacher Leadership*

Leslie J. Chamberlin

"Who wants to be like you?" is an unsettling question that every teacher needs to ask himself from time to time. Perhaps few teachers can be a prestige image for everyone of his students but he may have certain capabilities in the science laboratory, in the gymnasium, in the shop, or on the playing field that will enable him to provide a good example for many of them. Certainly each teacher should strive to be an honest, authentic, genuine, unique person and thereby encourage his students to do the same. Schools need to make the most of their natural prestige figures that they have on the staff.

No God-Like Qualities

Studies to determine the personal qualities of successful teachers tend to give the impression that a good teacher is a superperson with godlike qualities. We all know, however, that teachers are just plain people. In fact most people teach in some sense during some part of their lives. Successful professional teachers are distinguished, however, by both the kind of qualities they possess and the degree to which they possess them.

There is no one characteristic or group of characteristics that make for leadership or successful teaching ability. No single quality will enable an observer to select a particular teacher as a leader. No hereditary or environmental background will assure that a person will have leadership qualities. Leaders conform to no single pattern. Most educators would concur in the belief that teacher leadership can be acquired. Few people develop leadership qualities overnight. In teaching, the leadership relationship is built over a period of time as the teacher and class work together.

✗ Traits of the Successful Teacher

A survey of the literature seems to indicate that the most successful teachers exhibit some of the following traits to some degree. As a person he

1. Shows willingness to maintain contact with children over long periods of time.
2. Doesn't feel that every student must like him.
3. Has ability to absorb negative, even hostile behavior; presents an accepting attitude toward all children.
4. Doesn't use those for whom he is responsible to work out his own problems.

*Reprinted from *Education*, April/May 1969. Used with permission.

5. Has average or above intelligence but knows his own limitations and works within them.
6. Has good physical, mental and emotional health.
7. Shows willingness to serve others with a sense of humility and modesty.
8. Has courage when standing up for what he believes to be worthwhile; is a person of integrity and good judgment.
9. Has ability to express ideas clearly in speech and writing.
10. Has ability to organize and delegate responsibility.
11. Has ability to obtain cooperation by making others feel important.
12. Has a definite life purpose and objective.
13. Has the ability to face reality with imagination and self-confidence.
14. Has a good sense of humor.
15. Has enthusiasm in combination with plenty of energy.

Y As a teacher he
1. Understands that methods of raising children differ from one culture to another.
2. Understands that economic and social differences effect the development of the individual student.
3. Understands that children have a "culture" all their own and attempts to relate to it.
4. Is sensitive to the basic needs of children, both physical and psychological.
5. Attempts to understand how children learn.
6. Is interested in all children, both the good and the troublesome.
7. Attempts to provide a classroom atmosphere that is free of tension and conducive to teaching and learning.
8. Tries to be fair, impartial, and consistent in dealing with children.
9. Is primarily a pupil-centered thinker, not subject-centered.
10. Provides for individual differences in children in every way possible within the working situation.
11. Is a multi-media teacher (book-blackboard radio-T.V.-films, etc.) who makes use of the best teaching media available.
12. Plans and prepares what is to be taught thoroughly.
13. Works at establishing and maintaining good working relations with co-workers.
14. Has a working knowledge of the activities and services of the psychologist, psychiatrist, social worker, counselor, school physician, and school nurse.
15. Does not hesitate to use the services and facilities of the school system and community in solving difficult problems; has a team outlook; doesn't try to go it alone.
16. Uses test data from all sources in the scheduled test program and supplements this on an individual basis when necessary.
17. Uses the schools' cumulative records for the purpose of knowing his students.
18. Realizes that a teacher must play many roles in fulfilling his duties and plays all parts with interest and fulfills his role as a teacher.
19. Listens and says what he must say as simply and quickly as possible. Words, words, words are sometimes the teacher's worst enemy.

Tried and Proven Suggestions

Teachers differ one from another in every respect imaginable. There is no pattern, outline, or mold to which all good teachers conform. However, in the matter of maintaining satisfactory discipline, it seems that there are a few traits that are fairly common to most good teachers. A teacher can do much to help establish a favorable school atmosphere and thus help to prevent undesirable behavior.

He must maintain a certain reserve in new situations until he becomes acquainted. In most cases it is necessary to be firm at first rather than to permit students a large degree of freedom. Being popular with the students should not be a major goal of the teacher.

He must be influenced by his students in the same manner he expects them to be influenced by him. The teacher must consider the students' point of view and attempt to deal with all problems in their situational context.

He must attempt to develop a working understanding with his class about areas of authority by developing classroom and school behavior standards cooperatively with his students. The teacher must be consistent in maintaining and enforcing the agreed upon standards.

He must permit students to suffer the consequences of their decisions where they have been given the opportunity to make a decision. If on rare occasions it is necessary to interfere, a complete explanation should be made as to the necessity for taking this action. In most cases, however, students should be left alone to enjoy their efforts and accomplishments.

He must accept and appreciate each student as a human being and always attempt to maintain a positive and instructive attitude toward all students. He must view misbehavior objectively, not person-ally; he can reject the misbehavior without rejecting the misbehaving child as a person. He must recognize misbehavior as a symptom and seek out the true problem as well as dealing with symptoms. He must treat all pupils at all times in a professional manner as individuals of worth and dignity.

He must be observant and notice behavioral patterns of adjustment that seem to be heading toward undesirable behavior or perhaps delinquency. Students with such behavior patterns if identified early can be studied and possibly treated before serious difficulty develops. A recent report released by a United States Senate subcommittee on juvenile delinquency stated that one out of every ten children in the five-through-seventeen-years-old group showed behavior signs that warranted treatment.

The good teacher must learn to recognize "overloaded" or "symbolic" issues and to keep them in proper perspective.

When "contagious" misbehavior develops, sort of a yawning reaction, he must try to stop the source, not the last person in the line.

He must realize that a teacher's public praise is not welcomed by every student. Try to express approval in a time, manner, and place acceptable to the individuals concerned.

He must try to become sensitized to the proper "timing" for handling disciplinary situations. Most mistakes made by teachers in working with misbehaving children are errors in timing.

Most teachers plan carefully for the teaching-learning situation; yet they generally conduct a hit-or-miss program in planning for possible disciplinary situations. It is better to "be a leader" than to be led by developing predicaments. In attempting to maintain satisfactory classroom control, there is no substitute for forethought. But over and above all other things there must be something about the teacher—a personality leadership, a *charisma.*

In good teaching situations the whole often seems to be more than the sum of the parts. The factors taken separately could not bring about the climate for learning that the sum does. The proper factors must be present in the proper proportions for the right personalities. The teacher must be a leader to maintain such a situation.

Ruth Benedict in her book, *Patterns of Culture,* tells about a tribe of mild-man-nered, pueblo-dwelling Indians called Zuñi. The Zuñi are nice people who disparage personal authority in any shape or form. A person who wishes to be a "leader of his people" receives nothing but criticism from his fellow Zuñi. Perhaps there are too many Zuñis in the teaching profession. Too many teachers attempt to hold their position by "not making waves," being affable, or by running a popularity contest. The profession needs more people who are educationally and psychologically prepared to teach, people who can present the proper emotional and social example to the students in addition to providing satisfactory academic instruction.

The 4 P's of Healthy Classroom Discipline*
Marjorie Carr Smith

Every beginning teacher I know is worried, and a little scared, about discipline. Most of these teachers are not worried about subject matter or lesson plans for they are intelligent and feel that they can learn specific techniques. These young people tell me that no one in college seems to want to talk about discipline. Why? I don't know.

But hear what Dr. Harl Douglass, dean of the School of Education, University of Colorado, says in his book, *Teaching in Elementary School:* "Superintendents and principals attribute more failure of teachers to failure in this area (discipline), than to any other cause."

Young teachers have sat in college courses and heard educators beat around the bush with pedagogical terms such as social control, behavior patterns, group dynamics, democratic procedures. Probably they have participated in debates on such topics as teacher control versus self-direction, permissiveness versus autocratic control.

Please believe me, these are perfectly good terms. These discussions are stimulating to intelligent young people, but they do *not* tell the worried teacher much about how to get Johnny to sit down and keep quiet—at least long enough for her to get the day started!

We will risk the wrath of the theorists and say that healthy classroom control depends largely on personality (of the teacher); planning, principal and parents.

The Personality Ingredients

Be natural. Children can spot a phony as far as they can see one. They know when we are "putting it on," so why bother? Let's not be too severe or too cordial, too friendly or too aloof—let's not be too anything. Could we just relax and be ourselves?

I think this is as good a place as any to talk about one of the popular misconceptions floating around the teaching pro-

*Reprinted from *Ohio Schools,* October 1958. Used with permission.

fession. Some teachers have the idea they should be a "pal" to the children. I do not believe we should try to do this. Children need pals, yes—but pals their own age. You are the adult in the group. You are the leader. Unless you assume your rightful place as such, the children feel let down and disappointed. We will be warm, friendly human beings, but we will not be "pals."

Be consistent. Nothing distresses a child more than never knowing where he stands. Nothing undermines his security more than a teacher with widely variable moods. You know the situation—anything goes today; nothing is right tomorrow.

Must we be rigid in order to be consistent? Must we never give an inch or reverse a decision? Of course not. Consistency in routine matters, the things we must do over and over in the class, gives the child security for he knows what is expected and how to come through.

Be businesslike. Here I would like to look at another popular misconception about classroom discipline. Many young teachers coming out of teacher training institutions have the idea that it is the teacher's job to keep the children "happy." Furthermore, these same teachers feel that they are being "mean" to a child when they correct him, and "nice" to him when they allow him to run wild. Nothing could be further from the truth.

I don't think for a minute that our colleagues in the colleges are teaching these ideas, but I do think it is time for them to tell their charges, in no uncertain terms, that they are not entering a popularity contest on the first day of school, and that there are some more important things to think about than whether or not the children will be "happy" every minute.

Could we cultivate this attitude in our classrooms? "Here's a job to be done. Let's get busy and do it together." The togetherness is important—togetherness in planning, togetherness in working things out—but with complete acceptance by both teacher and child that it is our work.

Accent the positive. Most teachers know that in the practical life of a school some punishment is necessary. At the same time, as trained people, we must recognize that all punishment is negative and that we may never improve social behavior through its use. We will use it when necessary but always with discretion, and always knowing that it's just the beginning.

At the same time, we will accent the positive with praise, praise, praise. Does this mean that we'll give flowery compliments every hour of the day? No, it does not. The good teacher can praise with a nod, a look, a pat on the head, a smile, or a word as she goes by. There are many ways the teacher can tell the child that she approves of him. Look for these ways and beware of the undeserved compliment.

Change the pace. We have talked about a businesslike, consistent manner in the classroom; but remember there is time for fun and play, too. When it's time to play, let's play with the children. When something funny happens, let's laugh as hard as they do. When it's time for a party, let's make it the biggest and best party we can produce.

The good teacher learns to sense when she is "losing" the class. Any change of pace, any little surprise, will help you over the rough spots that happen to all of us. The light touch, instead of the pompous look, sometimes saves the day.

Watch your voice. Perhaps more than any other one thing, the teacher's voice can make or break classroom discipline. There are voices pitched too high, voices pitched too low, voices that advertise the teacher's insecurity. There are voices that create disciplinary problems where there are none.

What kind of voice should we have in order to have it help us? First, it should be clear. Second, it should be pleasant. Third, it should be firm. The voice is a wonderful organ. A great deal has been said about the well-modulated voice. If you have such a voice, use it—most of the time. But come the day when your voice seems to rise and rise, in spite of all you do, stop quickly, drop the pitch and volume and see what happens.

Try the reverse also. If you've asked a child to do something in a well-modulated tone—perhaps asked him twice—and he hasn't responded, try increase in volume and firmness. He will know that you intend to see that he does as he has been asked to do.

The Planning Essentials

Two phases of planning appear to have direct relation to good discipline. The first is planning classroom routines. Let's label some of the trouble spots in the life of the classroom and plan for these spots.

Trouble Spot No. 1. What do your children do when they enter the room the first thing in the morning? Bedlam, if bedlam we have, usually starts right here.

Children can and should start the day's work in a businesslike manner. As in an office, we want them to visit with each other and with the teacher, in normal tones, and to move about the room freely, but we want them to get ready to work, too.

The children can help you plan an acceptable routine. Guide them in listing a few simple rules. We will put our outdoor things away promptly. We will check to be sure the material we will need today is ready. We will look at the blackboard or bulletin board for any special jobs.

Caution: keep the list short. Children need to work on a few things at a time.

Trouble Spot No. 2. I have known teachers to keep children sitting quietly in their places until the class was ready to go through the ceiling. When I asked "why," the teacher answered, "I have such a time getting them down to work that when they are quiet, I dread letting them out of their seats."

Ah, what a vicious circle! For if they are kept sitting quietly for long periods of time, of course they burst out all over the place. Establish a routine for changing from group to group, from job to job. The children can help decide how to do it, but that doesn't mean that they will always remember to do it. It's the teacher's job to see that they do. They must be trained to care for routine matters with dispatch.

Trouble Spot No. 3. Moving about the building as a group requires routine planning with the children, also. We want to give them the reasons "why" whenever we can. The inexperienced teacher gets into very serious difficulties when she attempts to reason with children about every tiny detail of living every day. If your class trusts you, they should do many things simply because it's customary or because you asked them.

The second phase of planning that affects discipline is the planning of the work itself. This is not the time to discuss lesson planning as such, but I would briefly remind you that you must plan work on the correct level of difficulty.

Good materials help tremendously in this planning, but somehow you must accomplish this, whether or not you have adequate materials. You may have to beg, borrow or steal. You may get footsore tramping to the library. You may have to teach your program with the wonderful free materials our book companies and industries give away, but you must do it some how.

If the work is too hard or the vocabulary too difficult, your slow children will feel inferior and go looking for trouble. If the work is too easy, the bright ones will go unchallenged and bedevil you and their classmates. Don't forget, the squeaky wheel still gets the grease, and the teacher that wages relentless warfare on the budget maker usually gets part of what she wants if only to keep her quiet.

The first question asked is usually, "Where will I find the time?"

Try this. Resolve that you will spend all the time necessary for one month to plan, execute and evaluate a full, live program in your room based on properly graded materials. I'll wager that you'll be less tired at the end of the day, even if you work until midnight, than you were on the days when it was a battle all the way due to inadequate planning.

The Principal's Responsibility

Could we think now about how the principal can help in this matter of classroom discipline? At the same time I think we should consider the things that the principal *cannot* do.

Good teachers prefer to settle as many of their discipline problems as possible. They realize that no one but the teacher and the child living together daily can bring about real improvement in the teacher-child relationship. The principal can help but the teacher must *do*.

One responsibility of the principal is to provide an emotional climate within which the teacher-child relationship can flourish. Anything the principal can do to keep the morale in his building at a high level helps the teacher and the child.

One thing the teacher might do to help morale is to invite the principal to share in the children's activities once in a while. Have you ever thought that a principal misses the direct contact with the children? Have you remembered to show him the good things your class is doing? Do you ever think he might like to have children call on him as a reward rather than a punishment? He can sometimes help most by having the opportunity of "accenting the positive."

Just one more word about morale. Support your principal, especially in the eyes of the children. If only for selfish reasons, build his prestige with the children—then it will be there for you to call upon when you need a helping hand.

The Parents' Contribution

It seems to me, as I work with parents, that many are afraid of teachers. They aren't afraid of you as individuals, but they are afraid of the power you have over them through their children.

You may say, "I wouldn't be worthy of the title 'teacher' if I would take out on a child whatever I might feel about parents."

True, but just the same, in every parent's heart, there may be a little fear, a little anxiety about saying what he really thinks to you because you might take it out on the child. Time and again a parent has said to me, "Please don't tell Miss X that we talked. I don't want her to think I'm a complaining parent."

Second, I believe that we can do very little to help a child unless the parents are on our side. In order to accomplish this we may have to "take it" once in a while.

I can think of incidents in my own career when I might better have closed my lips and bitten my tongue. I might better have taken outright abuse from a parent than to strike back and antagonize the parent. Teachers are human, and our first reaction to unjust accusations or unreasonable demands is to say, "I don't have to take that from anyone."

But sometimes we do — for the child's sake. The child is the loser when teacher and parent disagree. How can you work with a youngster in school if he hears at home that the school is no good, the teacher doesn't know what she's talking about, and "that principal had better watch his step?"

Third, let's remember that every parent wants "something better" for his child than he had. It may not be the same thing that you, as a teacher want for the child, but that is beside the point. You want the parent to help you help the child so you will remember the parent may be afraid of you; the parent may be on the defensive — so be slow to anger; every normal parent loves his child.

If, in our relations with parents, we could remember these things always, we would find that most parents are our allies in this matter of healthy classroom discipline.

In conclusion, I would like to have you think about a question that was put to me at a discussion of this kind a short while ago. A teacher said, "How can we best help beginners who might have less trouble if we helped soon enough?"

Veterans Can Aid Beginners

The best answer is that the older teacher should *offer* to help. Make a new teacher feel free to come to you. My former students come back sometimes to talk over their first year problems. When I say, "But that's such a simple thing. Why didn't you ask the second grade teacher about it?" the answer is, "Oh, she always seemed to be busy with her own problems."

Of course every teacher has her own problems, but what could be more important than saving our young people for the profession? So we the older, the more experienced, the more skilled, will offer to help. Not just once but over and over. These young folks don't think they know it all, as we sometimes hear. Most of them are just plain scared, as we said in the beginning. Furthermore, they don't like to take every little thing to their superiors.

We hear a great deal today about people leaving our profession because of low salaries. I know that there are people who leave for economic reasons. But in my own experience I've never known a teacher who had a fine, satisfying relationship with youngsters who wanted to leave. In fact, you and I see teachers on all sides of us, making great personal sacrifices just to stay in this wonderful world of children.

So let's pitch in and help lick this bugaboo called discipline.

Discipline: Three F's for the Teacher*
Alvin W. Howard

Discipline is a major problem in virtually every school, and closely related is achievement. Basic to good classroom control, acceptable student conduct, and student achievement are three "F's" for teachers: firmness, friendliness, and fairness. Add to these consistency and preparedness, and you have the ingredients for successful teaching experiences.

The purpose of constructive discipline is to develop within our young people a sense of good judgment consistent with a de-

*Reprinted from *The Clearing House,* May 1965. Used with permission.

sirable system of values, leading to proper self-control and self-direction. People can not share or work together unless adequate standards of behavior, mutual respect and courtesy, and adherence to rules and regulations are present.

The teacher who lacks classroom control cannot function effectively, for the students' attention, interest, and application are prerequisites for learning. The experienced teacher recognizes that specific things should be done or not done in order to keep discipline problems to a minimum:

(1) Learn about the previous school experiences of your students through use of cumulative records and student folders. Be careful not to let a previous teacher's report bias you. The child is a year older and you are a different personality. Pay attention to attitudes revealed in written work and class discussions. Make note of important factors and incidents in the life of the child, family background, reasons for absences, and reports of special service people, if any. Remember each pupil is different, and be prepared to vary your approach.

(2) Your attitude is critically important, particularly in the cases of those students who, because of previous problems and failures, may regard all teachers with suspicion. Don't talk down to the class. They will know it and resent it if you become condescending. Work at being the kind of teacher that children like and trust. Be friendly and interested in each student, but maintain the reserve and respect you must have. We all want to be liked, but sacrificing respect in an effort to be one of the group will only lead to complete loss of control and ultimate classroom chaos. Remember firmness with fairness, sincerity with tact, humor without sarcasm. Be consistent. To expect one type of behavior today and another one tomorrow leads

only to confusion, discouragement, and frustration for everyone. Most students have a keen sense of fair play. If a student does something wrong, he expects to be punished for it, but he also expects every other student who does the same thing to get the same or equal treatment. The teacher must maintain her own poise and calm demeanor. Loss of temper, panic, and obvious anger lead to loss of respect in the students' eyes.

(3) Consider the environment in which you are working. A disorderly classroom invites disorderly behavior. Before class, make sure that your room is in order. Keep your bulletin boards attractive and change them frequently. Watch room temperature and ventilation. When a child is comfortable it is easier for him to be well behaved. Your own neatness and grooming, indicating pride in one's self and one's work, add to the general effect you are trying to create and maintain. Remember the importance of a pleasant voice and good enunciation.

(4) Thorough preparation is absolutely essential. A teacher who is thoroughly prepared knows what she hopes to achieve in her daily lesson, as well as what her long range goals are. She knows why this lesson is important and can explain its importance to the class. She knows how she intends to teach the lesson. A well organized outline of subject matter is only part of her preparation. There is a strong tendency on the part of too many teachers to rely upon lecturing. Plan varied activities and be flexible enough to permit alternate procedures. Well established routines minimize behavior problems. Group and individual tasks that give a student added responsibility for his own actions aid in development of good behavior. Every child needs a feeling of success in some activity. If a classroom is a place where a student meets

nothing but failure, he will soon seek other, less desirable, paths of recognition. Don't be afraid to praise good performance.

(5) Take a firm stand — but know what you are standing for or against. Establish policies for everyday procedures such as entering and leaving the room, sharpening pencils, and waste paper disposal. Some teachers feel that the class should participate in formation of behavior standards for everyday class living, while others believe that such policies should be teacher-constructed. Whichever method you choose, be sure that you and the class know what is expected. Work out beforehand the methods you will use in distributing and collecting materials, papers, and books. Again, forethought avoids problems.

6) Learn your students' names immediately. Misbehaving students have a sense of security in anonymity. Use a seating chart, although you may begin by letting students sit where they choose and, later, break up talky groups and move those children who appear to have a bad influence on each other.

(7) Make your assignments reasonable and clear, and be definite and concise in your directions. A hopelessly difficult assignment, or one which is so vague the students don't know where to start, will only foster frustration and rebellion. Put your assignments in writing, either on the board or on hand-out sheets. When writing on the board, avoid standing with your back to the class for any length of time. Whenever possible, have anything which needs to be on the board written before class. Start your class promptly and on time.

(8) Stand at the door at the beginning of the period. This gives you an opportunity to be friendly, greet your pupils, and exchange casual remarks. It also encourages students to get to class on time and discourages horseplay in the halls. It may well be considered as a real interest in your students and an effort to make them feel welcome.

(9) Be enthusiastic. The teacher who really believes that his lesson is important tends to be enthusiastic, and enthusiasm is contagious. If you appear bored and disinterested, you can hardly expect anything different from your class. An enthused student is not likely to seek troublemaking activities. To be dull is a deadly sin.

(10) Do something nice for your class occasionally. A class will usually support a teacher who shows an interest in them, and by doing something nice for an offender you may even shock him into acceptable behavior. Then, too, it may not necessarily be the child who should change. How about your teaching methods? Too talky? Too boring? And your personal relationships — too impersonal? Too cold? Too forbidding and distant? Too removed from the youngsters' lives?

(11) Never attempt to use threats as a deterrent. Clear explanations followed by action appear to be the best way for a teacher to show that he means what he says. Using idle threats as a disciplinary measure is a waste of time. What will you do if a student takes up the challenge? Never punish the whole class for the actions of a few — all that you will do is to lose the support of those who would have been on your side. Don't use school work as a punishment. By associating school assignments with punishment you are defeating your own purpose.

(12) Avoid arguing with your pupils. Discussions relative to classwork are valuable, but discussions that deteriorate into teacher-pupil arguments will only create ill feeling and unhappiness for both sides. Don't attempt to talk over noise. Trying

to compete with a room full of noisy students is a real mistake. Give everyone a chance to speak, and let your class know that you expect the same courtesy. As your voice goes up, so will the class volume. Try silence, stopping and waiting, and if this does not produce the desired result, speak directly to the offender. You may be able to control such rudeness merely by fixing your eyes on the errant one.

(13) Be as courteous to your class as you expect them to be with you. A request made with a smile is far more likely to be followed, and don't be afraid to say "Please." At the same time, allow the offender to save face. Failing to leave a way out for both yourself and the student can easily convert a minor problem into one which is serious.

(14) The use of detention as an effective punishment is highly debatable. A better method is to have a private conference with the student as soon as possible after the incident. Keep in mind, difficult though it may be, that it is barely possible that sometimes we are at fault, not the child. Our expectations may be off base. The cause of the misbehavior may be in our way of treating children. When you have such a conference, let the student talk. This procedure should follow immediately on the heels of the misdemeanor. This lets the offender and the rest of the class know that the teacher does not approve of the behavior. Some behavior problems may require depriving the student of certain privileges.

(15) Do not see and hear everything. Sometimes it is better to overlook an incident than to make an issue of it. However, if the breach is significant, you should not delay action. Call the student on it immediately.

(16) Never humiliate a child by a public reprimand. Publicly scolding a student not only will embitter him but sometimes enlists the rest of the class on his side, against you. Discipline should not be punitive; correction or adjustment should be your aim.

17) Avoid physical force. Laying hands on a pupil only proves who is stronger — and supposing you are not? A good teacher uses his mind, not his muscles, and never acts in anger.

18) Seek administrative help judiciously. Handle the normal range of misbehavior yourself, but don't hesitate to seek assistance for occasional problems that call for the skill of a specialist. By far the majority of classroom behavior problems may be avoided, but there will probably always be the small percentage of students who persistently misbehave. The teacher should know when to refer a problem to the appropriate counselor or special service personnel. Referring a student to the principal should be a last resort, and the principal should be made aware of the problem before the referral. Teachers who make a practice of sending students to the office are wasting the heavy artillery on small offenses. Furthermore, the principal cannot run your classroom from his office.

Responsibility for discipline is shared by all members of the school staff. The principal, as head of the school, sets the tone. In cooperation with the faculty, basic policies for discipline will be established, preferably at pre-school faculty meetings.

The weight of evidence would indicate that good school and classroom discipline and control depend primarily and continually upon the classroom teacher. A classroom teacher may reduce, if not eliminate, student behavior problems by following specific guidelines: consistency in her actions and standards; thorough preparation coupled with flexibility; and the three "F's" — firmness, friendliness, and fairness.

Beginning Teacher*

Carolyn Elizabeth Ward

IN TIME SMART

Are you suffering from boiler-factory nerves, headache, stomach ulcers, or heartache and dismay because you see your one last virtue — your deep love for kids — trickling down the drain? At times you almost hate them, and you complain that they've driven you to it. But secretly you have to admit that something is wrong — with *you*: Your classroom discipline is not only bad, it's just about impossible.

I was deeply discouraged one gloomy January day when my supervisor, Mr. Bishop, walked into my room to observe a reading class. The lesson I had prepared was good, I knew, but I panicked when the children started acting up, deliberately sharpening pencils, getting drinks, slouching in their seats, and laughing at the wrong times.

Mr. Bishop got up to go before the class was quite ended. All he said was, "I'll be back to see you at 3:30."

At 3:30 I didn't know what to expect, but I was not perpared for the straight, bald truth. "Mrs. Ward," Mr. Bishop began, "you don't have the first ingredient of a good teacher."

I seethed inwardly. How dare he say such a thing to me. I'd always loved and respected children; and, in my book, *that* had always been the first ingredient.

He went on: "The first ingredient is *good discipline*."

There was that awful word again. *Discipline*. How I hated it. Mr. Bishop continued talking, but I didn't hear a word. Finally he said, I'm going to stay here until you understand and accept the challenge of this problem. I'm going to keep talking

*Reprinted from *NEA Journal*, March 1968. Used with permission.

until something gets across to you."

"All right," I said, "I'm listening."

"Now let me add to your vocabulary," Mr. Bishop suggested. "Let's talk in a different way. You're allergic to the usual vocabulary. Here is a new word we're going to use — think about it: *Aware*."

Before long I was really listening. And I soon understood that in saying I didn't have the first ingredient of a good teacher he hadn't meant I didn't have any of the other ingredients.

"The very first thing you must do is make the children *aware* of you," he stressed. "Tomorrow morning, on the stroke of the bell, you stand up in front of your class with an interesting, well-planned lesson, and you stand there without any show of impatience or anger until every child is aware of you."

"Oh, yes!" I began defensively, I've tried that. They'd go right on making noise until noon unless I threatened them or offered a reward of some kind."

"Now wait. I didn't say 98 or 99 percent of the group. I said *every* child. And I meant 100 percent of the class. Children can't stand inaction for very long. If one or two are causing the trouble, patiently say, 'We're waiting for Jerome or Lila Bell.' And if the offenders don't quiet down, the whole group will start putting pressure on them. I don't care if you don't teach one thing tomorrow. Forget the subject matter; it will take care of itself later. But you make them *aware* of you. Agreed? They've got to look to you for action."

The next morning I stood my ground patiently until the class came to order. We had a good arithmetic lesson, and then I gave them a special treat for spelling — a well-organized spelling baseball game as a change from the usual spelldown.

The class was enthusiastic and soon decided to have a boys' team and a girls' team. I asked the boys to sit on one side of the room, the girls on the other. We chose pitchers and designated chairs for bases. A few of the boys made remarks about having to sit in a girl's seat, but they all sat down except Joe, a small boy who liked to keep the room stirred up.

For several seconds I waited patiently, looking at Joe, but he didn't budge. Don, the class leader, a good-looking, athletic boy who kept everyone charmed with his sense of humor, was silently amused at the prospect of a stall.

"We're waiting for you to sit down, Joe," I said quietly.

"I'm not going to sit down even if you try to make me," he asserted brazenly.

"That kid's going to be president some day," Don remarked.

The class laughed.

"I'm not going to make you sit down. You're quite capable of doing it all by yourself. We'll just wait until you do," I said.

"I won't, and you can't make me."

We waited. Several of the children said, "Oh, sit down. We want to play the game."

Joe finally sagged partway into the seat, and Don said, "He's sitting down now, Mrs. Ward. Let's play the game."

Calmly, I went back to see if Don was right. Those near held their breath for a minute, hoping and fearing there might be some action.

I walked slowly back to the front of the room, displaying no anger or impatience. "No, we'll have to wait some more until Joe sits down."

Others looked disgustedly at Joe and grumbled, "You're spoiling everything, stupid. Quit acting like a baby. *Sit* down."

When group pressure was with him, Don suddenly ordered, "Sit down, Joe, or I'll get you at recess!"

Joe sat down.

Hallelujah! I thought. Imagine having Don, who often made trouble himself, on my side for a change. Why hadn't someone told me these things before? Mr. Bishop was going to get a thankful earful from me after school.

We didn't get much academic work done that day, but the children became *aware* of me and my purpose in being there. From then on I was no longer a piece of furniture, a barking dog, or a lion tamer. I'd gotten smart in time to do some good.

✗ Classroom Control*
Leslie J. Chamberlin

While teachers might be reluctant to admit it, the problems of maintaining classroom control must be counted among the reasons why many leave their profession after only a brief stay.

It is not surprising, however, that too many beginning teachers find themselves facing serious discipline problems before they are ready for them.

*Reprinted from *Ohio Schools*, December 1967. Used with permission.

More than one out of every ten boys and girls in the 10-17 age group have police records and it is usually the beginning teacher who must deal with these youth in the classrooms. The general teacher transfer trend seems to be for the older, more experienced teacher with seniority to leave the so-called difficult schools.

Many of the young teachers who take their place are first-generation teachers with few people to provide counsel, encouragement, and vicarious experiences to help guide them. The beginning teacher who is assisted in adjusting to his new role is indeed the fortunate one. A district consultant or supervisor available upon call, a sincerely interested building principal, a department chairman, or even a more experienced teacher assigned to help the newcomer can be the difference between success and failure. Often, however, the orientation program involves no more than a brief explanation of daily procedures accompanied by a crystal clear warning that teachers who cannot maintain order in the classroom are considered incompetent.

The problems of classroom control can be a rude awakening for the beginning teacher who, almost without exception, comes to his first school system from a fairly desirable practice teaching experience. In the practice teaching situation, the student teacher has the supervising teacher to help him establish his authority and teacher identity. In most cases, the total school climate is one that is conducive to a good teaching-learning situation.

Too often, however, the beginning teacher's first assignment is to a school in an under-privileged neighborhood where he is left to sink or swim, to learn to keep afloat the best way he can in a school climate that places great emphasis on visible control and conduct. Thus, it is no wonder that many beginning teachers beat a path from their first classroom assignment to the psychiatrist's office, quit the profession as soon as possible, or are discharged at the completion of their first contract as being incompetent.

While the severity of disciplinary situations varies from child to child, group to group, classroom to classroom, school to school, and from neighborhood to neighborhood, several observations can be made.

In dealing with his students, the effective teacher must recognize that groups and individuals are the elements that compose any social order and that a child's world is no exception.

Everyone recognizes that groups could not be formed without individuals, but we frequently forget that the individuals that form the group are influenced by the organization they have created. This group influence on the individuals composing the group is a very real factor in student behavior. Whether the organization is a formal one (family, band, or class) or an informal one (gang, club, or neighborhood ball team), it will have an influence on the individual members.

Formal study of groups by teachers in the past has been limited. It is now recognized, however, that an understanding of the dynamics of group behavior is a basic essential to good teaching. A teacher's first contact with a student is usually as a group member. Even when working with only one child, the teacher must be aware that the student is also a member of many groups. He is not just a student but a member of a class, a team, or some other group.

Recognition of the individual's place within these groups is a vital first step in maintaining classroom control. Discipline situations usually focus attention on the misbehavior of one child. In many instances, however, the real source of the problem stems from group influence.

Group Influences

Even those behavioral problems which seem to be clearly centered around the behavior of one individual often cannot be solved or handled satisfactorily without a study of the group influences involved. Often it is not possible to completely understand a particular situation through a study of only one individual. If by careful study of the individual and proper action on the part of the teacher, the source of the child's misbehavior is found and corrected, the problem may not be completely solved in terms of group behavior. The previous misbehavior of the problematic youngster has had its effect on the group and will have a certain after-effect both on the individual and the class. The teacher will have to be aware of group reactions and influences to bring about a readjustment.

Teachers often overlook the fact that an individual student may be acting as a group member when the group is not actually physically present. Also, the relationship of one individual to other members within a particular group often changes as the group moves from one activity to another. The work relationships, authority relationships, social influences, and sex relationships change within the group.

Even beginning teachers soon realize that no two groups behave the same way although confronted with similar situations. In fact, the same group cannot be counted on for a similar response to different teachers.

The factors affecting the behavior of a group are numerous and diversified. In general, however, those factors affecting the classroom behavior of school children can be thought of as being related to mental, physical, social, or environmental problems. These are the things which have a bearing on the general level of behavior of a particular group. Every group has its normal behavior and this may or may not be considered satisfactory. Nevertheless, it is the "normal" behavior for the particular group.

Also present are conflict factors which may result in worse behavior than what is normal for that group. The classroom teacher may be able to correct these temporary conflict factors, whereas the behavior factors mentioned above usually require a coordinated action of many people and agencies if much improvement is to be accomplished.

Teachers need almost a sixth sense to anticipate trouble before it happens. Experienced teachers learn to recognize conflict factors as they begin to develop and by so doing, are better able to manage their classes.

Teachers must learn to think preventively about disciplinary problems. Naturally, not all disciplinary situations can be avoided or controlled by preventive techniques. Situations sometimes develop so rapidly or unexpectedly that the teacher can do little more than deal with them. It is best if the teacher has thought about the possibility of such a situation and has thought through various techniques that can be followed.

Opinions differ as to when a classroom situation should be considered serious. Most agree, however, that in terms of the trouble it can cause, there are three stages to the development of a serious disciplinary situation: whispering and inactivity; laughing, talking, the writing of notes, and horse-play; and the completely disorderly state which often involves tripping and punching and the throwing of missiles, catcalls, and open disrespect for the teacher.

In his efforts to correct the situation, the teacher should keep in mind that the seriousness of the problems he will face tomorrow may be lessened by the way he acts today.

If the teacher behaves in a professional way, he will:

—Never react to classroom malbehavior personally but preserve an objective point of view.

—Treat pupils in a polite manner at all times.

—Distinguish between the child and his behavior, rejecting malbehavior without rejecting the child.

—Try to locate the cause, not the symptom, of the trouble.

—Try to remember what it was like to be a child — insecure and full of doubt while wanting to succeed.

—Be reasonable, patient, and consistent.

—Choose his words carefully, remembering that his special choice of words will be an important factor in motivating a response from the children involved.

—Take a diagnostic look at the whole situation and do some thinking about the future.

It is a poor practice to scold a misbehaving child in front of his classmates. Arranging for a child to be "alone" for a time sometimes solves the immediate situation and provides times to delve somewhat deeper into the trouble.

One thing that a beginning teacher must come to realize fairly early is that some problems cannot be managed by the classroom teacher alone. A fruitful first step to try when confronted with a serious disciplinary situation is to contact the child's home. Often a short note to his parents, a brief phone call, or, if necessary, a short visit to the home will bring the family and school into close cooperation in attempting to solve the problem. It is important that the teacher be acquainted with the various services provided by his school system for attacking serious classroom situations. Over and beyond this, the teacher should be familiar with the various agencies and individuals in the community as a whole that can be brought to bear on a problem which the teacher feels is too serious for him to handle alone.

There are times when the pupil should be sent from the classroom at once and without many words. Some caution must be exercised, however. A child should be sent from the class only when the best interest of the class demands it. If he is sent from the room as a temporary measure, this should be understood by all concerned. And before sending a child from the class, the teacher should consider the various alternatives.

The beginning teacher must recognize that good classroom discipline is a climate composed of many factors. The teacher's understanding of the group structures involved in his total classroom is one such factor. He must also have an understanding of the general economic and cultural background of his students, their religious beliefs, their home environment, their neighborhood environment, and other circumstances of their lives.

But over and above these things, there must be something about the teacher — a personality leadership, a charisma — if a really good teaching-learning situation is to be established.

The importance of the teacher's attitudes and behavior in setting a good example for the students cannot be over-emphasized. Children behave so much like the adults around them that it is at times almost comical. Anything we do before children — for good or ill — remains with them longer than an adult can imagine.

The good teacher realizes that modern discipline, which emphasizes self-control and self-direction, is one of the most difficult things a child must learn to master in our changing social framework. By providing a learning situation that is free from serious distractions, the teacher can make a contribution toward the student's development.

Chapter IV

Discussionette

1. What can a teacher do to help students who have limited abilities for success?

2. What are some advantages and disadvantages of providing "social periods"?

3. What qualities, in your opinion, distinguish successful professional teachers?

4. Which traits are most important for successful professional teachers? Least important?

5. Do most beginning teachers really understand group behavior?

6. Is enough time spent in education courses on effective discipline for new teachers?

7. Is it easy for new teachers to keep the 4 P's in mind?

8. Which of these ideas would work well in elementary, junior high, and high school situations?

9. How can cumulative records help you with your students? How can they hinder or hurt relationships?

10. Why is it good to have policies for everyday procedures?

11. What are some nice things you can do for your class occasionally?

12. Which of Easton High School's hints on classroom control to new teachers are most valuable? Would you add any?

13. Is a thorough knowledge of subject matter adequate in establishing classroom discipline?

14. Are some teachers teaching around discipline problems rather than attempting to treat these problems?

Discussionette Words and Concepts

learning style	teaching	interest level
anticipating	caring	enthusiastic
courteous	sense of humor	interesting
leadership	charisma	psychology

Try to use these words.

Try to explain these words.

Try to relate these words and their concepts to current or emerging educational patterns regarding the teacher's role.

CHAPTER V

﴾ THE ADMINISTRATOR-SUPERVISOR- ﴿
PARENT ROLES

INTRODUCTION

THERE ARE MANY PEOPLE who do not work in school classrooms who are directly concerned with school discipline. These people include school administrators, supervisors, and parents who play either a direct or indirect role in forming and carrying-out school discipline policies. School boards, superintendents, principals, parent-teacher associations, etc. quite often develop rules and regulations regarding the operation of schools yet are not directly involved with students. Usually these groups assist in the formulation of school disciplinary policies, but do not directly work in the situation where their problems develop.

Since these groups assist in policy formulation, but do not carry out the actual discipline procedure, teachers should be knowledgeable of their role and influence. This chapter will assist the teacher in developing a better understanding of these groups and their motivations.

Teachers, at times, do not understand the role of these community groups and communication problems can develop. The best way to avoid these communication problems is to understand and work with these groups and their motivations.

The Schoolboard and Discipline*

J. B. Johnson and R. B. Lynn

It is not the function of the board of education or its individual members to help a classroom teacher decide when Bad Boy Bill should be moved from the back row to a front seat where he may be more easily watched.

It is the function of the board to give firm backing to teacher, principal, and

superintendent in disciplinary matters and to expel Bill if his antisocial behavior progresses — or regresses — to the point where such action is needed.

Also, the board should not tolerate disciplinary measures by school faculties which are unfair, discriminatory, or of a nature that will not develop high morals, good school spirit, desirable attitudes, and good citizenship.

*Reprinted from *NEA Journal,* September 1958. Used with permission.

Stated another way, the board of education is a policy-making body. It should not be expected to solve disciplinary problems, but must enunciate policies and insist upon practices which will help develop in pupils desirable attitudes, school and community pride, self-respect, dignity, and responsibility.

This means that the board must recognize that administrative policies within the various schools are controlled by, or result from, the curriculum that is offered.

The board, therefore, can best fulfill its basic purpose and do most to prevent the development of disciplinary problems by providing the most nearly adequate educational opportunities possible.

In our opinion, to do so requires a program that includes:

—Good teachers, adequately paid

—Classes of reasonable size

—Adequate supplementary and enrichment materials

—Grouping of students according to their ability

—Counseling and guidance

—Facilities for recreation and physical-education programs

—Parent-teacher co-operation

—Reasonable lines of communication for school employees, pupils, and parents

—A strong academic and vocational program

—Adequate classroom and work space

—Inschool time for teacher preparation

—Community support of the schools' cultural subjects, such as art, music, and language.

However, even if all these desirables could be provided, we would still not have a formula which would guarantee that disciplinary difficulties would not arise. And if they did, their solution would still require good judgment, reason, co-operation, and give-and-take by all parties concerned.

Nor does "all parties concerned" mean just the recalcitrant pupil, his teacher, principal, superintendent, and school board.

The board of education and the school officials should not attempt to replace the parents and other agencies. While board and school must assume their share of responsibility for behavior problems, they should expect the home, the church, and the community also to accept a fair share of responsibility.

The board of education should co-operate with such community groups as the Scouts, the Y's, the park board, the recreation department, and the churches in an effort to provide for the general welfare of all pupils and to keep disciplinary problems to a minimum.

The Role of the Principal in Discipline*
Robert J. Chamberlain

Before considering the effective role of the principal in dealing with the discipline problems of a school, it is necessary to digress long enough to look at some of the techniques which the classroom teacher may very well find useful. Even prior to this investigation, let us consider some of the specifics which are encompassed by the word discipline. Herein we find truth, promptness, kindness, protection of smaller people, helpfulness toward older people, respect for property, respect for privacy, and respect for personality.

*Reprinted from *NASSP Journal,* September 1959. Used with permission.

Classroom Techniques

Too often we look at a discipline case as being the immediate action of an incorrigible student. On occasion this may be true, but generally it is not so. Rather, we need to look upon discipline as a long-range teaching situation, even as we consider the teaching of English or arithmetic over a period of several years. The intricate involvements of good discipline are learned by trial-and-error, through persistent and conscientious teaching, even as good sentence structure and correct spelling come about after several years of training. Thus the class teacher needs to develop a philosophy of tending to help the students with personal problems, rather than letting frustration ride rampant because all matters of discipline cannot be immediately eradicated. Fundamentally, as good future American citizens, students need to learn that whatever they do in life and wherever they do it, they will always have a boss. Where could there be a better place to learn this than in the classroom. In fact, as teachers, we would be derelict in our duties not to teach this basic tenet. Considering this, then, we must look upon the teacher as the boss in the classroom. How can this fact be disseminated without saying as much in words?

1. The first day of school is tremendously important. This is the time when students enter the classroom with a "let's see" attitude. Teachers should be quick to capitalize on this occasion, particularly by being well prepared, mentally alert, and by displaying an air of genial authority. The old adage that first impressions are lasting ought to be carefully observed.

2. Students eventually respect most those teachers who demand respect and discipline. I remember very well recently interviewing some of our former students who were completing their first year of college work. In questioning them as to which high-school teachers contributed most to their training, the answers were almost unanimously the ones who enjoyed the reputation in school of being "hard." As teachers, we need to consider most the type of discipline which will be best for the students in the long run, not what will make the students like the teacher most now.

3. I am convinced that students have a keen sense of fair play. Certainly this virtue strikes at the very heart of all of us, and we may easily over-look this matter in too-quickly dealing with a discipline situation. A moment's hesitation, or even better, deferring action for a few hours or until the next day may avoid the irreparable harm caused by an inadequate decision wherein the elements of fair play have been violated.

4. Good judgment dictates that a teacher should not make threats to students that he cannot carry out. This may very well be another case of the teacher's issuing an ultimatum at the pitch of a discipline situation. In making a threat and failing to carry it out when the occasion demands it is to lose prestige and command of an entire class, not only with the student involved. It is well not to be too specific in saying what will happen if so and so occurs.

5. If we are to teach discipline and good order, we must first set the examples. One technique of producing this effect is to maintain excellence in the physical appearance of the classroom. Such things as paper on the floor, ill-kept bulletin boards, and disarranged shelves suggest a lack of good order to students entering the room. It is only reasonable then that they should assume that the teacher will be equally careless in matters of discipline. The pace is set before the tardy bell rings. We have

only to think momentarily of how quickly we form opinions of people by their manner of dress and initial appearance. Students react similarly to the physical appearance of the classroom.

6. How often teachers have gone on a campaign against a particular rule infraction, only to let it drop for perhaps a week or so and then wonder why the irregularity re-occurred. Again, the necessity for consistency. Whatever minimum standards are set, they should be maintained. It is well at this point again to emphasize that we should not undertake to correct more irregularities than time and good judgment permit. It is important that students do not build up the idea that the discipline which is being exacted today will be forgotten tomorrow.

7. Frequently, occasions occur in the classroom when the teacher's immediate reaction is to dismiss the student from the room. This is a dangerous practice. Whenever this is done, the teacher loses a certain measure of her prestige and future effectiveness. She is in effect saying to the class, here is a situation I cannot handle, and as such, admits defeat. Such action is tantamount to chalking up a win for one or several students. The psychological effect becomes increasingly worse with each repeated performance. We realize, of course, that the time comes occasionally when immediate dismissal is imperative. In such an event, the student's eventual return to class ought to be a meek, humble, and not-easily-forgotten experience.

8. Finally, I would urge that not too great a fear of the principal's office be built up in the minds of the students. The principal should be looked upon by the student body as a friend and confidant to an even greater degree than he is recognized as a distant and evil monster. Good judgment by teachers in their references to the principal's office play an important part in this mental characterization.

The Principal

We come now more specifically to the point of what the principal can do to insure the best possible discipline practices in the school. We are considering here not only the principal himself, but also the assistant principal or any other officer of the school who is charged with the responsibility of discipline. The need for constant vigilence is a paramount factor. The principal must be the pace setter. Just as students respect the exacting teacher, so do teachers recognize this quality in the principal. Discipline must be a co-operative effort on the part of faculty and administration. We might list these points in some detail.

1. It is the professional obligation of the principal to back the teacher in his decisions, and thus maintain the respect and prestige of the classroom teacher. In order that the principal can do this, the teacher must be careful not to say or do things that do not lend themselves to administrative backing. Such things as striking a student, threats of violence or expulsion, or destroying a student's work are difficult for the principal to enforce when the issue is brought to the office. These situations become embarrassing for the principal to unravel however desirous he may be of doing so. Preventive measures such as a faculty directive or discussion session should eliminate the occurrence of the aforementioned problem. The teacher is dependent upon the principal to give continuity and backing to his efforts to enforce discipline. Cooperation at this point will convey the notion to the teacher that he and the principal are playing on the same team.

2. It is imperative that, when a student is remanded to the office, he be given an opportunity to tell his story to a seemingly

impartial and sympathetic audience. A decision, however, based upon the student's version will generally prove to be an unwise one. Frequently, upon this first listening one might easily wonder why a student was dismissed upon so slight a provocation. As soon as possible the principal should confer with the teacher, at which time it will usually be found that the incident in question was only the culmination of a series of prior acts of misconduct. Armed with this new evidence, the principal is then in a favorable position to pursue the situation with the student on a basis of "let's talk about everything that has happened in class."

3. A situation similar in nature to the previous discussion is one in which a parent telephones the principal to relate a discipline situation as told to him by his youngster. Here again, unless one is wary of the impending proceedings, he may question the action taken by the teacher. The principal must immediately remind himself that a defensive action is being presented for which there must have been a justifiable cause. The purpose of such a call by the parent is to form a commitment by the principal that the teacher acted unwisely and without adequate cause. If such an implication is given by the principal, he will have literally "pulled the rug from under one of his staff members" without hearing the teacher's story first. At this point, the principal must be a very good listener, as the parent will only be satisfied by having his say. The only wise answer will be a promise to confer with the teacher as soon as possible and call him back shortly. Not only should the principal get the facts on the immediate situation, but also investigate all previous acts of misconduct as long as the student has been in school, together with his grades in relation to his academic ability and his attendance and tardiness record. These facts may come in handy to strengthen the school's point of view.

4. In order that adequate records are available for cases such as the one just mentioned, it is necessary that a system of referrals and filing be maintained in one central office. Merely to inform a parent that his son has been a discipline problem for a long time and suspension may be likely is not enough. He may then counter by asking for specific instances. If the principal can pull out an index card or file folder and recite exact instances of misconduct, the teacher involved, and the date of the offense, the parent can do nothing but respect the integrity and efficiency of the school. The parent will usually go over to the side of the school at this point and promise co-operation. To bring the parent along, the principal should assure the parent that he has the best interest of the student at heart and by a co-operative effort probably a solution can be worked out that will be for the best interest of the boy. This, the parent will understand. A technique which is probably not used enough is that of calling the parents in for an interview. By doing so he sees that the principal is not the ogre that the student has described him to be.

5. Occasionally a teacher who has dismissed a student in utter desperation and disgust is surprised to find that the trip to the office did not result in the loss of a limb and, therefore, the principal did nothing about it. It must be remembered that when a teacher does send a student out for discipline action, he inherently expects something to happen. The principal has an obligation to let the teacher know what action was taken. Physical action being out of the picture, we need to look at more civil types of reprimand. If this is a repeated case, it might be well to send

the youngster home and request he return with his parent. When mother or father are asked to come to school, something is likely to happen. By having one or both parents present, together with the offender, the elements of pride and shame can be brought into play. It may be pointed out to the student that the only thing that parents live for is to see their children grow up and be the type of person in whom they may take pride. The student may be questioned as to just what things he has done while being in the school of which he can be proud. (With such a student, he usually finds it hard to name one.) The point may be pursued of listing the blessings which this student has, such as good health, parents, a free country, the economic necessities as contrasted with others within the building who are struggling against the odds of a broken home, incurable disease, a crippled body, *etc.* This line of reasoning almost always forces a feeling of shame not only upon the student, but also with the parents.

6. Certainly various buildings place some emphasis on different items of conduct such as gum chewing, types of haircuts, belts in trousers, punctuality, *etc.* In order for a school to be successful in the pursuit of one or all of such items, there must be uniformity of action by all teachers. A violation of any of the stated regulations should be picked up by any teacher in any part of the building. By having everyone work on these things, the burden does not fall upon a few. Also, by a lack of uniformity of enforcement, certain teachers may take a "what's the use" attitude in feeling that they are fighting the battle alone. It becomes the responsibility of the principal constantly to remind teachers of their obligation to be alert for offenders, and to impress upon them that, by everyone working, the job is made easier for all.

7. All of the foregoing items could be placed under the caption of citizenship. This is a job for everyone in the building all of the time. A school is known for the type of discipline it exacts and the citizenship it stresses. The time to get discipline is before it is violated, and nothing takes the place of constant hammering. This may take the form of awards, citations, assembly programs, public address announcements, and other novel recognition activities. The rewards of stress on good citizenship are numerous; to overlook this quality breeds discipline problems.

Primer for New Principals*

Gerald DeWitt

The new principal, facing a new school situation, a new community, and new colleagues, has mixed emotions of anticipation and anxiety. To do his job well, he needs sufficient time for pre-evaluation and pre-planning in order to develop guidelines for his first year. Four critical areas which will dominate his thinking will be the school's organization, the curriculum and instruction, the communications program, and staff and student morale.

Overall Organization

The school administrator's first function will be to define his own role and the roles of his associates in written form, describing each area of responsibility. These descriptions will not only detail the roles of other administrators, department chairmen, counselors, class and club sponsors, and

*Reprinted from *The Clearing House,* September 1965. Used with permission.

so on, but also delineate those of non-certified personnel.

Through a review of existing written materials, the new principal will gain an insight into past school organization and procedures. Following conferences with key personnel, he must decide which regulations he expects to continue, which he prefers to hold in abeyance before making a decision, and which he prefers to change immediately. A word of caution: immediate changes should be kept to a minimum and inaugurated only after careful consideration.

He should study the school calendar carefully to learn the type, quality, and balance of the school's activities.

He will want to determine the status of student government and compare it with his own defined attitudes in this area. Through school publications, he will familiarize himself with the student leaders and, if at all possible, invite them for pre-school conferences.

The new administrator will also review and evaluate the assignments, organization, and leadership of the custodial and secretarial staffs.

One of the crucial areas is that of scheduling. If, on arrival, he finds his work completed, he will familiarize himself with the procedure. If scheduling has not been done, he will duplicate the efforts of the previous year after surveying the curriculum, staff, and facilities. He will make few changes until he is completely familiar with the school situation.

If the school is involved in data processing, the newcomer will study carefully the operational procedures and services rendered. He will check the data processing calendar to insure that it has accuracy and balance and that it permits sufficient time for efficiency of operation.

Other organizational problems will include reviewing the attendance system and its relationship to good public relations, checking the plan for calling substitute teachers, analyzing the system of staff and student parking, and devising a method for the secure accounting of school keys.

Curriculum and Instruction

The new principal must provide *immediate* leadership for his faculty, so that together they will continually seek ways of providing students with meaningful educational experiences. He will determine the status of the curriculum developmental structure by analyzing the curriculum, department by department.

He will share his curriculum philosophy with his staff and work with the faculty, as a whole or in groups, in making a continued evaluation and revision of existing curriculum offerings.

The improvement of instruction, as important as curriculum improvement, rates high on the new principal's list of priorities. After consultation with department chairmen, he will establish his plan for such items as schedule of class visitations, follow-up procedures, methods of rating, and so forth.

He will plan in advance for specific in-service workshops, the orientation of new teachers, the use of consultants and guest speakers, and carefully structured faculty meetings, which will emphasize improved instruction.

The observant principal will acquaint himself thoroughly with the facilities, equipment, and supplies of the school plan in order to determine their effect on quality instruction. He will then initiate recommended changes, inspections, repairs, cleaning, and rearranging.

Communications

The principal will realize that his success or failure in a new situation may be determined by his ability to communicate his philosophy to the patrons, staff, and student body.

By reading and analyzing the written communications and minutes of the previous year, he will know his school and, at the same time, become aware of areas where communication revisions and refinements are needed.

Soon after his arrival, he will meet with P.T.A. officers to discuss the year's program. In order to advance his own educational philosophy, the principal may want to suggest such additions to the established program as a school-to-home publication, a study group, a college night, or a career conference.

Throughout the year the newcomer to the principal's position will be constantly alert to ways of informing the certified and non-certified staffs of his desires. Channels of information may include the faculty meeting, staff newsletter, use of the public address system, and meetings with groups such as department chairmen, counselors, student government sponsors, class sponsors, and student leaders.

Although the principal will be eager to provide opportunities for developing his philosophy, describing his organizational procedures, and revealing his future hopes, he will also want to encourage patrons, staff, and students to inject their democratic thinking into developing a school philosophy and improving operational procedures. For such purposes, he may want to introduce the suggestion box, informal coffees, a faculty bulletin board, or personal conferences.

Individual conferences with staff members should be scheduled in the spring. Although time-consuming, these face-to-face communications are the most successful means for attaining desired goals.

Other communication areas which will demand the attention of the new principal include school records, bulletins, handbooks, student publications, and assemblies.

The school record system must be checked to insure its accuracy and its provision for an efficient way of reporting information to students, parents, colleges, and prospective employers.

Faculty bulletins deserve attention to make sure that they are informative, accurate, concise, and inspirational.

Decisions will be made as to the areas to be covered by handbooks. Possibilities will include a curriculum handbook, with subject numbers, titles, and descriptions; a teacher's handbook containing philosophy, procedures, and policies; a substitute teacher's handbook; a student handbook; a registration handbook; a job description handbook; and an awards handbook.

The school publication will be reviewed in light of established guidelines pertaining to editorial and photography policies and manner of portraying school life.

Another question which must be answered is whether the assembly program meets its educational objective through a balance of programs in number, kind, and quality.

In fact, no aspect of communications is too small to escape the attention of the principal who is establishing a successful administration.

Attitudes and Morale of Staff and Students

The development of positive and cooperative attitudes in both staff and students is of prime importance to the new principal. He cannot become so bogged down with organizational and procedural details that he is limited in his personal opportunities to influence his colleagues and the student body. Too often they are unaware of what the principal stands for and, what is more tragic, are not particularly interested.

A semi-open door policy is a recommended procedure for the new principal, so that his faculty can see him and talk with him, thus building a feeling of security regarding what he is and what he stands for.

Early it is necessary that the new principal take time to know his staff, to become familiar with items that are important to his teachers—their names, birthdays, families, interests, defeats, and accomplishments. This can be done by verbal comment of short personal notes or letters. A principal who is interested in his staff will encourage teachers, by his example, to be equally interested in their students.

The school head will be responsible for leadership in a preventive program in school discipline. This involves the provision of well-informed homeroom and classroom teachers, quality assembly programs, a positive cocurricular program, and an active student government.

The new principal will provide opportunities for the involvement of students in service projects, student conferences, and leadership activities. At all times he will encourage each student to achieve his potential.

After reviewing the rules and regulations of the school, he will make the necessary adjustments so that they are reasonable, yet firm. Above all else he will define his plans for the execution of these rules with a firmness and consistency that will insure a feeling of security on the part of staff and students.

The opportunity for students to develop self-discipline will be one of his greatest challenges. He will give serious thought to the possibility of creating honor study halls and endorsing dignified organizations such as the National Honor Society and an awards system that recognizes students for service, good character, and leadership in the school.

The new principal can, through careful analysis and appraisal, and by including his colleagues' opinions in addition to his subjective judgment, design for himself and the school a plan of gradual change which will instill in the students, staff, and community a new enthusiasm for learning. He can do this only by giving close attention and considerable time to the projects described here, which will enable him to get a closer look at what is being done in his school—and at what he intends to do about it.

A Principal Looks at Discipline*
Delmar H. Battrick

Since the beginning of education, there have always been good teachers; for them, disciplinary problems have been rare — unless the teachers were faced by classes of unmanageable size. They are the teachers who like children and who inspire them to learn by opening new vistas of knowledge for them. They are the teachers who have infinite patience with the slow learn-

ers and the capacity to challenge the quicksilver minds of the gifted.

In contrast to these teachers, we have those for whom formal discipline, strictly and authoritatively administered, serves as a cover-up for their own shortcomings. As better-qualified teachers continue to re-

*Reprinted from *NEA Journal*, September, 1958. Used with permission.

place the rigid, authoritarian type, many of the disciplinary problems of today will disappear.

A part of the required "equipment" of any good teacher is a thorough knowledge of the physical, mental, and emotional growth patterns of the youngsters under his charge. The teacher's ability to command respect stems from this basic knowledge of the individual, combined with a mastery of the subject matter he is to teach.

In our school the toughest discipline problems, I believe, have been solved (or prevented) by trying to create a school climate which radiates friendliness. This friendliness must exist between administrators and teachers, teachers and students, and students and administrators. It must result in a desire on students' part to protect their school's good name by positive acts of good citizenship.

We have used student councils, clubs, and other student-directed activities to assist students in exerting their leadership ability toward imroved school morale and good citizenship.

Our teachers have developed a high standard of classroom control by creating an atmosphere where the moral tone is exceptionally high.

Ruth Baker teaches eighth-grade English. One of her main concerns is the mental and emotional growth of her students during this stormy period of physiological change. The boys and girls like her, and the feeling is mutual.

Part of her success as a teacher is due to her well-organized plan of procedure. Her room is immaculate — bulletin boards, cupboards, window shades, all give the impression that orderliness and careful planning are a part of her teaching.

Early in the semester, simple, routine classroom requirements are discussed and accepted. Miss Baker is quick to spot student leaders and to delegate responsibility to them. Identification of potential trouble makers also comes early in her plans, and she soon holds private conferences with these students to encourage a good attitude and to help in their adjustment.

Miss Baker's early courses in the psychology of the adolescent taught her to look for the underlying cause in most undesirable behavior, since behavior is only a symptom. This understanding leads her to use test records and other guidance data on her students as she evaluates their individual growth.

Another teacher, George Martin, whose field is industrial arts, has a particular fondness for boys who are sometimes classified as "square pegs."

Ron and Phil were two such boys who, because of repeated failures, had become rather serious discipline problems. When assigned to shop, they showed no interest in producing anything either for themselves or for anyone else.

A request from the vocal-music department for a hi-fi record player intrigued Mr. Martin. He decided that if the physics department could assemble the amplifier and speaker, his boys could produce a creditable cabinet. When he suggested the project to his woodworking class, he was pleased to find that Ron and Phil showed an interest.

With his encouragement and instruction, a beautiful cabinet was made by these two boys, who worked long hours after school to have it completed by the end of the semester. In the process, they worked cooperatively with two boys from the physics class. The finished product, admired and enjoyed by all, is a particular source of pride to Ron and Phil. Incidentally, their discipline problems diminished.

Gene Thompson was labeled a bully and

a perpetual source of trouble to all his teachers. When he was assigned to a sophomore art class, Marion Jones, his art teacher, soon realized that imposing the prescribed art course on Gene would accomplish nothing.

After winning his confidence, she found he had an interest in oil painting. By developing this interest and providing him with special equipment and instruction in this medium, Miss Jones not only developed Gene's talent but helped him become better adjusted as an individual.

Of basic importance in this whole problem of helping students grow toward responsible citizenship is an understanding of adolescent youth in general and of the individual home situation in particular. As Luella Cole has said in her book, *The Psychology of Adolescence:* The teacher should know that "much adolescent restlessness and inattention are due to muscle cramps, the ravenous appetite, and the glandular developments of the period." The teacher "is likely to waste his energy on useless efforts at discipline. The awkward, the inattentive day-dreamer of 16 cannot be cured of his characteristics by either extra assignments or sarcasm, but in the course of time he will grow out of these annoying manifestations."

Family influences and methods of discipline used in the home may vary to such an extent among members of a single class as to be a major factor in class discipline. Various of our students have encountered such diverse types of home discipline as severe corporal punishment, scolding, contrasting one child's behavior or achievement with that of another, deprivation of privileges, bribing, threatening, rewarding, appealing to affection or reason, and allowing children to suffer the natural consequences of their acts by exercising no parental control whatsoever.

Taking a cue from the last-mentioned approach, the principal can pass the problem of discipline entirely to his teachers by letting them simply make the best of it. On the other hand, he can encourage his entire staff to work together in solving their problems.

The principal is in a position to help develop a citizenship policy based on the best thinking and experience of students, teachers, and parents. His teaching staff will vary greatly in natural ability to handle discipline problems. That is why he should work through key people to instill a basic philosophy of good school citizenship. Among other things, he can have frequent conferences with boys' and girls' counselors and home-room teachers. They can help him keep a constant check on how the school citizenship program is going.

In school, as in the home, there is no substitute for talking things over with the people most directly involved in a problem. It is often effective for the principal to undertake this himself. At other times, he will call on whichever staff members represent his most direct link with the students.

I think many teachers will find helpful the following "Tips on Classroom Control," based on a list which appeared in the April 1958 *Bulletin* of the Minnesota Association of Secondary-School Principals.

—Move about the room frequently.

—Use your eyes. Look at all parts of the room regularly.

—Word questions clearly and insist on clearly stated answers.

—Allow for supervised study time in class.

—Make all assignments and explanations clear and definite.

—Establish classroom regulations by the end of the first week of the semester—what students may do and what they may not do.

—Have an understanding with the principal about what types of discipline problems should be sent to the office.

—Don't make a major issue out of trivial offenses.

—Don't accept impertinence.

—Don't talk too much, too fast, or too loudly.

—Avoid group punishment for the mistakes of individuals.

—Avoid threats you cannot enforce.

—Look for ways to relieve or prevent tensions in the classroom by varying your methods, e.g., introducing guest speakers, films, tape recorders, field trips.

And my final tip is this: Remember, your principal's major job is to help you improve your teaching. Use his help whenever you need it. He will appreciate your asking him.

The Beginning Teacher and Classroom Control*

Carl H. Peterson

One of the primary concerns of secondary school administrators is the ability of new teachers to maintain proper classroom control. In larger urban high schools in particular, where the student is apt to be somewhat more cosmopolitan, many young teachers find to their surprise that the young "adolescents" sitting in their classrooms are as worldly and mature as the teacher.

At Easton High School, an assistant principal is given responsibility for the professional growth of new teachers in matters of curriculum, teaching techniques, and classroom control. Since Easton expects each of its eighty-four classroom teachers to be capable of maintaining proper classroom discipline under normal conditions without outside assistance, it is considered important that new teachers receive proper guidance at the outset.

The first step in Easton's program is to see that each new teacher consults several books on adolescent psychology, available in the school library, with the thought that the craftsman must know the material with

*Reprinted from *The Clearing House*, Sept. 1960. Used with permission.

which he is working. If possible, these materials are made available to the teacher during the summer.

With the start of school, the administrator charged with the supervision of new personnel meets frequently with them during the first few weeks of the term. At these meetings the teachers are encouraged to ask questions and to share their feelings and experiences with other new staff members. One of the primary purposes of the frequent get-togethers is to create in new teachers the feeling that they are part of a friendly group and that they have not been left entirely to their own devices at the beginning of their teaching careers.

In addition to frequent informal meetings, where the administrator acts as an adviser and guide rather than an authoritarian figure, he also visits classes frequently, but for short periods of time. The reason is obvious. Long visits, where the observer sits through an entire class, often tend to unnerve rather than reassure a new teacher. Short, spot visits, however, where the administrator drops in briefly, serve to reassure the teacher that he is not, after all, quite alone, and that help is available in case he needs it.

The frequent sight of an administrator strolling casually into the room has an additional benefit. High-spirited members of the student body are less apt to take advantage of an untested staff member if they know that an administrator who has "been around" as much as they have is apt to catch them in an unwise act.

"Testing the new teacher out" was how one student rather lamely explained to me his overt misbehavior, in a recent closed-door disciplinary session. Little did the student know, perhaps, that his remark was a rather neat summation of what the adventurous student, in his classroom misbehavior, is attempting to do to the neophyte teacher.

In order that the testing-out period be of as short duration as possible, each new teacher at Easton is given eleven concrete suggestions for obtaining student-teacher rapport. The suggestions are based on the fact that there are certain things which a new teacher does, or does not do, which materially affect his chances of establishing, or failing to establish, rapport with his pupils.

Lacking experience, many young teachers become overdictatorial, meting out punishment for every tiny infraction. To an age group whose primary urge is to move toward independence, this is anathema. Resentment soon flows wholesale, and the battle is taken up in earnest.

Other young teachers move in the opposite direction. Believing in a democratic classroom atmosphere, and wishing to gain the good will of their students, they fail to assert themselves in the slightest degree. Unfortunately, adolescents, though seeking freedom and independence, usually lack the maturity to function effectively in a lassez-faire atmosphere. Consequently, bedlam soon reigns, and the teacher's days become one exasperating effort after another to hold the line. In addition, control

once lost becomes extremely difficult to regain.

The eleven suggestions for establishing and maintaining proper classroom control, given to all new Easton High School teachers, are outlined below. It has been the author's experience that the new teacher, following these precepts, gains a feeling of confidence in his ability to handle adolescent behavior sooner than if he had been left entirely on his own. In addition, older teachers often benefit from a reassessment of the basic techniques essential to the maintenance of a harmonious teacher-pupil classroom relationship.

Hints On Classroom Control To New Teachers

1. *Be businesslike.* The students will be watching you to see what kind of person you are. Remember that first impressions mean a great deal. If they size you up as a mature, confident person who knows what he is doing, the battle is half won.

2. *Be prepared.* High school students are quick to note indecision, vacillation, and unpreparedness on the part of the teacher. Start each lesson on time and know what you are going to say and do.

3. *Keep your lesson and presentation interesting.* Bored students often get into trouble. Interested students seldom do.

4. *Know when to overlook.* Don't seek trouble. Overlook small things which are unintentional and do not matter.

5. *Know when to assert yourself.* This is one of the most important principles in maintaining proper classroom control, and the place where many young teachers err. Every experienced teacher (and every student) knows that for the common good, there is in every democratically run classroom an invisible line beyond which students must not pass.

(a) Distinguish between unintentional and intentional pupil misbehavior.

(b) Distinguish between pupil discussion and pupil argumentation.

(c) Distinguish between pupil humor and pupil insolence.

Once having decided that a pupil's action falls into one of the three latter categories, deal with the situation immediately. Remember that, as a teacher, you too have certain rights. Do not be afraid to assert yourself. Your students will respect you for so doing.

6. *Do not bluff.* Students are quick to see through and lose respect for the teacher who continually threatens but who does nothing about pupil misbehavior. Such a teacher is fair game for a roomful of high-spirited adolescents. Once you have decided that chastisement or punishment is merited, administer it matter-of-factly and return to the lesson. (*Important:* Experience has shown that some students, if not all, have an amazing facility for assuming an air of injured innocence when being reprimanded by, or after receiving a disciplinary ninth period from, a new or beginning teacher. Your school administration assures you that this is perfectly normal, and asks you to remember that students respect a teacher with strength of mind and character. Once having decided that a student deserves disciplinary action, stick to your guns. When administrative backing is needed, it will be there.)

7. *Be consistent.* Do not suppress certain pupil actions one day, and tolerate them the next. This leads to pupil insecurity and distrust of you as a teacher and person. Let the pupils know what you will and will not stand for, and your disciplinary problems will be few and far between.

8. *Be fair.* Treat all pupils alike. There is no place for favoritism in the classroom.

9. *Do not pretend that you know everything.* Simply because you are a teacher does not mean that you must always be right. Your students already know that you are not infallible, and will respect you if you say, "I don't know; let's look it up."

10. *Get to know your students.* One of the basic needs of adolescents is a need to conform. Perennial discipline problems are nonconformists, and most are in need of outside help. A series of afterschool conferences with an interested, understanding teacher can do much to help such students find and accept themselves. A teacher who takes the time to know and understand his students usually finds that his job has become more interesting and that his major disciplinary problems have a way of disappearing rapidly.

11. *Keep your sense of humor.* One of the most important things a teacher can bring to class with him as he attempts to relate effectively to the varied adolescent personalities which fill his classroom period by period is a sense of humor. Students look forward to their classes with mature, confident teachers whose cheerfulness and humor combine to make the lesson both interesting and worth while. In addition, humor has saved many a classroom situation from becoming needlessly embarrassing or difficult for both pupils and teacher. The teacher who combines firmness with a sense of humor to fit the occasion is hard to beat.

Practical guideposts such as the foregoing, designed to aid the new teacher in securing and maintaining an optimum pupil-teacher relationship, combined with frequent, friendly supervision and advice, do much to ease the strain of teacher adjustment during the all-important opening weeks.

As most administrators will agree, the teacher who has the class under control early in September is quite likely to be the teacher who has the least problem, disciplinewise, in June.

Antisocial Behavior: Whose Fault*

Joseph Resnick

Considerable controversy exists as to where blame should be placed for a child's antisocial behavior. There are those who would stress that the child is primarily at fault. Others place the responsibility on the parents. Consideration has also been given to the school, the neighborhood, and heredity as influencing factors.

The statement that there are no delinquent children, only delinquent parents, is open to serious question. This view assumes that a parent could do better if he merely decided to do so. Such an assumption appears unwarranted. Can we take for granted that the parent knows what is best and can apply his knowledge? The circumstances in which the parent lived as a child and as a youth have served to mold him so that his own fears and insecurities become a part of him. Actually society as a whole is responsible for delinquent behavior since both the parent and the child are its products. The parent who has suffered repeated failure as a child and has been embarrassed because of the unkind remarks of his classmates as a result of being oversized for grade placement could hardly be expected to look enthusiastically at the school situation and urge his own child to attend. Such a parent might also think of educators as a prisoner might regard a warden, as one who assigns unpleasant and uninteresting tasks.

Parents usually do the best they know how at the time. While their methods may not be what the teacher feels he would have followed, nevertheless the procedure decided upon is what the parents felt needed to be done to meet the problem.

In every adult the cumulated incidents of his earlier life influence present conduct and behavior. The individual against whom, in childhood, society has discriminated because of color, religion, nature of his birth, extreme poverty, physical defects, or similar factors over which he has had no control, bears within himself a wound or scar which has never quite healed. These basic elements reveal their presence by rendering the person more sensitive to criticism, by giving him a tendency at times to become easily discouraged, and by increasing the speed with which he reacts to situations related to many youthful experiences, thus revealing anxiety. A knowledge of the factors which affect the adult's behavior serves to disclose the cause for present conduct and draws aside the curtain which hides the reason for undesirable behavior. When the cause for wrong behavior is known, sympathetic understanding usually replaces a desire to blame the individual.

If a child feels loved and wanted in his home, and recognizes that his parents care for each other, errors in child rearing usually do not create emotionally disturbed behavior which is serious. Similar mistakes in child training, without the common bond of mutual love, could arouse feelings of insecurity, with the accompanying accumulation of nervous tension which might find a release in various ways, such as fighting, stealing, tearing books, or carving a desk. The child tends to discount the incidents which are unpleasant if he feels that beneath the firmness is someone who is sympathetic and vitally interested.

Vivian, a girl of twelve, came to the writer's attention because of her slow learning ability. The results of an intelli-

*Reprinted from *The Clearing House*, October 1957. Used with permission.

gence test showed an I.Q. of 70; yet the child was pleasant and well adjusted to peers and adults. A conference with the mother, who had not finished elementary school, indicated that the home was stable and that treatment of the daughter involved an obvious showing of love and affection but also, at times, considerable firmness. Corporal punishment was administered when the mother felt it was needed. Sending the child to bed early when she misbehaved was a part of the disciplinary procedure. Apparently the child was making allowances for her mother's treatment and felt no bitterness, as indicated by her remark, "I really get it when I don't mind." In the school, the child was given classwork on her level of ability and related to her daily life experiences in order to arouse interest and effort. The practical nature of the school program had also served to bring achievement and praise. This child showed that when personality needs are adequately met, the result is usually a happy, well-adjusted individual.

Most misbehavior arising in the classroom may be regarded as normal in nature. Usually the reason for the misconduct can be disclosed in conferences with the child regarding his classwork, interests, and home life. Where antisocial behavior develops, it means that the child lacks techniques which will enable him to solve successfully his personal problems.

The Part the Parent Plays*

James M. Patterson

If the typical parent has not thought too much in the past about school discipline, he is thinking now. Headlines like these have compelled him:

TEEN KILLER OF 9 CAPTURED

2ND SCHOOL GIRL ATTACKED,
YOUTH SEIZED IN BROOKLYN

ROWDYISM IN SCHOOLS:
IS IT COVERED UP HERE?

SHOULD SCHOOLS KEEP
TOLERATING PUNKS?

Of course, there should also be headlines to tell us that the young punks are not typical—that they represent only from 1% to 3% of our young people.

By the time delinquency has become a statistic, it has also become largely a matter for the courts. Home and school must concentrate on preventing the delinquency

*Reprinted from *NEA Journal,* September 1958. Used with permission.

rate from rising and must redouble their concern for discipline in everyday life.

Here parents have the primary responsibility. A Chinese philosopher once said that parents who are afraid to put their foot down usually have children who step on toes. Because of strong parental influence, delinquency is almost unheard of in our Chinese-American communities.

Parents set the standards of conduct that their children carry over into the schools. I know of an instance in which a teacher was making a survey on delinquency. One Saturday night she called a number of parents to see if they knew where their children were. The results were disappointing—the first six telephone calls she made were answered by children who did not know where their parents were.

Teachers have a right to expect parents to teach acceptable standards of conduct and to set acceptable examples for their children. Simliarly, parents have a right to expect the school to uphold and not undo the moral lessons taught at home. I was shocked once to see my seventh-grade son displaying unsportsmanlike conduct on the school playground. The teacher was letting him get by with conduct that we would not have permitted.

Personally, I believe that self-discipline is the goal to strive for. Self-discipline is the result of guided practice and good examples. Teachers, administrators, and parents must set good examples. And they must not allow situations to exist which give youngsters the idea that bad conduct pays.

"What happens to boys who tell lies?" the Sunday-school teacher asked.

"They get into the show for half price," the boy replied.

The same kind of impression may be created when the class troublemaker is permitted to drop a tough course and substitute an easy one, because that looks like a reward for misconduct.

Teachers must be alert and consistent, also, about maintaining the thing we call fair play. My boy's main gripe is the unfairness of punishing the entire group for the misconduct of one member.

I believe that discipline and education go hand in hand. Good teaching prevents new disciplinary problems from developing and decreases those that already exist.

Here let me repeat my belief that education must take place at home as well as in school, and should be a continuous process in both places. If we want our youngsters to grow up able to steer a straight course, then home and school must give them the experiences that will develop the gyro we call character.

Too many people talk about *building* character. They want it built at once; they are too impatient to wait for it to *grow*. Well, it can't be built. *It must grow. In the atmosphere of freedom, cultivated by practice, fed by example, watered by desire, and warmed by the sunshine of recognition, character grows.*

This is our most important crop which you, the teachers, are cultivating, and which America and the free world will harvest. As a parent, I applaud your efforts. What's more, I'm hoeing right along beside you.

Chapter V

Discussionette

1. Discuss problems of discipline which may be brought before the board of education.

2. Is it reasonable for boards of education to establish discipline policies for schools?

3. Discuss how effective citizenship leads to effective discipline.

4. Is it true that the time to establish discipline is before it is violated?

5. What can be resolved if an administrator and a teacher have different feeling on discipline?

6. How can an administrator involve staff, students, and the community in establishing appropriate discipline?

7. What can an administrator do so people tell the administrator the truth rather than what the people think the administrator wants to hear?

8. Can "friendliness" resolve many discipline problems?

9. Discuss the tips given for classroom control.

10. How can the school and the home work together help children who demonstrate antisocial behavior?

11. Is misbehavior normal in children?

12. What can the home and school do to prevent the delinquency rate of young people from rising?

Discussionette Words and Concepts

communication	back-the-teacher	management
guidance	in loco parentis	dress codes
cooperation	home-school carry over	morale
educational program	citizenship	activism

Try to use these words.

Try to explain these words.

Try to relate these words and their concepts to current or emerging educational patterns regarding the administrator-supervisor-parent role.

PART III

UNDERSTANDING THE TECHNIQUE

CHAPTER VI

PREVENTIVE DISCIPLINE

INTRODUCTION

THE TEACHERS WHO LEARN to avoid, prevent, or control classroom situations which lead to disorder, discourtesy, or inactivity not only improves his effectiveness as a teacher, but also his job security and chances for future progress.

Good preventative disciplines requires and emphasizes self-control and self-direction from the students in the management of their own discipline. However, adequate classroom control develops when appropriate measures are taken by teachers which help to insure success.

It has been said that "an ounce of prevention is worth a pound of cure" and this is definitely true of preventative discipline. The wise teacher can direct an effective program by anticipating and planning the educational program around preventative techniques. Thus, if appropriate prevention is taken in the classroom, it is unlikely that disciplinary problems will develop.

Positive Discipline*
Foster F. Wilkinson

Research has pointed out many times that poor discipline is the factor that causes most teachers to leave the profession of teaching.

The Program

A. Have the instructional program so carefully planned that there is no time for major problems to develop.

1. Account for each minute of the day in your plans.

2. Provide optional activities and experiences for pupils who have time to spare.

3. Encourage the pursuit of individual problems, projects, and research.

B. Explain each new phase so thoroughly that pupils will not need to flounder in carrying out experiences.

1. Tell the what, where, when, how, and why of the activity.

2. Answer questions before the activity is started.

C. Organize the class as a democratic and social group.

1. Plan with the pupils what can and cannot be done, as rules for the class. Keep them where pupils can be sent to study them.

2. Elect officers and committees, and change them regularly.

*Reprinted from *Instructor,* February 1971© The Instructor Publication, Inc. Used with permission.

3. Alternate the responsibilities of the room among all members.

4. Plan as many phases of the program with the pupils as feasible.

5. Allow the children to plan some activities on their own.

D. Evaluate your teaching and pupil relationships constantly.

1. Make a detailed study of each child.

2. Allow time for pupil conferences and individual conferences each day. This may come before or after school.

3. Smile at each pupil at least once daily.

4. When days go badly, check to determine whether your plans were adequate. Chances are that they were not.

5. Set your standards slightly above what you really expect.

6. Be firm but fair in your pupil relationships.

7. Strive to make each child responsible for his own actions.

E. Anticipate possible trouble spots before they develop.

1. Idle minds should be put to work.

2. Separate habitual trouble-makers.

3. Isolate sources of misconduct immediately.

F. Handle cases of misbehavior as smoothly as possible.

1. Remain calm and unemotional yourself.

2. Give the pupil a chance to explain his actions.

3. Make a detailed study of the *real* cause behind the act.

4. Associate the punishment with the deed.

5. Continue your regular program as though nothing had happened.

G. When punishment is necessary remember these do's and don'ts.

DO'S

1. Explain thoroughly the reasons for the punishment.

2. Insist that the pupil concerned suggest some punishment for the misconduct (which may or may not be followed).

3. Allow some time for the pupil to think about his deed.

4. Become familiar with any board of education policies regarding discipline and punishment.

5. Associate as closely as possible the punishment with the deed. The following are suggested measures to use:

a) Pupil writes a paragraph explaining what happened.

b) Pupil reports to the class on what happened and why.

c) Pupil stays after others have gone to complete work not done during time wasted.

d) Pupil makes a report to the parents and has them call the teacher or principal.

e) Teacher isolates the child who has abused his class membership, preferably away from the room.

f) Teacher makes problem assignments to be solved, in cases of legal infractions.

g) Teacher uses physical punishment only when the pupil responds to nothing else.

DON'T'S

1. Children who misbehave should not be put in the hall to waste time. Many times this child only wants a break from the class routine.

2. Pupils who misbehave should not be put in front of a class to entertain.

3. A pupil should never be turned over completely to another person for punishment for an offense. The teacher should always accompany the child in conferences with principals, counselors, or parents.

4. Never embarrass a child as punishment. This only causes resentment and future problems.

5. The class should never be punished

as a group just to catch a single guilty child. Group pressure may be employed rather, to enforce rules.

6. Do not look upon a child's misbehavior as a personal affront.

7. Do not carry grudges against children for any length of time.

8. Do not discuss problems of discipline in public.

Any cases which do not respond to the above program need clinical assistance. Teachers are not qualified to analyze such problems.

Discipline and Preventive Techniques*
Leslie J. Chamberlin

The teacher who learns to avoid, prevent, or control classroom situations which lead to disorder, discourtesy, or inactivity not only improves his effectiveness as a teacher but also his job security and chances for future progress.

Good teachers realize that modern discipline, which emphasizes self-control and self-direction, is one of the most difficult things a child must master in our rapidly changing, complex social framework. These teachers realize that any contribution they may make toward students' development of character, good citizenship, and self-control depends largely on their skill in managing pupils in a manner which conforms to a psychology of self-direction.

Adequate classroom control involves:
1. providing a learning situation that is free from serious distractions;
2. establishing and maintaining respect for authority in the classroom of the school;
3. attempting to develop student ideals, interests, and skills which contribute to self-control and good citizenship;
4. presenting a dynamic, but not dominating, sympathetic, and pleasing teacher personality to the pupils.

What can the teacher do to provide a learning situation free from serious distractions which maintains respect for authority and contributes to self-control and good

citizenship?

The teacher must realize that problems will not occur if they are not allowed to develop. Establishing mutually meaningful standards is the foundation of good discipline.

Therefore, early in the school term the teacher and the students should discuss the standards which the group will accept. This prevents many problems resulting from ignorance of what is acceptable, from carelessness, or from just seeing how far a student can go.

An effective teacher must:
1. be free from any driving need to be liked by all of the students;
2. accept the role of the parent figure;
3. realize that boys and girls do not want to be given absolute freedom to do whatever they please;
4. be consistent in upholding the adopted standards.

Specific routines will help students take care of many recurring classroom situations. The teacher must accept and perform his part in these routines.

For example, it is a good idea for the teacher to meet his classes at the door of the room every day and each new class period. This permits him to supervise his corridor and to greet his pupils as they come into the room. To be effective, however, the teacher must be at his post regularly.

Routines dealing with book and paper

*Reprinted from *School and Community,* October, 1961. Used with permission.

distribution, making assignments or giving directions, student seating, and forgotten articles must be worked out. In fact, all small details must receive careful consideration.

Often teachers use student monitors in connection with these various routines. This practice is educationally sound, but a teacher should exercise care since the efficiency of the monitor program depends on the selection of reliable children.

The monitor's function should be carefully defined as assisting the teacher and nothing more. Until controls are established, it is well for the teacher to limit the number of simultaneous classroom activities and to handle most of the details himself.

An inexperienced teacher may want to avoid certain teaching procedures, such as group work and other activities which require a good deal of self-control on the part of students, until he becomes more skillful in maintaining good control.

Keeping a class constructively busy has much to recommend it as a policy of maintaining satisfactory classroom discipline. A five- or ten-minute assignment written on the board each morning encourages classes to enter the room promptly and to get to work quickly. Such morning work also enables the teacher to attend to the latecomers individually, to make last plans for the day and to complete many other daily duties.

This policy of keeping students busy with interesting, well-planned assignments applies to the last few minutes of the school day, also.

Often teachers talk too loudly, on too high a pitch, or simply too much. Good teachers learn to listen to themselves, stop talking, and then to continue in a more conversational tone that is free from anger, annoyance, or anxiety.

Children resent being yelled at or screamed at and often will be hostile as a result. Many successful teachers use signals such as the classroom lights, a small bell, or putting a finger to the mouth to request silently that everyone lower his voice.

Teachers need to remember that children's attention spans are short. Often when children work on an activity too long, restlessness and noise seem to grow spontaneously. This should be considered when planning lessons, but should it happen during a lesson, the farsighted teacher should start a new activity before the noise gets out of hand.

Since many discipline problems arise when a student or a few students cannot do an assigned task, the teacher should try to individualize instruction whenever possible. It is better for the less capable student to complete a modified version of the general assignment than for him to drift into a disciplinary situation.

In the classroom, easily recognizable rewards should follow approved behavior without delay. The wise teacher gives recognition to his students whenever possible for their superior work or behavior.

A child who is hungry or tired is apt to become a discipline problem. The teacher should analyze his class periodically as to proper rest and diet.

Being aware of certain physical and/or mental defects can help a teacher avoid many difficult classroom situations. The school's cumulative records help a teacher learn about a child's physical and mental status.

All teachers sincerely interested in providing a good teaching-learning situation should welcome constructive supervision.

Supervision encourages the teacher to try for better classroom control. It sometimes calls attention to previously unnoticed or flippant or sarcastic remarks or unfriendly looks on the part of the teacher.

Supervisors may notice antagonistic or rebellious pupil attitudes as a result of teaching techniques which invite disorder. If this information is presented to the teacher in a professional manner, he then has an opportunity to take corrective action before serious situations develop.

In summary, proper classroom organization improves the teaching-learning situation by saving time and energy, helping preserve order, and contributing to char-acter development. Good teachers devise definite modes of seating pupils, recording attendance, directing traffic, distributing and collecting materials, arranging and caring for equipment, regulating light, heat, and ventilation, and for seeing that desks and floors are kept neat.

Preventive measures help keep problems from occurring, but when serious discipline problems do develop they should be dealt with objectively and firmly without rejecting the misbehaving child as a person.

Tips for the Beginning Teacher*

Martha W. Hunt

May an old hand give a beginning teacher some tips about keeping classroom discipline? I have found these procedures helpful:

Learn names. Whenever possible, be familiar before your first class session with the names of your students and with the pronunciation of each name.

Look over the permanent records. Foresight is better than handsight. The records will give you clues to students' hearing and vision defects or other physical ailments, family relationships, and emotional disturbances which affect learning rates. IQ scores will give some indication of whether or not students are working to capacity. If not, trouble will probably develop sooner or later.

Check the classroom environment. Have the temperature and ventilation as right as you can make them. Draw shades to cut out glare if necessary, but be sure there are no dark corners. See that classroom furniture and accessories are in order and that no seats are placed so that students have to face the light.

Watch seating. Big students should not block the line of vision of smaller students. Place students with defective vision or faulty hearing near you.

Plan the lesson. Be ready to use the first minute of class time. If you get Johnny busy right away, he has no time to cook up interesting ideas that do not fit into the class situation.

Learn symptoms of illness. Misconduct often has a physiological basis. Learn the meaning of a flushed face, reddening and watering eyes, a skin rash.

Deal with individuals. Instead of having an entire class sit around marking time while you reprimand one offender, arrange to have a private appointment with him outside class.

Practice marginal vision. You can learn to see out of the corners of your eyes.

Mind your manners. Student behavior often reflects a teacher's good or bad manners.

Don't stay glued to your desk. Move about. Sit in the back of the room when class reports are being given—it accents student responsibility.

Use a bit of ritual. I find code signals

*Reprinted from *NEA Journal,* September 1958. Used with permission.

handy. In my school, gum chewing is forbidden, so I give a person-to-person reminder by sign language. I rapidly close and open my thumb and forefinger (imitating jaw motion), and then, like a baseball umpire calling out the runner, I motion with my thumb toward the wastebasket.

The class is not distracted; I wait until I catch the eye of the offender, give my code signal, and let the business of the class go on. For talking or whispering, a finger on my closed lips may be enough. Codes are short cuts, and can save time and energy if introduced with good humor.

Relate learning to life plans. The sooner you know the career plans, interests, and even the hobbies of your students, the more successful you will be in directing all their energies into constructive channels.

Be yourself. Pick up ideas wherever you can, but be yourself and teach in the way that is right for you.

Secondary School Discipline*
Dale Findley and Henry M. O'Reilly

Probably no one single issue recently has been of more concern to principals than the matter of student behavior. Of late the principal's authority has been seriously challenged. At least what principals have held to be their authority has been challenged.

In order to help children and youth develop the intellectual and moral discipline essential for being free people, we as adults and school administrators have to exercise discipline of mind. We must think through carefully and clearly what we mean by discipline, what kind of discipline we want, and by what methods we can best achieve it. (1, p. 1)

In the face of uncertainty many persons tend to regress to simple and primitive ways of dealing with difficulties. In times of strain and anxiety there are demands for speeded-up action. Patient educational procedures in the making of complex judgments, are likely to be neglected. Instead, people begin to look for a less thought-requiring procedure. Some begin to look for a scale in which there is a prescribed form of punishment for every specific mis-

demeanor. Others advocate such coercive techniques as return to "woodshed" whippings, military marching in schools, more drills in the 3 R's, or fining the parents of children who get into trouble. These solutions are unappealing to most of us because they do not teach children the right ways of behaving when coercion is removed. It is because of such confusions that we as administrators must examine very carefully the concept of "discipline" and our own practices with the children and youth of today. (1, p. 2)

There are mainly three different ways teachers talk about discipline. First of all teachers refer to the degree of order we have established in a group. Secondly, teachers define "discipline" as not the order we have, but the trick by which we have established order. And the third way teachers commonly use the word "discipline" is special ways of enforcing discipline by punishment.

Administrators must decide what goals we expect discipline to attain. Discipline is always connected with a goal or purpose. Individual discipline is often thought of as an organization of one's impulses for the attainment of a goal, while group dis-

*Reprinted from *American Secondary Education*, December 1971. Used with permission.

cipline demands control of impulses of the individuals composing a group for the attainment of a goal which all have accepted.

Formulating A Philosophy of Discipline

In dealing with discipline and the adolescent in high school we must be prepared to change with the times and with changing conditions. Discipline, along with all other aspects of school life, is a changing phenomenon, reflecting the rapidly shifting community scene today. Policies relating to discipline often become outmoded. School regulations, like city statutes, become anachronisms with changing conditions. Thus policy evaluation and policy formulation become a continuous problem.

In formulating a philosophy of discipline the principal's role is one of advisory to the school board. Formulating school discipline policies is a legal function of school boards. While it is true that the power to make policies are vested in the school board, recent history has seen changes wherein popular participation in policy formulation has broadened considerably. School boards have become sensitive to the desires of the people and have listened thoughtfully to interested groups of citizens, teachers, and to their administrators. There is a good deal of truth in the notion that America's schools are as good or as bad as the people want them to be. (2, p. 135-136).

A principal and school board must remember that in our society and in our schools the individual citizen is granted certain inalienable rights, among them life, liberty, and the pursuit of happiness. (3, p, 33). In light of recent court decisions it is very important that school boards act with reasonable exercise of their authority. The recent court decisions have tended to restrain the school from exercising many of the forms of control over student conduct which it and the community formerly accepted as normal and proper. But whatever the reasons for these legal actions may be and whatever their outcomes are, the impact of court decisions relating to control of student behavior is felt more immediately and heavily by the building principal than by anyone else in the administrative or teaching hierarchy.

It is worth mentioning at this point that some states have policies on school discipline which must be followed by local school boards. However, even when the state outlines school discipline policies, there is usually a degree of freedom, which permits the community to handle certain local problems.

The principal must take the lead in promoting a positive approach to discipline. To do this, the principal must be aware of the factors and practices that aid in developing good behavior patterns in schools. Lawrence E. Vredevoe, in his "Third Report on a Study of Students and School Discipline in the United States and Other Countries," indicated that practices that students and teachers believe to be most successful in developing good teacher-student relationships do not differ in size, location, or composition of the student body. In Vredevoe's report the schools selected as being representative of the best citizenship and teacher-student relationships, had the following common practices:

1. There was an understanding and apparent recognition of the purposes and values of the standards and rules in force by faculty and students.
2. Emphasis was placed on self-discipline by teachers and students.
3. Good citizenship and conduct were characteristic of the faculty as well as the student body. Courtesy, con-

sideration, respect, professional dress and manner, and good speech were practiced by faculty members.

4. Standards and rules were subject to review and change, but were enforced until changed by due process.
5. The emphasis in treatment of all discipline cases was on the individual involved and not the act. This represents a significant change in the past 50 years. Today's society is more concerned with the transgression than the crime.
6. Students could expect fair but certain reprimand or punishment for violation of rules and standards.
7. The punishments meted out were fitted to the individual rather than the transgression.
8. Faculty and students cooperated in establishing, maintaining, and revising rules and standards.
9. The program was challenging to all groups. (4, p. 216-17).

The kind of discipline which works in a democracy is self-discipline. Such discipline begins at the earliest years with external authority imposed by parents and teachers and is gradually relaxed as the student finishes the secondary school. From a sociological and psychological base, discipline is a learning process whereby the individual progressively learns to develop habits of self-control and recognizes his own responsibility to society. (3,-p. 334).

Generally speaking there are three to five percent of the student body on whom corrective measures must be used, the general emphasis in schools should be on the prevention of misconduct and education toward self-control. (3-p. 334).

Walter E. McPhie indicates that methods of preventing problems of control are divided into two categories: (1) things that should be done, and (2) things that

should be avoided.

"The following things should be done: use personal experience as a guide in identifying students as discipline problems, talk informally with the students at the beginning of the year about classroom procedures and expectations, permit students to see classes they choose, learn the students' names early, begin lessons promptly, be enthusiastic, provide each student an opportunity for success, admit error, make assignments reasonable and clear, occasionally do something nice for your students, and, above all else, be alert. The following things should be avoided: don't try to buy popularity, don't be a comedian, don't talk through noise, don't enter into arguments, and don't do things for students that they can do for themselves." (5, p. 82-91).

The individual teacher is very important in school discipline. The better the teacher is in his preparation, teaching technique, personality, etc., the less likely are student concern problems to arise. It is sometimes helpful to remember that many discipline problems can be solved through preventive correction by the teacher instead of a control penalty on the student. (6, p. 22).

The specific causes of student offenses related to specific instances are many and varied, but most discipline problems can be attributed to a few fundamental reasons. Some of these are as follows: lack of general training and development, lack of interest in course work, poor teaching, poor school organization, unsatisfactory home conditions, lack of social adjustment, bad associates, physical defects, lack of responsibility, adjustment to adolesence. (3, p. 337).

The school is a society in which the students and teachers interact with each other for a common purpose. Freedom exists but with it comes great responsibility, and as in all societies, there is a need for restrictions. Whenever restrictions are levied to govern the behavior of a group, rewards and penalties are necessary to support the restrictions. These restrictions should be spelled out in the student handbook so the students have full knowledge of the existing rules. (3, p. 339).

Teachers and principals in the more difficult schools may long at times for autocratic methods of keeping order and forcing obedience that were available to the schoolmasters in earlier times. But even if today's students would submit to the harsher disciplines of the past, these methods would hardly suit the goals of modern education. The old disciplinary procedures served a society that held submission to authority to be a prime goal of childhood education. Today the ideal product of the mass schooling system is expected to possess an independent mind and a cooperative spirit, traits not likely to flourish in an atmosphere of institutional coercion.

Fear of the rod in traditional American schools was a major instrument of student discipline. Infliction of physical pain was justified on the same grounds as were the harsh penal codes of the day for adults. "Fear was conceived as the only force which would make men amenable to dominion . . . It was natural (to believe) that children, too, should be controlled by violence or the threat of violence." (7, p. 643).

An historian of childhood, Philippe Aries, has traced the great change in educational style that took place between the late Middle Ages and the 17th Century, from a comradely association of teachers and learners to prisonlike schools where "the birch became the mark of the schoolmaster . . . the symbol of the subjection

in which he . . . held his pupils." (8, p. 644). Thus a humiliating disciplinary system—whippings at the master's discretion became widespread in schools in Europe. The American colonists, coming from a land where flogging had become common in schools, took it for granted that corporal punishment would be used to control the children in the schools they established in the New World (7, p. 644).

The children in pre-Revolutionary America suffered not only pain of the flesh, but the tormenting threat of eternal damnation. A catechism told him he would be sent down to an everlasting fire if he were naughty. Evangelist preachers told the child that he was born sinful and graphically described what awaited them in the afterworld. This repressive attitude toward life, this insistence on conformity to a moral and ethical code based purely on religious sanction, was naturally reflected in the colonial schools and in the discipline of children. (9, p. 42).

The libertarian ideas and the humanitarian movements of the 18th and 19th centuries were slow to overcome the authoritarian spirit that still prevailed in schooling of the young. Though whipping posts and other harsh instruments of adult punishment gradually disappeared the tradition of the rod remained fixed in the educational practice. The Rev. Francis Waylaid, president of Brown University expressed the prevailing view in a public address in 1830, "it is the duty of the instructor to enforce obedience and the pupil to render it." (7, p. 644).

Even Horace Mann, who crusaded during the 1930's against excessive application of corporal punishment, did not approve of abolishing it altogether.

The pros and cons of corporal punishment have been debated for years. And corporal punishment never quite dies as an educational issue. However, corporal punishment hardly presents itself as an answer to the disciplinary problems of the schools of today.

Such devices as detention periods have been initiated for the disobedient child. However, upon taking a close look at detention periods it appears they are not correcting the discipline problems of the times either. We must stress the prevention of student discipline problems. With the many social changes in the past decades we can see that the authoritarian atmosphere of the public school classroom is disappearing. The teacher is still the boss in the classroom, but the prevailing principle on discipline leans more toward a cultivation of self-discipline than toward rigid conformity to specific rules of conduct. Advances in the study of child psychology and the measurement of intelligence, growing recognition of emotional factors in learning, the rising influence of the scientific spirit, and the declining influence of Puritan morality over public education have all helped to free the student from the stern discipline of earlier times. (7, p. 646).

Other types of punishment in common use in American school districts for student misconducts are the reprimand, conference, detention, fines, suspension and expulsion.

The reprimand is the most common device and the one most frequently resorted to as first choice of a teacher. If administrated calmly and without the heat of anger it can be very effective.

Strictly speaking, the pupil-teacher conference should not be listed as a punishment device, but we must admit that it can have overtones of punishment when it is held after school as a result of the misbehavior. For one thing, the pupil is forced to remain after school for the appointment. This can be a very real punishment in itself if the student works after school or if he takes a bus. The conference can be a most effective means of getting to the bottom of misbehavior.

Another popular device, as old as education itself, and one which has met court approval is "staying after school—detention." As was mentioned earlier, many schools have abandoned detentions completely because it appears that detentions have only annoyed the annoyer and didn't get to the root of the problem. Also, it is very difficult to assign certain punishments in the form of hours of detention to certain misconducts.

Fines are sometimes used in schools for certain adult type offenses like damaged books or failure to return books to library. However, principals should be aware that the courts have not looked with favor upon fining students without an alternative punishment such as the legendary "Ten dollars or ten days." The principal who excludes a pupil for failure to pay a fine and for which no alternative is offered, is on dubious ground if the matter goes to court.

It sometimes becomes necessary to exclude a student from class (suspension) for more than one day, this is entirely up to the principal. Suspension should be regarded as a fairly drastic punishment since it involves a definite academic penalty. However, in a school where students would rather be out of school than in, it hardly seems much punishment to suspend them from school.

Expulsion is the responsibility of the school board and should only be enforced if offense is grave enough.

To summarize, the principal shares with parents, guardians, teachers, district personnel, social workers, policemen, and juvenile judges the responsibility for teacher self-control and administering discipline to youth. The schools should supplement the role of parents and other agencies when these other agencies have a major responsibility in providing both teaching and corrective measures. The school has the major responsibility when the violation takes place within the framework of the schools program. It is important for the principal to understand the theory of effective discipline as well as the practical aspects of administering discipline.

A student, like other citizens in the community, has freedom, but the freedom is tempered by the responsibility that is involved in any given situation. In a free society restrictions are necessary to define the limits of both freedom and responsibilities. Because there are people who forget, or who place other values ahead of society's accepted values, or who are completely unwilling to accept responsibility, it is necessary to have penalties. Corrections should just be educative in nature to bring about self-discipline. But there are times when a penalty must be issued for control purposes. The principal should administer penalties that are in keeping with the nature of the violation; they should be administered as soon after the violation as possible. The penalty should be one that the principal feels just and at the same time can be successfully imposed.

Although corporal punishment has been in schools as long as schools have existed, the use of corporal punishment today is still a serious matter for the principal. Some states permit corporal punishment; other states do not. States that do permit corporal punishment do not make it mandatory. The teacher and the principal are still liable for their actions. As far as possible, both the teacher and principals should find other satisfactory penalties that will accomplish the same result as corporal punishment.

Presently we are facing many conflicts in the acceptance of new modes of maintaining student discipline. The consensus is that changes will come about nonetheless, and that when the schools have actually become better adjusted to the needs of the students, in both their instructional and their disciplinary functions, the anger and the alienation that lie behind adolescent violence will recede from the foreground of public education. (7-p. 652).

A proposal for the development of an effective discipline program

1. Provision should be made for involvement of the student governing body in the development of procedures to handle discipline matters.

   (a) Decisions relating to the extent of student involvement in the development of school rules and regulations should be made.

   (b) Decisions must be made relating to the extent of student involvement in the enforcement of school rules and regulations and the punishment resulting from the infraction of school rules and regulations.

2. The total faculty and staff must be involved in the development of the discipline program. The principal and his administrative staff must rely heavily on the teachers and supporting staff members to assist in carrying out the discipline program. It cannot be emphasized too strongly that the whole curricular program has a very important affect on the discipline program. A relevant curriculum can prevent many discipline problems.

3. The total program for handling discipline problems should be written. Caution should be exercised in the development of rules and regulations to insure enough flexibility to allow students to feel

that they are being handled as individuals rather than inanimate objects. An appeal procedure should be established that allows students a fair and equitable hearing concerning their case. Time and money for supplies to develop and print the entire program should be allocated. All students, staff and faculty should receive a copy of the program.

4. The emphasis of the total program should be on prevention of misconduct, therefore, the principal must make an analysis of the cause of the misbehavior.

  (a) Consideration must be given to the conditions which led to the misconduct.

   1. What type of attitude do students have toward their total school experience.

      a. Do students feel teachers and administrators are "against" them?

   2. What type of home background does the student have?

   3. Was the misconduct an individual matter or was a group involved?

   4. Is this a first offense or a repeat offense?

   5. What facilities and services do you have available in the school system to provide assistance to the student involved so that he may adjust or so that the causal factors of misconduct may be removed?

   6. What evidence exists to suggest that the student has achieved success in some way at school?

5. A periodic review of all rules and regulations should be undertaken to determine if the objectives of the discipline program are being met. Some record should probably be kept of the nature of offense and the disposition of the case to facilitate this analysis.

Bibliography

1. Sheviakor, George D., and Fritz Redl. Discipline for Today's Children and Youth. Washington, D.C.: Association for Supervision and Curriculum Development, National Education Association, 1956.

2. Larson, Knute G., and Melvin R. Karpes. Effective Secondary School Discipline. Englewood Cliffs, N.J.: Prentice-Hall Inc., 1966.

3. Ovard, Glen F., Administration of the Changing Secondary School. United States: The MacMillan Company, 1969.

4. Vredevoe, Lawrence E., "School Discipline— Third Report on a Study of Students and School Discipline in the United States and Other Countries," Bulletin of the N.A.S.S.P., March 1965.

5. McPhie, Walter E., "Discipline Problems: an Educational Malignancy," Bulletin of N.A.S.S.P., December 1961.

6. Brown, Edwin John, and Arthur Thomas Phelps. Managing the Classroom—The Teacher's Part In School Administration. New York: The Ronald Press Company, 1961.

7. Shaffer, Helen B., "Discipline In Public Schools," Washington, D.C.: Editorial Research Reports, 1969.

8. Aries, Philippe. Centuries of Childhood. First Vintage Edition, 1965.

9. Falk, Herbert Arnold. Corporal Punishment: A Social Interpretation of its Theory and Practice in the Schools of the United States, 1941.

Classroom Control in the High School*
Emelie Ruth Dodge

*Reprinted from *NEA Journal*, March 1958. Used by permission.

As I stood before my first eleventh-grade English class seven Septembers ago, a full-fledged teacher at last, I enthusiastically looked over the 30 pupils whose lives I was going to mold, and my heart sang, "Mine! These are mine! I can do anything I want with them!"

This power-mad era in my life was brief, but it was years before I realized that behind the silence and order of my first day of school were concealed 30 scouts reconnoitering enemy territory. In my case, the report must have gone back, "Sitting duck!"

I was unprepared to cope with problems in classroom behavior. I knew the history of educational philosophy; I was familiar with educational terminology; I accepted the principle of permissive atmosphere. But no textbook or lecture had dealt with flying missiles, strange noises from unknown quarters, out-of-control discussions, chronic tardiness, impertinence, effrontery, or any of the other devices for retarding classroom progress.

"Discipline," in its connotations of demand and punishment, of autocratic authority, went out of style about 25 years ago. But because to teach remains the paramount purpose of teachers, and since this purpose cannot be accomplished without classroom order, "discipline" is still necessary altho it wears a new and prettier dress. We see it walking abroad as "control."

Superintendents demand teachers who can control students; boards of education dismiss teachers who lack classroom control.

What, then, can new teachers do to deal with problems of classroom control? Teachers colleges and textbooks have some helpful general discussion of the matter, altho they seldom go into detail about methods. Articles in education journals may be useful, and advice from experienced teachers can provide aid.

However, since the very same classroom problem rarely arises twice, a pat answer or case history isn't much value. Furthermore, each teacher's personality has a different impact on students, and, therefore, each teacher is forced to discover his own particular way of handling a problem.

I have found that the most sensible way to handle the matter of classroom control is by not allowing problems to develop in the first place.

My brief but potent experience has revealed some general procedures which boys and girls have seemed to find fair and logical, and which I find helpful in preventing unpleasant classroom situations.

Several recent surveys of what students consider as the characteristics of a good teacher list fairness as a first requisite. This sounds simple. However, fairness involves constant vigilance on the teacher's part, careful attention to consistency, faithful warning in advance, and several weeks of patient waiting while the students test and observe.

To say that a teacher is fair neither convinces students nor makes it true. Having dealt with adults for years, students have learned that adults are inconsistent, inattentive, moody, and capricious.

Adults have severely punished youngsters on one day for an offense which, on another, merely receives a reprimand. And knowing that every grownup has a weak spot, youngsters have coaxed their elders into or out of decisions, have gotten away with deeds under the noses of preoccupied parents and teachers, have successfully and fraudulently appealed to the sympathy of adults to win their desires.

In short, boys and girls are what they are because of what adults, advertently and inadvertently, have taught them in classrooms and out.

If you want to build a reputation for fairness among your students, these principles may prove valuable to you:

Don't threaten unless you can, and intend to fulfil the threat. Don't promise unless you can, and intend to, fulfil the promise. It will take only one unfulfilled threat or promise to assure your boys and girls that you are no exception to their rapidly crystallizing conviction that adults are three-quarters hot air.

Don't break a rule for anyone unless the entire class can see that it is an emergency. There are times when exceptions must, of course, be made; but when these cannot be postponed and handled in private conference, the class should be allowed to see that an exception is necessary.

Stick to school rules yourself. Frequently, it is not required that you observe them; however, do not break rules or equivocate before your students. If an assembly seems a waste of time, you can accomplish no good by going to sleep, "cutting," or being obviously bored. If there is a tardy bell, observe it yourself. Don't wander into your classroom late and expect your status to excuse you.

Always tell students the truth. It is better to say that you don't think they need to know than to risk being caught in even the most innocent and generous lie, and you will be amazed at how much the class can accept and understand.

Your students will hang around after school to talk things over and will seek your advice on the most personal matters once they decide that you are honest. But if you are to win their confidence, don't condemn too quickly their sweeping generalizations or their denunciation of the institutions most of us cherish. They must question everything. *Let them!* You and I have decided what we think about a good many things. They have that same right.

But when they ask you what you think, tell them the truth.

Keep your classroom rules short and simple. Don't establish long lists of dos and don'ts, but make five or six basic and inclusive statements and then stick to them.

Always make your demands clear to everyone ahead of time. Don't give a pupil a chance to say: "But I was absent the day you gave us that!" Write your requirements and assignments on the board to be copied into notebooks, or give out mimeographed sheets. Then make absolutely certain that these instructions are understood.

The students' second requisite for a good teacher is knowledge of subject matter. If your boys and girls respect you as a person who knows what he's talking about, who is widely informed, and who works hard and consistently at his job, your problems in discipline will be fewer.

Come to class each day prepared to utilize every minute of the period. As I think over the unpleasant situations I've experienced in class, I find that they almost invariably occurred because the students were not really busy.

At least three different types of activity during one 50-minute period, such as a spelling quiz, a 15-minute discussion, and a short lecture, will provide variety and will keep students too well occupied to engage in class-disrupting entertainment. Always plan more than you can do in a period, so that if you see signs of boredom and restlessness, you can switch your activity and again avoid difficulty before it occurs.

In spite of all this golden advice, you will probably find some disciplinary situations arising in your classes. These are best handled unobtrusively on an individual basis.

Don't *ask* a student if he will stop an

annoyance. He will feel compelled to answer you, and the answer will probably be impudent. Simply *tell* him to stop whatever he is doing and then go on with what you were doing at once without waiting for a retort.

Any red-blooded student is aware that his friends are watching to see what will happen. If you give him the slightest opportunity to answer back, he will simply have to do so. Don't appeal to him by suggesting or implying that he is different from the others, that he has more ability than the others, or that he may expect sympathy because he has a problem at home. Young people want to be treated as individuals, but not singled out as different—even if they are.

I have found that normal teen-agers deeply resent special treatment. For the most part, they do not understand why or how they get into painful situations, but they feel that in treating them as psychological cases, teachers and deans are exhibiting a total lack of understanding and are making a crisis out of a crocus.

Many high-school students will play on the sympathy of their teachers at every opportunity, and later kill themselves laughing at the teachers' credulity. This arouses students' contempt, which writes finis to classroom control.

Your consistent refusal to accept late work or to make exceptions on the strength of tales of woe will be accepted with sheepish grins if you turn them away with, "Stop it! You're breaking my heart!" Parrying with a light and slightly flippant touch is often successful, as long as your foil is not dipped in the acid of sarcasm. Refusal to take a wheedling student seriously does not mean letting him—or the class—think you're ridiculing or belittling him.

You should try to be pleasant, you may be amusing, but always be firm. Any new group of students probably will not accept the fact, at first, that you mean what you say. They will continue to search for weaknesses. Expect, too, that you won't be able to be perfectly consistent all the time.

But if students know that you are trying to be fair, if they can respect your knowledge and industry, and if they feel that you sincerely like them, they will be less interested in humiliating or annoying you, in retarding class progress, or in seeking amusement of an unpleasant nature during class time. In fact, given the right classroom climate, self-discipline will flourish in a gratifying way.

Students will feel increasingly secure in your presence as they become more sure of their ground. When they know what to expect, they will feel happier and more comfortable, and so will you.

Discipline in a Large Junior High School*
Walter M. Jackson

Situations which arise in the junior high-school disciplinarian's office range from petty theft to fighting; from lewd actions to decks of cards; from profanity to truancy; and from disrespect to insolence. Each time an event demands punitive ac-

*Reprinted from *NASSP Bulletin,* October 1963. Used by permission.

tion, the circumstances can be similar or different, depending upon the situation and the people involved.

Fairness and Consistency

Indeed, the word discipline has many connotations which can be expanded into a complexity almost beyond belief. Obviously, there are no "pat" answers or phrases to solve all these problems. Simple words such as "behave yourself" or "you know you shouldn't do that" more often than not fall on uncomprehending ears.

Although situations may vary, certain constants exist. First and foremost of these is fairness and consistency. The junior high school student has a keen sense of fair play. If he does something wrong and is punished in a certain way for it, then he expects every other student who does the same thing to get the same or equal treatment. This is as it should be. Young people, though they may have violated some rule or acted in a juvenile manner still have certain rights which should not be violated. You must respect their rights if you demand or expect respect from them in turn.

Thoroughness and Accuracy

Another constant which the disciplinarian must keep in mind is that of thoroughness. *All* the details of a situation should be gathered *before* a course of action is decided upon. Then, and only then, should punishment be meted out or parents consulted. The reasons for this are obvious. Parents will want to get the complete facts for their own satisfaction. If the facts which they gather are different from yours, they will expect explanations.

It is good to have your "ammunition" ready, but even better to have it accurate. If you have gathered all the information available on a particular matter and have dealt with the incident objectively using only concrete facts then you will be on sure ground. Your thoroughness and objectivity will win the respect of both parent and student as well as teachers involved in particular cases. In addition, your thorough investigation may alert you to other problems in the making and thus offer the opportunity to take preventive measures.

Virtually all misdemeanors which reach the disciplinarian's office are serious enough for parent notification. A telephone call, if possible, is best followed by a letter. This way, the parent gets a verbal explanation of the difficulty and the letter gives you a written record of the call.

Parents should confer with you as soon as possible. Procrastination on the part of school officials or parents only delays the inevitable. Also, time tends to minimize the impact of certain offences. Probably the greatest justification for parental conferences in matters of discipline is that you are able to explain personally the school's position on such matters.

Suppose a student is allowed to smoke at home. His parents even buy his cigarettes. Yet, at school this is a violation of rules. Consequently, he is caught between permission of parents and nonpermission of the school. This is where the personal conference is most important. The school official can explain the school's position and give the reasons for school rules.

Records

Another aspect of disciplinary action in the junior high school is that of keeping adequate records. Many problem children are chronic in their misbehavior and adequate notes of violations, notifications (telephone or letter), conferences, and punishments are mandatory. This gives the disciplinarian an accurate and up to date account of the history of the individual. It does not have to be a long dissertative type of record. Simply a few notes, on five by eight cards and kept in an alphabetical file, may suffice. These notes will be of great importance when preparing a referral or a resumé, or when holding parental conferences.

In addition, all correspondence concerning a case, as well as referral copies, should be placed in the student's permanent folder. It is also of prime importance to confer periodically with the school guidance people so that they may be brought up to date on a particular case. However, this information should be handled discreetly and it should not be used as a door opener in future interviews.

Issuing threats as a deterrent is a pitfall which should be avoided. Never tell a student what will happen to him if he does a certain thing. For instance, if a student is truant, a threat of suspension for future truancies is not the answer. Better to get to the bottom of the problem. He may take the challenge and you will then have no recourse except to suspend even though this might not be the best course of action.

The success of school discipline depends on the teachers with the administrative force acting as a guide or helper. Teachers should get official backing on breaches of discipline. On the other hand, teachers must be properly oriented as to their position in matters of discipline. What to do? How to do it? When to take action? These are questions which must be answered, particularly for the new teacher. It would be wise to devote some pre-school orientation time to these topics. This will eliminate many future misunderstandings between faculty and administration. Along this same line, it is wise to occasionally devote time in a teachers' meeting to disciplinary problems and necessary changes in procedures or policies. Remember that school discipline control depends initially on the teachers.

It is good to use teacher appraisal in parental interviews, as teachers usually know the student better than the official school disciplinarian. Their word is especially useful in dealing with parents when a student is having difficulties with more than one of his teachers.

Lastly, keep a sense of humor. Although many situations are grave, it is always best to look for some good in people and to see the humor of a situation. A school disciplinarian can become extremely cynical in his daily dealings and a sense of humor can help.

It might even be wise to set aside a day when only *good* pupils are sent to the office. Pupils who have done something outstanding can help keep the school disciplinarian's perspective much brighter. Some would consider this foolish, but if analyzed from all angles, it has merit. Above all else remember: (1) Investigate thoroughly; (2) Don't make snap judgments; (3) Be firm, be fair; (4) Keep adequate records; (5) Look for the good in students; (6) Keep your sense of humor.

Classroom Control—58 Successful Hints Offered to Beginning Junior High Teachers*

Edward Brainard

First-year junior high school teachers need definite assistance in developing a realistic attitude toward effective classroom control. This fact suggests orientation meetings conducted by the principal, teacher self-evaluation, and a resource of successful ideas which minimize problem situations in the classroom.

The paramount concern of most beginning teachers relates to classroom control.

*Reprinted from *Education*, May 1964. Used with permission.

These teachers often do not realize, as do experienced junior high school teachers and administrators, that much student misbehavior can be avoided. A learning situation lacking student discipline and cooperation is less than effective.

Working with several first-year teachers is a formidable task for the junior high school principal, as such teachers need his tactful assistance in order to establish a personal attitude toward classroom control and ascertain the school's attitude toward discipline.

How can the junior high school principal assist beginning teachers in developing effective classroom control at the outset of the school year? Periodic meetings with new teachers are of supreme importance for creating an understanding of the school and its students. In addition, a written resource of ideas can highlight orientation discussion sessions and valuably assist the new teacher in developing teaching plans for the first weeks of school. Such teachers can refer to such a list of ideas as they actually plan for instruction.

The following list of suggestions is given to first-year teachers at Lakewood Junior High School for individual use. Use is also made of this list in group discussion at orientation meetings and during individual principal-teacher conferences.

Successful Hints on Classroom Control

Effective student classroom control is partly teacher attitude, desire, and positive action. Circle the response which describes your procedures.

A. Developing a positive teacher attitude toward discipline

Yes No 1. I use preventive discipline. That is, I attempt to recognize and identify problems before they develop.

Yes No 2. I am friendly, but firm with my students.

Yes No 3. I, not the bell, dismiss class.

Yes No 4. At the start of the school year students gain permission to leave their seats when they desire to sharpen pencils or get special materials.

Yes No 5. I am consistent, impartial, and fair in operating my classroom.

Yes No 6. I believe I cannot sit at my desk and still know what is going on in my classroom.

Yes No 7. I display a sense of humor.

Yes No 8. I operate on the assumption that the student wants to do the right thing.

Yes No 9. I am available to students before and after school to help or "just talk."

Yes No 10. I do not allow students to talk while another student or I am talking.

Yes No 11. I show sincere enthusiasm for the subjects I teach.

Yes No 12. I know that a neat room and personal appearance give students the idea of orderliness.

Yes No 13. I do not lose my temper.

Yes No 14. I insist on my students maintaining high standards in their work ad behavior, but my standards are realistic for the age group and are obtainable.

Yes No 15. I do not accept impertinence.

Yes No 16. I make no punishments I cannot enforce, that are unrealistic for the age level, or are not carefully thought through.

Yes No 17. My class can move from one room to another without disturbing other classes.

Yes No 18. I attempt to build the ego of each student.

B. Managing the classroom

Yes No 1. While I take attendance or perform other necessary duties at the outset of each period, my students are working independently.

Yes No 2. After giving directions and during supervised study, I move about the room observing the effectiveness of directions given. In addition, this minimizes student frustrations, hostility, discouragement, and quitting by those having difficulty with the assigned task. By noticing these difficulties and giving assistance, I avoid many behavior problems and provide a more effective learning situation.

Yes No 3. I have established routines for collecting papers and distributing materials.

Yes No 4. If some students often cause problems before the class period begins and the passing period ends, I stand near the doorway so that I can supervise both the hall and my classroom.

C. De-emphasizing behavior problems and situations

Yes No 1. When a student misbehaves in class I divert the class with a discussion question and talk to the student individually in a quiet whisper instead of making a scene and, therefore, focusing the class's attention on misbehavior.

Yes No 2. When I change a student from one seat to another, I notify the individuals concerned either before or after class. Except in emergencies, I do not make changes during the class period as this only emphasized problem situations.

Yes No 3. I do not allow misbehavior problems to become acute before seeking assistance from the administration.

Yes No 4. I praise my students as a group and individually for good work.

Yes No 5. I never argue with a student before the class.

D. Fairness in handling discipline problems

Yes No 1. I do not punish an entire class for the actions of a few students. This is unfair in the opinion of students and helps to destroy an effective teacher-student relationship.

Yes No 2. I do not discipline an individual in front of the class. This focuses attention upon misbehavior and hurts the student's ego.

Yes No 3. I do not embarass students in front of the class. I treat them as I would want to be treated.

Yes No 4. When my students misbehave I do not give extra homework as punishment.

Yes No 5. I do not scold, shame, or use sarcasm in disciplining students.

Yes No 6. I do not make major issues out of trivial offenses.

Yes No 7. My students understand the fairness and reason for all established standards.

Yes No 8. When a student, after being corrected for misbehavior, attempts to do the right thing,

I praise or otherwise encourage him.

E. Effective planning relates to good classroom control

Yes No. 1. I provide a variety of learning activities.

Yes No 2. During each class period we have more than one type of activity. Rarely do I use an entire period for group activity as students get restless without a change of pace.

Yes No 3. I realize there is no one "best" teaching method. Methods and learning activities are many and varied.

Yes No 4. I adjust my daily planning to the students' span of attention.

Yes No 5. I provide supervised study periods during which I move about the room giving individual assistance.

Yes No 6. My homeroom has a purpose, is definite, instructional, and regulated as to the time it will take a student to complete the assignment.

Yes No 7. I believe that by having each class period well organized I not only provide a better instructional program by utilizing the entire period, but discipline problems are minimized as there is little pupil inactivity.

Yes No 8. During same class periods I provide at least one activity in which all students can experience success. Then I praise them for their good work and talk to the "slower" students and major discipline problems individually about their success on the exercise.

Yes No 9. I make the classroom attractive by having effective bulletin boards using materials related to classwork. Student work is also displayed.

Yes No 10. I provide means for giving students responsibility. For example, bulletin boards can be planned by students.

Yes No 11. I make use of available library materials.

Yes No 12. Periodically I tape record a class session so I can evaluate the effectiveness of my procedures.

Yes No 13. I am patient with my students. I am willing to reteach, without resentment, concepts which were not understood when first presented.

Yes No 14. I avoid actions which cause student frustration and anxiety.

Yes No 15. During each class period I summarize or have students summarize the day's learnings.

Yes No 16. The work that I assign is within the power of the students, provided they make the necessary effort.

Yes No 17. My daily plans are in conjunction with teaching units.

Yes No 18. I teach my students how to study so that homework assignments are effectively completed.

Yes No 19. I do not take for granted that students already know certain concepts. I use pre-tests or other procedures to ascertain what is already known.

Yes No 20. When a class gets restless and noise seems to grow spontaneously, I do not scold the class, but instead provide for a change in activity.

Yes No 21. I give directions one step at a time. I avoid long and detailed directions.

Yes No 22. I use the chalkboard and other visual aids to help present and review concepts and directions.

Yes No 23. I avoid the lecture method of teaching.

Your Score: If you answered all items "yes," you are developing positive attitudes toward classroom control.

Chapter VI

Discussionette

1. Do teachers usually work at the source of the discipline problem?

2. Do you accept or reject the suggestions for adequate classroom control?

3. Are most teachers willing to accept the suggestions given by the author to be an "effective teacher"?

4. What examples of good human relations techniques are in this article?

5. How can you make your subject matter contribute to your pupil's needs and attitudes?

6. When is behavior due to being "uninformed" as compared to "norm-violating?"

7. Is ignorance an excuse for inappropriate behavior?

8. How can you avoid having problems develop in the first place?

9. Why would normal teenagers resent special treatment?

10. What "rights" do junior high school students have which should not be violated?

11. What can teachers do to help students avoid misbehaving?

Discussionette Words and Concepts

compensation	feedback	readiness
individualized learning	counseling	personality
mutually accepted standards	restrictions	philosophy
consistency	student rights	preparation

Try to use these words.

Try to explain these words.

Try to relate these words and their concepts to current or emerging educational patterns regarding preventive discipline.

CHAPTER VII

❦CORRECTIVE DISCIPLINE❦

INTRODUCTION

THE OVERALL GOAL OF SCHOOL DISCIPLINE is self-directed student behavior; however, short range corrective measures must be taken by teachers to handle immediate problems. To effectively handle the short range corrective measure, teachers should know who was involved, how the situation started, what actually happened, and base their action on this information.

Most discipline problems develop on a spontaneous basis and there is not usually much time to think about the proper action to take. Thus, if teachers can develop corrective techniques in advance and anticipate certain courses of action, solutions for the immediate problem can be anticipated. This is not to infer that a huge list of problems and appropriate actions by teachers need be developed; however, a few courses of action can be projected which would probably resolve most situations.

This chapter gives concrete suggestions for teachers in the area of corrective discipline which can provide teachers with insight into potential problem areas.

Disciplining the Pupil*

Carlos de Zafra, Jr., Richard Berndt,
and Elizabeth Mitchell

(1) Good group discipline and good disciplining of the individual supplement each other. Even a normally well-behaved individual is tempted to exhibit improper behavior when something goes wrong with control of the group of which he is a part. As you perfect your group discipline, individuals who are potential behavior problems are more likely to fall into line and to work constructively.

(2) Judicious seating arrangements are a specific tool for good discipline. They

can both prevent and cure certain discipline situations:

(a) When pupils enter your classroom for the first day of school, let them take whatever seats they wish. Potential troublemakers often take rear seats, and a few front seats are usually left vacant, if there are more seats in the room than there are pupils. Then casually fill the vacant front seats with reluctant back-seaters, and the pupils themselves have unwittingly helped you to head off trouble before your class has even

*Reprinted from *The Clearing House*, September 1962. Used with permission.

146

begun! You want the troublemakers right under your nose.

(b) If pupils with physical handicaps have not themselves taken appropriate seats, appropriate reseating should be done as soon as you are aware of these individual needs.

(c) It is well to have the front desk in the middle row unassigned. This can then be used during the year as a "hot seat" for the immediate alleviation of discipline problems (also as a collection and distribution center and as a convenient place to rest your own weary bones!).

(d) After two warnings, break up "talky" combinations and groups of pupils who are inattentive and/or bent on sabotaging the class's progress.

(3) Never threaten or punish an individual (or a group) in anger. Suspend sentencing until both you and the pupil can view the case in perspective. You might ask the pupil what *he* would do if he were in your position. Have him *understand* the purpose and the justice of the punishment, if punishment is necessary.

(4) Try to get at the cause of antisocial behavior. Some of our best guidance is done by classroom teachers whose sympathetic concern encourages pupils to talk with them and unburden their troubles. The teacher may be able to identify himself with the pupil from personal experience, or at least help the pupil to analyze his own case objectively. Hand-in-hand fulfillment of an improved pupil "image" *could* be the turning point in a youngster's life. There have been cases where a teacher was the only real friend a pupil had, and pupils have been known to be eternally grateful.

(5) It has been known to happen with an individual offender that when the teacher has unexpectedly done something especially nice for him, he has been so taken by surprise that his antagonism has collapsed!

(6) It is an old, often effective technique to give an individual pupil responsibility for remedying among his fellow pupils the very offense for which he is remiss; e.g., the boy who litters the floor is given the responsibility for encouraging others to keep it clean, the straggler is delegated to keep other pupils in line, etc. The creation of a proprietary interest in the class by a pupil may be achieved by his acceptance of *any* responsibility for the class as a whole.

(7) If unacceptable behavior is widespread in your group, concentrate on the ringleader, if there is one. If you can win him over, you may regain control of your class.

(8) Refrain from using penalties which are personally and publicly humiliating to a pupil.

(9) Each pupil is different from every other pupil. Not all pupils respond in the same way to the same technique. Be sure that your approach (and punishment, if necessary) fits the *offender* as well as the offense. This requires sensitive insight. (You must also avoid favoritism! This can be a real dilemma. Use your best judgment.)

(10) Action is often more effective than words. For example, there are pupils who may try to catch up on their reading or homework for other classes during your class period. Simply take the "foreign" material without comment. The pupil must then come to you to get back his book or assignment. This can be more effective than having him listen to a disciplinary "lecture" from you while he is surrounded by sympathetic peers in class.

(11) Try "silence" as a means of checking one or two misbehavers in an otherwise

well-disciplined group. Stop dramatically in the middle of a sentence and wait for them and the group to sense the reason.

(12) You may wish to communicate with the parents of chronic misbehavers. Parents are sometimes more cooperative than you expect. It is advisable to discuss such communications with your department head, the counselor, or the adviser before proceeding.

(13) If it seems advisable to enlist parental cooperation, it is sometimes effective to have the pupil write a letter to his parents informing them of his unsatisfactory citizenship and stating his intentions concerning his actions in the future. Request that the letter be returned to you with his parents' signatures.

(14) Good discipline, group or individual, is seldom accidental. It requires planning. The following is a suggested sequence of steps, a sort of "defense in depth":

(a) "Call" a pupil on unacceptable conduct in class if it is a significant breach. Don't delay action in the case of individual misbehavior which is constantly annoying to the group and to you. That which is annoying today may result in havoc tomorrow.

(b) If such breaches recur, move pupil immediately to the "hot seat" (front seat of middle row, which is kept unassigned for just such emergencies). Then speak to the offender privately after class to achieve his understanding of the situation and intention of doing better. (When it is necessary to reprimand a pupil severely, it is usually best to do it in private; to do so in front of his classmates may elicit sympathy on his behalf and/or build his prestige among his peers.)

(c) If breaches of good conduct continue, move pupil to a special seat in rear of room for isolation until he is ready to be "readmitted" to class, or to a new permanent seat in front under your more immediate supervision.

(d) By now, you should make a point of getting all information available about the pupil. Make use of guidance and department files. Consult counselors, former teachers, and/or advisers. A "u" (unsatisfactory) in citizenship may well be justified by this time. You may also wish to contact the parents (see #12, #13).

(e) If unacceptable conduct continues, have pupil stand outside your door and report to you after class. (Charge pupil not to stray from the door. Never send more than one pupil out at a time). You might exact a promise of acceptable conduct *in writing*.

(f) If unacceptable conduct still continues, and you feel you have exhausted your own resources, it is now time for referral to the adviser, vice-principal, or principal with a case history from you. Readmission to class should be probationary.

(g) Further evidence of incorrigibility calls for a return of the pupil with documentation to the administrative officer who readmitted him to your class on probation. Parental conference, psychiatric analysis, a change of teachers, dropping the subject, and/or suspension from school by the principal is at last called for.

Corporal Punishment: Relegated to Last Resort Discipline, Survey Shows*

L. C. Hickman

Chicago — A box on the ear or slap on the rear rarely occurs in classrooms today. Although 49 states permit pupil punishment in schools, districts approach it warily, according to a survey of schoolmen undertaken by McGraw-Hill World News. Some districts ban it, but most restrict it to "last resort" situations, spelling out in careful detail how and when it may be applied and padding it with safeguards to protect both punisher and pupil.

The case against pupil punishment rests on many grounds, from the philosophic to the pragmatic.

Some schoolmen argue that physical reprimands are ineffective responses to difficult or antisocial behavior.

"We feel corporal punishment is not the solution, but merely compounds the problem in many situations," commented a Georgia schoolman. "It is the written policy of the board to search for the cause of maladjustment rather than to suppress the symptoms."

"Fear tactics," said an Illinois superintendent, "are not consistent with the self-control we are trying to develop in the children."

The pragmatic arguments against corporal punishment observe that the problem is not the children but the parents.

"Parents do not have the emotional maturity to permit others to administer corporal punishment," replied a Utah administrator.

"It's not worth the chance you take. I don't make enough money to get involved," admitted a California principal.

Even schoolmen who oppose corporal punishment in principle tend to support it as last-resort discipline. The prevailing view in public schools: Corporal punishment is not wise; where permitted, it is not recommended; when used, it is only after all else has failed; when applied, it must be administered carefully.

Written Rules

Indiscriminate punishment is out. Rather than take incidents as they come, most superintendents and boards of education have decided the best approach is a firm set of written rules.

In Kansas City, Mo., punishment may be given only when parents previously consent. It can be administered only by the principal — in the presence of a witness who is a member of the school staff — and a written report of the incident must be sent promptly to the superintendent's office. Punishment must never be inflicted by striking on or about the head.

The four key points in Kansas City's rules are almost always found in the rules of other districts. This coincidence is not accidental; rules are purposely designed to protect both punisher and pupil.

Parental Knowledge: In most systems, parents must be informed. Minneapolis, Birmingham, Ala., and Bellevue, Wash., require approval before punishment. DeKalb, Ga., recommends parental approval. Berkeley, Calif., requires only that parents be informed.

Adult Witnesses: In Glendale, Calif., two witnesses are required. Normally, witnesses are to be school staff members, though Indianapolis requires only a "professional person," and Fargo, N.D., and Beverly Hills, Calif., call simply for "one person."

*Reprinted from *Nations Schools*, December 1965. Used with permission.

Written Report: A record of the punishment and the warranting incident is widely mandatory. The punisher normally completes the report for filing in the principal's office or routing to the superintendent's attention. In Portland, Me., the report must be filed within 24 hours. In San Francisco, reports are sent to the superintendent monthly.

Below-Neck Punishment: The head is taboo. Many districts expressly forbid head shaking, ear boxing, and face slapping. Others make it off limits by deleting it from lists of punishable zones.

Over the years, it has not been uncommon for parents to bring legal action against disciplining schoolmen. Sometimes these are civil actions, for damages; sometimes, criminal actions, for assault and battery conviction. Requiring parental knowledge, administrators seek to involve parents in the punishment and prevent later complaints. Witnesses can provide verification of the events (what spanked Johnny tells his mother later may stray from the truth), and written reports assure the facts are recorded. Shielding the head minimizes physical danger; it's a sensitive area and making it off limits protects both child and teacher.

Who Administers It

A school system permitting punishment usually specifies who can give it. In many cases, it is the principal only. Explains Marvin T. Nodland, superintendent of schools, Sioux City, Iowa: "We don't permit teachers to strike youngsters. That's to prevent a case of a teacher suddenly becoming angry and striking a child on the moment's impulse."

Some systems permit the principal to delegate his right; others, such as Detroit and Indianapolis, specifically grant the right to classroom teachers.

In districts where punishment is prohibited or reserved solely to the principal, teachers are not entirely without the right to use physical force. State laws recognize the right of self-defense and the obligation of teachers to protect pupils in their care. Many districts separately include these instances in their rules.

"Stipulated regulations should not be construed in such a way that a teacher couldn't exercise physical contact if he is being threatened." (Kansas City, Mo.)

Kinds of Punishment

Usually rules state only that punishment should be "reasonable," "not excessive," or "not undue."

Sometimes, punishment is specifically prescribed: spanking with open hand (Berkeley, Calif.), paddling hands or rear (Pittsburgh), ruler raps (Birmingham, Ala.). Sometimes, it is specifically proscribed: no violent jerking, pinching or kicking (Biggs County, Ga.), no slapping, pinching, hairpulling, swatting (Tucson, Ariz.), no boxing ears, slapping face (almost all districts).

Rules in all districts make it clear that punishment must never be administered in anger or malice.

When Applied

The consensus: Apply corporal punishment only as a last resort. It should come at the end of a long trail of efforts to correct behavior. The first steps should be counseling and parent conferences — in heavy doses.

"We feel we are an educational institution, not a penal institution, and if a child doesn't intend to behave, we suspend him from school until he brings his parents for a conference," said an Iowa administrator.

"We'd want to involve the child's parents immediately," reported an Illinois superintendent. "The second thing we might do would be to either contact the school social worker to get his evaluation, or we might have the child tested by a qualified psychological examiner."

Most districts authorizing punishment permit it in all grades. Some, however, draw distinctions:

Punishment is permitted in elementary but not high schools in Oakland, Calif., Wichita, Kan., San Antonio, Tex., Fort Sam Houston, Tex.

Punishment of female students is not permitted in Baltimore County, Md., Oakland, Calif., Converse, Tex.

Some districts elaborate the exact circumstances under which punishment may be applied:

"Corporal punishment shall not be inflicted on students who have committed an offense for the first time. Nor shall it be inflicted for any other than overt behavior." (San Jose, Calif.)

"Corporal punishment might be used in the following cases: insolence and other disrespect toward superior; fighting or causing physical injury to others, or inciting violence; using profane or vulgar language; drawing or possessing obscene or indecent literature; destroying or defacing school or personal property; disobedience to reasonable demands; disorderly conduct, smoking, possession of tobacco or alcoholic beverage; forgery; truancy and habitual tardiness; misrepresenting the facts." (El Paso, Tex.)

Future of Punishment

Most districts are content with their current stand on punishment. Changes in the last few years have been made occasionally. Usually these introduce punishment where previously banned or replace informal rules with a written code.

The militancy of teachers in negotiation has resulted in some increased power to punish. Milwaukee, San Francisco, Kansas City, Mo., and Detroit have taken sterner punishment positions because of teacher pressures. In 1965, the Illinois legislature passed a law permitting spanking; in signing the bill, Governor Otto Kerner said its purpose was "to provide a defense against harassment suits brought by parents."

How Detroit Handles Corporal Punishment

General Statement

The policy in the Detroit schools is to provide school conditions, conduct school operations, and develop relationships between teachers and pupils, and among pupils that contribute to orderly operations with as much freedom of expression and activity as will be conducive to the growth of individual responsibility and self-discipline.

There is no formula by which teachers can have appropriate disciplinary action for immature, co-operative children who are well and without special emotional strain, that also will hold when the teacher is confronted with an emotionally disturbed youth or a group of adolescents seeing how far they can go in making life miserable for a teacher.

It is a general policy to expect that teachers will maintain discipline by means other than the use of corporal punishment. This policy does not prohibit corporal punishment but does restrict its use, in accordance with the following provisions, to these cases in which there is no adequate substitute treatment.

Definition

The term "corporal punishment" shall be understood to mean any use of physical force by a principal or teacher upon a pupil.

Legal Aspects Of Corporal Punishment

Under Michigan law the teacher is considered to stand in loco parentis with respect to his pupils while they are under his charge. The teacher thus, in loco parentis, may punish a pupil for acts that are detrimental to the good order and best interests of the school. The punishment administered must not be cruel or excessive and must be proportioned to the gravity of the offense, the apparent motive and disposition of the offender, and to the size, sex, and physical strength of the pupil, and must not be such as to cause lasting pain or injury. The teacher may not act wantonly or from malice or passion.

School Administration Of The Discipline Problem

Principals are responsible for the maintenance of proper discipline in their respective schools as they are responsible for every other aspect of the school program.

Principals should, therefore, inform their teachers that corporal punishment may be used, within the legal limits outlined above, in those emergency cases which, in the judgment of the teacher, require such immediate action for the preservation of proper order in the class or school, or for the protection of the pupils, teachers or school in general.

Teachers will receive full support of the principal and the central administration in any action taken by them pertaining to discipline provided they act within the above dened limits. This support shall include defense of the teacher's action by the principal against complaints of parents as well as legal assistance by the central administration in the event that a criminal complaint is made or civil court action is instituted for damages.

Prohibited Disciplinary Action

Punishment which, in the judgment of the Superintendent, is more severe than that which might be administered by a reasonable parent; which is cruel or excessive; which is more severe than is indicated by the gravity of the offense, or the apparent motive and disposition of the offender; is excessive with respect to the sex, size, or physical strength of the pupil; which results in lasting pain or injury; or which is administered wantonly or from malice or passion, is prohibited in the Detroit schools.

Clear Understanding Of Policy Necessary

It is essential that a clear understanding should exist between the principal and the teachers in each school concerning the above policy. Principals should, therefore, discuss this important matter with their teachers frequently enough to ensure that all are well informed on this phase of the disciplinary problem. The principal should be informed promptly by a teacher when incidents occur which require the use of corporal punishment. This will permit principals to be of greatest assistance in working with parents and the teacher for a full understanding and solution of the problem. —*Reprinted from the Detroit Teachers Handbook.*

How the Law Looks at Corporal Punishment
Lee O. Garber

Although legal principles concerning corporal punishment haven't changed much lately, the laws in some states have.[1] For districts that wish to review or establish corporal punishment procedures, here are 10 legal guidelines to keep in mind.

1. A board of education may enact any reasonable rule or regulation concerning corporal punishment, unless it is forbidden to do so by state statute. Only one state, to the best of the writer's knowledge — New Jersey — forbids corporal punishment by law.

2. A teacher may administer corporal punishment if there is no prohibiting board rule or state statute. If prohibitions exist, teachers must abide by them. Not too long ago an Indiana court indicated that a board rule depriving teachers of the right to use corporal punishment might be held invalid if the state statute specifically stated that the teacher stood *in loco parentis* (in place of the parents) to his pupils.[2] It took the position that the rule could be depriving a teacher of a statutory right — which the board had no right to do.

3. The person administering punishment must not be motivated by anger or malice. If he is, he may be considered guilty of assault and battery.

4. Punishment in all cases must be reasonable. If it isn't and a child is injured, the teacher may be held liable. (However, if a child has a physical defect of which the teacher is unaware and this defect is aggravated by punishment, the teacher will not be liable if the punishment was reasonable.)

5. The courts, in determining what is reasonable, consider various factors: the nature of the punishment, the nature of the offense committed, and the age, sex and physical condition of the child. Punishment suited to a 16 year old boy obviously might be considered unreasonable if given to a first grade girl.

6. A teacher may not punish a child who refuses to obey a rule when disobedience is required by the parents. Also, in some jurisdictions, a teacher may not punish a child who breaks a rule later held to be unreasonable. In most jurisdictions, however, it will be held that if the teacher was not aware that the rule was unreasonable, he would be exempt from liability even if he punished the child moderately for breaking the rule.

7. A teacher stands *in loco parentis* to pupils even though statutes do not specifically so state. This is a rule of common law, universally accepted.

8. Though a teacher stands *in loco parentis*, he does not occupy a parent's exact status. His authority is more limited. For example, certain parental punishment, while harsh, might not be declared unreasonable; but, if it were administered by a teacher, a court might hold it so. In other words, a parent has more control over the child than a teacher.

9. Because the teacher standing *in loco parentis* has authority, he has responsibility to the child too. It is assumed the teacher will see that the child is protected from harmful incidents.

10. A teacher's authority over a child extends from home to home. This means that a teacher may punish a child for things done off school grounds and out of school hours if the punished offense was related to the school's welfare and morale. This does not mean, however, that a teacher is responsible for the child from the time he leaves home until he returns. He is responsible only while the child is under his supervision.

[1]Garber, Lee O.: "When Is Corporal Punishment Legal?", THE NATION'S SCHOOLS, vol. 100, pp. 100, 104, 106. April, 1960.

[2]Indiana State Personnel Board *v.* Jackson, 192 N.E. (2d) 740 (Ind.).

Let's Stop This Nonsense About Student Dress*

John A. Stinespring

We are constantly hearing educators rage and storm about the problem of student appearance. Teachers demand that the school (meaning the principal) set some real standards of propriety and decency that students will have to obey. Faculty meetings are filled with apparently serious and frequently heated discussions of whether or not students should be permitted to go without socks, of whether culottes are shorts or skirts, and so on.

The problem is not really student appearance at all. Every teacher can agree that there is such a thing as inappropriate and indecent dress, even if the exact dividing line between decency and indecency is nearly impossible to define. The real problem is the desire of teachers to have someone prepare a lengthy list of precise rules that they can then enforce without the need of making judgments.

Principals who prepare a list are in danger of putting themselves and the school in a ludicrous position. Rules have a tendency to become more and more detailed and less and less useful as demands for clarification occur. The result of this process is likely to produce such rules as follows:

A girl's skirt must be long enough to touch the floor when she is kneeling.

Boys' shirttails must be tucked in unless the shirt is specially designed to be worn on the outside.

Boys' hair may not exceed three inches in length.

Such rules are perhaps reassuring to those teachers who would rather use a ruler or protractor than their brains for decision making, but they deserve the ridicule and resentment that students will show for them. Furthermore, a principal who enforces rules of this sort may find himself facing a parade of students sent by teachers who want him to confirm their measurements and "do something" with the culprits.

Schoolwide dress codes will become outdated by rapidly changing styles that will make the codes obsolete as soon as they are published. This means, of course, that teachers will ultimately have to exercise judgment themselves and apply a much more general standard of the following sort to each individual case:

Is the appearance of a student in my class so out of line with accepted standards of decency or appropriateness that he will degrade himself or detract from the process of education in the class? Will bringing this to his attention help him, the class, or the school enough to warrant the time and effort required to do it?

Teachers may object to this kind of procedure, since it could put them in the awkward position of enforcing "high" standards while other teachers who are "lax" gain favor with students. It would be unprofessional for a teacher to succumb to the student objection, "The other teachers let us." Teachers will have to be sufficiently secure in their judgment to resist submitting to what students report "everyone" is doing.

A poorly substantiated assertion often heard in discussions of this subject is that student appearance sets the tone for the school and that students who are required to look neat and well-groomed will behave better and be more serious about their school work. This assertion may well be true. But the people who promote this

*Reprinted from *NEA Journal,* February 1968. Used with permission.

unproven claim typically fail to include other related effects.

It is equally possible, for example, that rigidly enforced appearance rules will interfere with other important goals of education. A teacher may feel obligated to enforce a rule on a student who is a potential dropout and consequently drive him to quit. A teacher who is trying to develop rapport with a student may find that enforcing the rules interferes with a more important educational goal.

Teachers should be grateful to be freed from the need to enforce picayune dress codes. They should welcome the opportunity to communicate with their students in a private and matter-of-fact discussion about appropriate attire. When treated individually and with respect, students will respond favorably and the appearance problem should recede into the background.

Dress Codes: We Forget Our Own Advice*

Morris J. Weinberger

A parent is talking to a high school principal, concerned because his daughter is acting strangely: new and "different" friends, school truancy, and disobedience at home.

The principal, from his store of experience and knowledge, speaks calmly and with reassurance: "Relax, Mr. Jones. Adolescence is a normal time of rebellion and testing of new behaviors. If you deal with her patiently and with understanding now, you'll find her basic qualities are still there and will still control your child when the chips are down."

Later that same day, a teacher refers a boy to the principal for what she terms "bizarre" behavior: Bob has come to school with long hair and the beginning of sideburns and a moustache. He refuses to go home to shave them off, and he is dressed like a "hippie."

The principal, from his store of experience and knowledge, speaks to the student with patient firmness: "John, I'm certain that someday you'll understand that every society must have rules to regulate what individuals do for the good of all. You know our school rules on hair and accep-

*Reprinted from *The Clearing House*, April 1970. Used with permission.

table dress were adopted after careful thought, and yet you deliberately break them. We must keep up our standards — either you will conform to our rules, or you will be suspended until you do!"

Is the principal being consistent, or is he unknowingly caught in conflicting expectations? To the parent, he can be the understanding and flexible student guide, while to the student he feels it necessary to steadfastly stand for the greater values of society. And further, there is something about what is dramatically visible to those in authority which makes student dress variations less understandable or tolerable than similar behavior variations which are more subtle but may be more serious.

In the ever increasing frequency of conflict over high school dress codes, it appears as though some very simple but basic truths are being overlooked. Educators who have used these truths to counsel teachers and parents at other times, now forget them in their own reaction to what appears to be a moral issue.

Yet, it is obvious that this issue is but another variation of the age-old conflict between the needs and the rights of the individual as compared to those of a larger society. It is complicated by the age of the students involved, the school tradition of *in loco parentis*, and the persuasive attitude that direct control of thoughts and desires is somehow possible (although we really know better). Because of these factors it is very difficult for educators to implement beliefs about student development that might almost be automatic in another context. Most educators agree upon, but often forget about, these following points:

(1) Adolescence is a period of experimentation during which various adult roles are "tried on," even if only mentally, as the adolescent attempts to find out who he is.

(2) The kinds of feedback the adolescent gets during these years is extremely important to him as he decides about the "real me." Feedback from peers is much more important than feedback from adults, the latter frequently serving as a negative orientation.

(3) The more restrictive and the more visible (i.e., more often used, or referred to) a rule is, the more it is essential for the adolescent to test the rule deliberately, if only vicariously through the actions of another.

(4) Many fads are characteristic of this role experimentation and hence most of them come, are embraced enthusiastically, deeply, and even exclusively for a time, and then quickly go to be replaced by another equally important "in" symbol. (Witness the fickle loyalty to top recording stars or to make-up styles.)

(5) When any individual devotes an enormous amount of his personal emotion (his psychic energy) to defending his actions or beliefs, it can no longer be a fad to him. For now, the very defense causes it to become an important issue to him or else he has to admit to being wrong — in public. This is difficult for anyone, and impossible for most teen-agers.

(6) Much parental (and educator) retreat to morality as the reason for a belief or action is more related to tradition and the status quo, and to the sin of disobedience toward a person who has their best interests at heart, than it is to morality in either the religious or sociological sense. It is difficult for adults, also, to back down and admit a change of mind.

(7) American society is going through a more intense self-examination of values than ever before. One of the major points of consideration is the role of the individual in an increasingly mechanistic social order. A growing depersonalization is felt by modern man as the influence of first business, then unions, and more recently government reaches inexorably into daily life, with the recent spectre of the computer as an agent of future control adding to his feelings of alienation. Thoughtful adult discussions and analysis of alienation in the mass media has, in part, shaped student action to attempt to be one's own man.

(8) Some rebellion in adolescence is not only a normal phase but a necessary one as the individual marshals his forces to assert his independence and become his own man. To deny legitimate questioning and experimentation on sheer moral principle, without a full hearing and discussion, only confirms the sense of alienation felt by the individual and his need for rebellion.

(9) Yet, when all is said, there is still a basic kernel of reality that demands of responsible authority in all institutions, including schools, that they safeguard the goals of their institution. This means that school officials must control student actions which are truthfully injurious to the individual or to the larger school, or which are truthfully interruptions of such a quality as to hinder learning. This latter reason is

most frequently advanced, and yet educators frequently find out that real learning occurs during the solution of chance problems. This would appear to be a sufficient reason for us to be quite permissive if we truly desire a pluralistic society and not merely a conformistic melting pot.

What ought a school administrator do then? As is so often the case in our profession, we most often get into trouble when we overreact to a problem before the problem really exists. If the above general principles appear to be valid, then why don't *you* really take a look at the issue again? Reexamine *yourself* and your basic values — your beliefs about how students learn and incorporate change within themselves.

If individuals, and school faculties, will proceed on their best knowledge in advance of a critical problem, they will undoubtedly handle this issue far better than in the reactive mode, after the controversy hits their school. Considering the number of articles interpreting recent court decisions that tell us that students do have real legal rights, which are more often being recognized by the courts, surely educators will not choose to risk an issue being taken to court — especially when legal precedent is against them.

In this matter, as in many others, the enlightened action appears to also be the most educational. The student body could be realistically involved in mutual problem solving over enough time for the issues to be thoroughly discussed and even minority positions examined for whether the wishes of the majority deny minority rights. When students are treated with respect for their judgment, they most frequently respond with mature action (although not perhaps in the first blush of trying their wings — we often need to have patience through their testing of our trust in them). Minimal rules developed mutually, not just by students or faculty, will be better understood and more easily complied with. Democracy really can work if we believe in a pluralistic society, the worth of the individual, and give people a chance to really try it.

Yet, this is one of the many issues in which no one solution is right for all. Beware of cure-all advice from Mount Olympus. Instead, make an honest effort to listen, understand, and help students solve the real problems of their immediate life. Education is still a rewarding, if at times demanding, vocation.

Practical Suggestions for the Novice Teacher Concerning Discipline*

Warren William Bell

Many teachers say one of the hardest tasks they face is maintaining good classroom discipline. Certainly it is one of the most important aspects of teaching. Regardless of how much the teacher knows about his subject, it's impossible to teach inattentive students. The teacher who lacks classroom control cannot function

*Reprinted from *NASSP Bulletin,* October 1971. Used with permission.

effectively because the student's attention, interest, and application are prerequisites for learning. Studies have shown that the primary reason for teacher failure is not lack of knowledge in his subject area but his inability to maintain control of the classroom.

Discipline is training to act in accordance with rules; it is instruction in the correct method to conduct one's self. It also means punishment inflicted as a means of correction and training.

Too often discipline is imposed simply to punish a student, but this should never be the case. Since the desired result of discipline should be improved conduct on the student's part, it should be applied only to correct — never to punish. It should be administered in a firm and just manner, for the purpose of developing within the student a sense of good judgment consistent with a desirable system of values, leading to proper self-control and self-direction. Needless to say, good judgment, self-control and self-direction aren't developed overnight.

One would think that this aspect of teaching would be thoroughly covered in college and university education courses, but that is not always the case. Many times it is covered superficially, and too often the beginning teacher finds that the theory that was stressed in college does not work when put into practice.

What is the best method to achieve good classroom discipline? Unfortunately, there is no simple answer to this question. What works for one teacher may not work for another. Perhaps that is why college professors emphasize theory rather than trying to present practical solutions to behavioral problems.

Suggestions For Maintaining Control

Since the teacher's effectiveness is so dependent upon his ability to maintain good classroom control and since each discipline problem must be dealt with individually, the following suggestions are made in an attempt to help the novice teacher.

1. Learn your students' names immediately. Very seldom do teachers encounter any real discipline problem the first week of school. If you can call each

of your students by his first name by the end of the first week of school, you will automatically eliminate many problems. A way to accomplish this is to allow the students to choose where they want to sit but require them to sit in the same seat for the first week. Tell them the reason for the requirement. Students respect a reasonable rule but rebel against an arbitrary one. Then pass out a sheet of paper to each row of students, have each pupil sign his name, and then take the first and last five minutes of each period during the first week to call roll. As you do so you should try to associate each face with each name, and then practice calling students by name during the remainder of each class. Thus, by the end of the week you should be able to call each of your students by his first name.

2. Learn about the previous school experience of your students through the cumulative records, but be careful not to let them bias you. Visit with the counselor; one of his primary objectives is to help you do a better job of teaching. One of the main reasons such records are kept is to help you assist each student in achieving his maximum potential. In order to do this, you must know where to start and then build from there. If you have a student who has a history of being a behavioral problem, the cumulative records should also include valuable information as to how you can best cope with him.

3. Develop to your fullest extent qualities which in themselves will aid in the prevention of disorder: self-confidence, a sympathetic understanding of and liking for young people, a sense of humor, and a sense of justice and fair play.

4. Always be prepared for class, as idle time is playtime. Thorough preparation is absolutely essential, but don't allow your lesson plans to serve as a straightjacket.

Make your classroom an interesting, meaningful, and vital place to be. Don't assign busy work; if you do, students will soon learn what you are doing, become bored, and create their own activity which you probably won't condone.

5. Make your assignments reasonable and clear. Be definite and concise in your directions. Write them on the chalkboard and suggest to your students that they keep an assignment notebook.

6. Know your subject, but don't make the mistake of thinking that the goal of teaching is to have your pupils learn all that you know about it. Your challenge is to see what contribution your subject can make to their needs and abilities.

7. Establish a business-like atmosphere in your classroom. Be a sharp dresser and stand at the door at the beginning of each period. This gives you an opportunity to be friendly by greeting your pupils and exchanging casual remarks. It also encourages students to get to class on time and discourages horseplay in the halls. Then when the bell rings, close your door and start class promptly.

8. Be prepared for the unexpected. A good disciplinarian anticipates problems before they occur.

9. Keep rules to a minimum. However, if you find they are necessary, be sure your students know them. If you expect your pupils to behave in a certain way, tell them so, and explain the reasons why. A class discussion of these rules can be enlightening both to you and your class. You may discover that some of them have no real purpose, in which case you should be willing to cancel them gracefully.

10. Be consistent. When you reprimand an action one day and ignore it the next, students don't know what to expect. As a result, they'll often try it again to see if they can get away with it. They are also quick to see and resent the basic unfairness of inconsistency.

11. Don't make threats that you cannot enforce, or your word will mean nothing.

12. Never punish the entire class for the actions of a few. Not only is it unfair to the innocent, who will harbor resentment, but it is also educationally unsound and indefensible.

13. Control your temper, but if you lose it have the student stand in the hall (or back of the room) until you cool off. Thus you will avoid saying or doing something you will later regret. When you lose your cool you lose your ability to solve the discipline problems sanely, rationally, and thoughtfully. A cardinal rule to remember is, "Never say anything to a student that you would not say while in the presence of his parents."

14. Watch your tongue. Humiliating a child by a public reprimand is seldom a wise method of discipline. A tongue lashing may end the disturbance — but at what cost!

15. Change the routine. Do something nice for your class occasionally. Rearrange the room and use your bulletin boards as instructional tools. Ask your class for different ideas, but remember that, as the teacher, you must be in control and make the final decisions.

16. Be as courteous to your class as you expect them to be with you. Establish a good teacher-student relationship as well as a good peer relationship among class members. Let the students know you like them. Look for things to praise, especially in students who are discipline problems. Accept them as worthwhile, in spite of their misbehavior. Disapprove of the act, certainly, but not of the individual.

17. Be careful not to become buddy-buddy with your students. The striving for popularity is perhaps the biggest pitfall a

beginning teacher must overcome. Your goal is respect, not popularity. (You will find that if they respect you, they will probably like you.)

18. Learn the pupil's problems. It may be more important for you to find out something than to do something. Look for the reasons behind misbehavior. It often stems from the fact that the curriculum — or the teaching approach — does not interest your pupils.

19. Don't make study a punishment. The teacher who keeps children after school to study mathematics or write an essay, as a penalty for misbehavior, is saying: Study is an unpleasant thing. There is no joy or satisfaction in it. It's so painful that I use it as a punishment." This hardly creates a thirst for learning in youngsters.

20. Don't be afraid to apologize if you've treated a pupil unjustly. You'll gain, not lose, the respect of the class for admitting your error.

21. Don't be afraid to use the telephone. This is one of the most effective, yet little used, means of obtaining assistance in dealing with a disruptive student. Most parents will support the teacher but they can't if they are unaware of what is going on. In most cases, a call home will solve the problem.

22. Avoid arguing with students. Discuss differences of opinion in private. Class time is instruction time.

23. Walk and talk among the students.

24. Don't see and hear everything.

25. Be enthusiastic; it's contagious.

26. Avoid physical force; use your mind, not your muscle.

27. Don't try to do the impossible. Some students have emotional problems only a better trained person can solve. When a youngster is a constant troublemaker and all your efforts to help him fail, perhaps you should refer him and his parents to a psychologist, psychiatrist, or to an agency which provides such services. There are limits to what a teacher can do in child study, diagnosis, and treatment.

28. Keep administration informed when dealing with a problem student, but seek administrative help only after all other means have failed.

Unfortunately, there is no one way to maintain good classroom control. However, the teacher who possesses good judgment and is firm, fair, and friendly will very likely be successful.

Corrective Discipline*
Leslie J. Chamberlin

The unpleasant experiences of teachers who have not learned to cope with classroom situations that lead to disorder, discourtesy or inactivity often cause them to leave the profession.

Even experienced teachers who change locations find they must adjust their usual disciplinary techniques to the new children and situation if they are to continue successfully. Serious problems may develop

even when the teacher consistently uses preventive disciplinary techniques, and such situations must be dealt with by the teacher.

But when is a classroom situation considered serious?

There are three stages to the development of a serious disciplinary situation. They are: (a) whispering and inactivity; (b) laughing, talking, writing notes and horseplay; (c) the completely disordered state which often involves tripping, punch-

*Reprinted from *School and Community,* December 1961. Used with permission.

ing, throwing missiles, catcalls and open disrespect for the teacher.

Whenever a classroom situation reaches stages "b" or "c", it can be called serious, and the teacher should take definite steps to restore order.

The teacher should try to resolve the problem before involving the principal or school administration. Too often teachers think that bringing the principal into the situation helps solve the problem, although at times it only complicates the solution.

The teacher needs to look at the whole situation and try to locate the cause, not the symptom, of the trouble. To do this effectively he must:

(1) distinguish between the child and his behavior, rejecting malbehavior without rejecting the child as a person;

(2) never react to classroom malbehavior personally but preserve an objective point of view;

(3) try to remember what it was like to be a child, insecure and full of doubts and wanting to succeed. With this understanding, communication becomes easier. When the teacher cannot communicate with a child, he should turn the problem over to someone else.

One of the best methods of securing the cooperation of a particular child or a small group of children is to contact the child's home. A short personal note from teacher to parent, a brief phone call or even a short visit to the home by the teacher makes the home-school relationship closer. With the sincere assistance of the home, few school problems remain serious.

There are times when a pupil should be sent from the classroom and without many words. A written slip should be kept ready for such occasions. A good practice is to say just a few words to the child at the door to let him know why he is being sent out.

Sending an offending pupil from the room, usually to the principal's office, is one of the most frequently used methods of classroom control.

To insure that the practice is not overworked, a teacher should follow these principles:

(1) Send a child from the room only when the best interest of the class demands it.

(2) Follow the accepted policies and procedures for his particular school which govern when and how to send a pupil to the office.

(3) Whenever a pupil is sent from the room as a temporary measure, everyone concerned should understand this at the outset.

(4) When the teacher wishes the principal to handle the problem, this should be made clear and all the circumstances surrounding the issue should be put in writing.

(5) Before sending a child from the room, the teacher should consider using various alternate disciplinary approaches.

Sometimes just arranging for a child to be alone for a short time solves the immediate situation and gives the teacher time to delve deeper into the trouble. Sending the child on an errand, assigning a special project or just asking him to stand in the hall or somewhere away from the class are useful techniques.

Generally speaking, it is a poor practice to scold a misbehaving child before his classmates. A better procedure is to ask politely and firmly that he stop this behavior and tell him you will talk with him about it later.

At times it is wise to shift the classroom arrangement by asking the misbehaving child to change his seat. This immediately creates a new setting in which to continue.

Whenever discipline is discussed the use of corporal punishment is considered. Teachers, parents, administrators, the courts and others agree that corporal punishment should rarely be used and that it should be administered reasonably.

In most school systems corporal punishment may be administered only when written permission from the parent has been secured and filed in the school office. With such permission, the teacher may administer the punishment only in the presence of the principal and is held accountable for the manner of punishment. Striking the head, slapping the face, box-ing the ears and similar means of inflicting pain are prohibited.

Career teachers say that thorough lesson planning, private conferences with students and parents and a careful study of the characteristics of the persons involved in the problem help them control pupils without resorting to punitive measures too often.

Good preventive techniques should be used. However, when discipline problems do develop the teacher should deal with them objectively and firmly and without rejecting the offending individual.

Chapter VII

Discussionette

1. How does the principle of "knowing yourself" assist teachers in establishing more effective discipline?

2. Might it be desirable to teacher training institutions to provide analysis or some similar cause in the curriculum for prospective teachers?

3. What rules are necessary, if any, regarding the use of corporal punishment?

4. Can parents, after previously approving the use of corporal punishment, prosecute a school employee for using "too much" corporal punishment?

5. Is corporal punishment, like capital punishment, becoming undesirable to use?

6. "How the Law Looks at Corporal Punishment"
   a. What was your reaction to this article?
   b. What is the purpose of this article?

7. How often today do extreme styles of dress disrupt classrooms?
   a. Should school boards and administrators, or student councils, develop student dress codes or should codes be eliminated entirely?
   b. Have most school dress codes changed with times?
   c. Are school dress codes usually worth the notariety which they have received?
   d. Why have some schools done away with dress codes?

8. Discuss other examples of what usually happens when the needs and rights of the individual come into conflict with the needs and rights of the community.

9. Have you had previous experiences with reverse psychology?
   a. Can reverse psychology backfire on the user?
   b. In what other situations might reverse psychology work?

Discussionette Words and Concepts

group dynamics	detention	conduct
peer pressure	physical force	restraint
morality	restrictive	dress code
mechanistic	relevant	role

Try to use these words.

Try to explain these words.

Try to relate these words and their concepts to current or emerging educational patterns regarding corrective discipline.

CHAPTER VIII

⟨⟨THERAPEUTIC DISCIPLINE⟩⟩

INTRODUCTION

TEACHERS WHO START OFF THE YEAR with appropriate discipline measures usually have more success than teachers who try to change their discipline after having made their first impressions. Most often a teacher's first impression will last for the entire school year and it is usually easier to loosen discipline procedure rather than to enforce stricter disciplinary measures.

Usually a teacher's first control with the student is as a group member rather than as an individual. Consequently, if appropriate group discipline is established it is logical that appropriate individual discipline will develop. However, the importance of first impression in dealing with groups is often overlooked and the emphasis has been placed on the individual. Teachers who understand and use group dynamics will usually be successful in individual discipline as well.

This chapter deals with effective therapeutic discipline for both the group and the individual aspects of student behavior.

Group Behavior and Discipline*
Leslie J. Chamberlin

Teachers deal with groups — assemblies, bands, choirs, classes, cliques, clubs, courses, divisions, ensembles, gangs, meetings, orchestras, organizations, staffs, and teams. The important word, however, is group. Teachers deal with individuals, of course, and must be very capable and knowledgeable in dealing with the individual student, but most often a teacher's first contact with the student is as a group member since the basic school organizational unit is the classroom group.

In the past, formal study of groups by teachers has been limited. The emphasis

*Reprinted from *The Clearing House*, October 1966. Used with permission.

during teacher training has been on the individual, which is very important and necessary. However, it is now recognized that an understanding of the dynamics of the group behavior is also very important. This article attempts to provide an insight into the behavior of school children in groups.

The Problem

In most discipline situations attention is usually focused on the misbehavior of one individual. In very many situations, however, the real source of the problematic behavior stems from group influence. The misbehavior of an individual pupil is fre-

165

quently a symptom of or reaction to group influence. The pupil may be acting out the feelings generally felt by the group, responding to certain pressures exerted by the group or attempting to fulfill certain personal satisfactions by gaining group acceptance or prestige. At times it is not possible to completely understand a particular situation through a study of only the main individual in a particular discipline problem. Until the situation is studied in terms of possible group influences, the true source of conflict may not be found.

Most teachers are aware that some youngsters become somewhat intoxicated as a result of group activity and they often attempt things as members of a group that they would never consider doing as individuals. Membership in groups require a certain kind of behavior. Unfortunately the required behavior may be completely at odds with what is considered satisfactory by the child's parents and/or teachers. Nevertheless, group pressures for compliance will cause one to behave according to the group's norms if he is to be accepted.

Even when the source of a disciplinary problem is actually only one individual the influence of the group must be considered. By careful study of the individual and proper action on the part of the teacher the source of misbehavior may be found and corrected. However, the problem still may not be completely solved. The previous misbehavior of this youngster has had its effect on the group and it will have a certain after-effect both on the individual and the class. The teacher will have to be aware of group reactions and influences to bring about a readjustment.

Teachers often overlook the fact that an individual student may be acting as a group member when the group is actually not physically present. This becomes clear when we begin to enumerate the many different groups to which one individual may belong. The average student is a member of a family, a neighborhood, a school, a class, an age group and sex group. In addition to this, he comes from a much larger group that has a particular economic, religious, social and ethical background. We can add that from time to time he may also be a member of a team, club, musical organization, clique or gang. To further complicate the problem, the influence from any or all of the above-mentioned groups can interact, off-set, or reinforce one another, at any time.

The relationship of one individual to the other members within a particular group often changes. As the group moves from one activity to another the work relationships, authority relationships, social influence relationships and sex relationships change within the group. One individual may belong to several sub-groups within any larger, more permanent group. These sub-groups are formed and re-formed according to the activity of the larger group. No two groups behave precisely the same way although confronted with like situations. What will be accepted from one teacher will cause trouble if tried with another and behavior that is overlooked by the group for one individual just won't be tolerated for another.

Obviously there are many factors that can effect the behavior of a group. If the teacher or administrator is to maintain satisfactory discipline in the classroom and within the school, an awareness of the effects of certain factors on group behavior is imperative.

Behavioral Factors

The factors that can effect the behavior of a group of children are so numerous and so diversified that it is difficult to place them in any simple, organizational form. For analytical purposes, however, four general categories will be used. Generally speaking, the factors that affect the behavior of classroom groups are related to (1) mental, (2) physical, (3) social, or (4) environmental problems.

Mental factors, for example, would be related to problems involving gifted children, mentally retarded children, emotional stability, the difficulty of classroom assignments as related to group ability, or the interest span of the children. In other words, those factors involving the intelligence level, creativity, emotional development, interest level, or attention span of the group.

The second category, *physical factors,* is concerned with things such as the children's chronological age, physical development, growth stages, sex relationships (that is girl to girl, boy to boy and girl to boy friendships), or those natural things that have to do with the child's body rather than the mind or spirit.

By *social factors* we refer to such things as the general feeling of security, feeling of belonging, acceptance by the group, proneness toward delinquency, private friendships, prejudice because of color, race, religion, and those things pertaining to the association of students with one another.

The term *environmental factors* pertains to the child's surroundings. Such things as the home, the school, the neighborhood, as well as the child's larger environment — involving the areas of economic status, and cultural and religious background — are the things which influence growth and character.

In discussing the four general categories just defined we refer to those things that have a bearing on the general level of behavior of a particular group. Every group has its "normal" behavior. This behavior may or may not be considered satisfactory, nevertheless it is "normal" behavior for that group. The behavior factors are the various things that help to establish this norm. When group behavior is worse than the usual norm for the group, something must be affecting it. We will call these temporary influences "conflict factors."

Conflict Factors

Conflict factors are closely related to the behavioral factors. The primary difference between the two is that a behavioral factor is something that has a long lasting general influence on the behavior of the group, whereas a conflict factor is something that brings about an immediate change in the normal behavior and may or may not have a long lasting effect on it. When describing environmental behavior factors it was mentioned that the students' classroom environment would have definite influence on the classes' general behavior pattern. Here we have reference to the usual or long term environmental characteristics of the classroom. From time to time a classroom may become very noisy because of an unusual amount of truck traffic; it may become too hot or too cold because of the temporary malfunction of the heating equipment; or the humidity within the classroom may become very uncomfortable because of weather conditions of the day. These temporary environmental factors or classroom irritants would be considered conflict factors because of their temporary nature. A teacher may be capable of correcting a conflict factor, whereas a behavioral factor would probably require the coordinated action of many people and agencies in order for much improvement of the situation to be accomplished.

Teachers need a sixth sense to anticipate trouble before it happens. Experienced teachers learn to recognize conflict factors as they begin to take form. They realize that situations which jeopardize classroom control vary from class to class, teacher to teacher, and from day to day. But they also realize that conflict factors are more likely to formulate under certain conditions. Changing groups, working on committee work, entering or leaving a classroom, distributing or collecting materials are a few of the activities which contribute to the development of conflict. Children's feelings, like the barometer, rise and fall with changes in the weather. An unusually windy day, a sudden snow, or an unexpected rain calls for special scheduling and planning. Because students naturally become keyed up immediately before the holidays or vacation time, the teacher needs to be especially alert for the formation of conflict factors on those occasions. The main job of the teacher in such situations is to keep the activities of the group in their proper perspective to the group's normal school activities.

In more general terms, conflicting factors usually develop because of resulting discord:

(1) from inter-reactions of group members.

(2) between the self-identification of group members and the symbols and/or persons representing the total group.

(3) from strained emotional climate connected with unusual weather conditions or anticipated holidays, etc.

(4) between the leader's self-identification and the group's current purpose and identification.

(5) between the leader's personal needs (that is, need for domination) and the group's willingness to fulfill these needs.

(6) between the leadership tactics applied and the group's organizational concept.

(7) between the private behavioral code of individual group members and the total group's behavioral standard, culture level or goal.

(8) from too great a difference between the difficulty of material to be studied, as related to the ability of the group, and the interest level of the materials to be studied.

(9) from teacher attitude in regard to what "must" be accomplished, and the ability of the group.

(10) between the basic needs of children — such as need for belonging, need for freedom from fear, and need for freedom from guilt — and the teachers' attitude.

Conflict factors, then, are those transitory circumstances that enter the normal behavioral pattern of a group of children, causing one or more of the group to deviate from what would be considered normal behavior.

Summary

Usually a teacher's first contact with a student is as a group member. In most discipline situations attention is focused on the misbehavior of one child, however, in many situations the real source of the problematic behavior stems from group influence. At times it is not possible to completely understand a particular situation through a study of only the main individual in a particular discipline problem, and the teacher will have to be aware of group reactions and influences to correct the situation. Generally speaking the factors that affect behavior of classroom groups can be thought of as being related to mental, physical, social, or environmental problems. These four factors refer to those things that have a bearing on the general level of behavior of a particular group. When group behavior is somewhat worse than the usual for the group, something must be affecting the group. We call these temporary influences "conflict factors." A teacher may be capable of correcting a conflict factor; however, a behavioral factor would probably require the coordinated action of many people if much improvement were to be accomplished. Experienced teachers learn to recognize conflict factors as they begin to take form. They know that conflict factors are most likely to develop under certain conditions and learn to anticipate them. By doing so, the teacher is better able to manage his class in a manner which conforms to a psychology of self-direction.

Delinquent Behavior*

Teen-agers kill teen-agers in New York City. A Senate subcommittee, headed by Thomas Hennings, Democrat of Missouri, begins study of juvenile delinquency.

The White House Conference on Children and Youth (1960) says juvenile crime is a problem in 45 out of the 50 states.

Such was the temper of the day when the Juvenile Delinquency Project made its second and final report to the National Education Association. The material that follows was drawn directly from the Project's second report, *Delinquent Behavior — Principles and Practices.*

Good teachers and good schools are cited as the "first line of defense against delinquency." Here are some suggestions on what the teacher can do about it.

The teacher's knowledge, interest, and concern for the pupils in his class go beyond the classroom; he is cognizant of the home and family backgrounds of his pupils and of the conflicting value systems reflected in their cultural milieu. (Because much of the information his pupils tell him and much of what he learns about their homes and family backgrounds is extremely confidential, he must maintain a constant sensitivity to professional ethics.)

The teacher makes provision for individual differences by using a wide variety of methods which may enable every youngster to achieve a measure of success.

*Reprinted from *Ohio Schools*, December 1959. Used with permission.

The teacher aims to involve youngsters in the solution of problems relevant to their age group. In order to insure development of self-discipline (an ultimate goal) the teacher provides opportunity for young people in school to make moral decisions with a minimum of school supervision and direction.

Even good teachers have disciplinary problems. But good discipline is more than keeping order in the classroom. Its ultimate goal is to help children develop self-control, self-respect, and respect for property and people around them.

Out of a bagful of tips on discipline published in the Project report, let's look at ten.

1. Make your instructional and other classroom activities interesting, meaningful, and vital.

2. Know your subject, but don't make the mistake of thinking that the goal of teaching is to have your pupils learn all that you know about your subject. Your challenge is to see what contribution your subject can make to their needs and their abilities.

3. Know the fundamentals of classroom management; seating, attendance details, promptness in beginning the work, being on time yourself, lighting, ventilating, and the mechanical details involved in efficient management. Use student help whenever possible. What if students do make mistakes occasionally?

4. Learn the pupil's problems. It may be more important to you to "find out something" than to "do something."

5. Know your pupils' backgrounds, interests, abilities, needs, and present levels of achievement.

6. Hold to "standards," but be sure they are standards which the pupil can meet.

7. Give some thought to your own personal qualities. Be firm, dignified, sympathetic, patient, fair, charitable, pleasant, calm, confident, and businesslike. Dress attractively and neatly, but not glamorously.

8. Know your pupils' names. Read Carnegie's *How to Win Friends and Influence People*. A good teacher is a good salesman.

9. Be willing to apologize to a pupil if you find that you have treated him unjustly. Don't try to "cover up" in order to "save face." A teacher loses nothing by admitting his error.

10. Control your temper.

As for the teacher's role in identifying early the child who leans toward trouble making, the report has this to say.

Delinquent behavior should not be regarded as a 24-hour malady. It rarely happens overnight. Many youngsters give some hints or signs well before a pattern of norm-violating behavior is thoroughly established.

The classroom teacher who, as a trained observer, sees the pupil for an extended period of time and who comes to know him intimately is in an advantageous position to identify those pupils who evidence need for emotional, psychological, or cultural support. Through early refer-ral of the delinquency-prone youngster to the appropriate agency, followed by special help and treatment, the teacher can achieve preventive action in the literal sense.

Two Points for Caution

There are many techniques for identifying the predelinquent but perhaps two points would be sufficient here:

In forecasting, the teacher should be alert to the problem of labeling a youngster "predelinquent," for there is a constant hazard of a self-fulfilling prophecy: the youngster will act out the role he has been given.

The teacher should be objective in observing and assessing the modes of behavior which are characteristic of youngsters from lower-class families. He should be on guard lest he misjudge an unfamiliar cultural pattern as a sign of potential norm-violating behavior.

Finally, the teacher has an important task in seeking help when confronted with a serious case of trouble making. The classroom teacher should not try to be all things to all pupils. There will be occasions when the teacher will need to lean heavily upon special service personnel — guidance workers, psychometrists, school nurses and doctors, psychologists, caseworkers, speech therapists, remedial reading experts, and psychiatrists. There are limits to what the average classroom instructor can be expected to do by way of child study, diagnosis, and treatment. Specialized professional personnel are needed to supplement and re-enforce his role.

The Disturbed Child in the Classroom*
Kay Tift

If you are assigned a student whose daily actions foul up the learning climate in your classroom, you must have feelings of frustration, and even of fury, at times.

The purpose of this article is, first, to reassure you that you are *not* inadequate because you wish the child would disappear forever and, second, to suggest specific ways for dealing with problems which arise because he does not disappear.

One note of clarification: If the comments which follow seem overly simple, it is because emotional illness is overly complex. Little attempt will be made here to analyze the causes of emotional disorder; rather, the goal is to provide practical suggestions for dealing with those surface behaviors which disrupt your classroom.

Try to visualize a "typical" disturbed child. DC is a ten-year-old whose social behavior much of the time is at a three-year-old level. The minute your back is turned he runs his pencil across a neighbor's worksheet, he dips water from the fishbowl into the clay barrel, or he shoves and trips others without warning. He keeps you on edge because of his destructive actions but masters just enough subject matter and conforms just enough to your demands to keep you from telling your principal: "Either he goes or I do." (You can't ask to have him transferred; the other teachers have DC's too!)

When you first get such a student, a useful step is to check with other staff members who have come in contact with him. Does your school counselor have a case record for him? Did *other* teachers find your DC disruptive in *their* group situations?

If their answers are No, put aside this article and, instead, ask a peer whom you trust to visit your classroom for a day. Tell him to observe *your responses* to the youngster, rather than vice versa. If your friend's findings lead you to seek guidance for *yourself,* be thankful for the experience!

*Reprinted from *NEA Journal,* March 1968. Used with permission.

As you acquire insights into your own feelings, everyone — especially you — will be the winner.

Once you feel confident, however, that *you* are not largely responsible for this "enemy" action in your classroom, take the next step of acquainting yourself with the general nature of DC's disease. What *is* emotional disturbance? Where does it come from? In what different ways does it manifest itself? For meaningful answers to these questions, try the following activities:

1. See the motion picture, *David and Lisa.* (Your principal might arrange a showing for his whole staff).

2. Visit an accredited school for emotionally disturbed children. (Observe there for a day and talk with different staff members.)

3. Read at least one book which deals with the emotionally disturbed child in the classroom. (In my opinion, one of the best texts to date is *Conflict in the Classroom: The Education of Emotionally Disturbed Children,* edited by Long, Morse, and Newsman. Wadsworth. 1965.)

As you follow up these suggestions, you will become increasingly aware that the behavior which angers you is a *signal* of an illness, just as red spots are a signal of measles. You will understand that a disturbed child does not have a disease of destroying property or hurting people; these are but symptoms of his emotional disorder. And you will be reassured, once again, that *you are not responsible for his illness.*

The completion of step one (ascertaining that you'll be part of the solution, not the cause of the problem) and step two (becoming aware that emotional illness has deep environmental roots, that it is very complex, and that you alone won't "cure" it) frees you to ask the constructive "How can I help this DC and thus help all of us in the group?" instead of the defensive "Why is he doing this to *me*?"

For a third positive step, read about the following classroom situations, imagining yourself as the teacher in each of the three.

SITUATION NUMBER ONE: As you sit with a reading circle, you see the children stop reading and begin to stare across the room at DC, who is drawing pictures on the floor with chalk.

Your response to help DC goes something like this. You say clearly, for all to hear, "DC, I'm unhappy because my reading students are looking at your pictures instead of at their books. Tim [Tim is a dependable "normal"] will you help DC erase the chalk from the floor and then you and he may carry some books to the library for me."

Comments:

1. DC is relieved because (a) his unacceptable behavior was clearly defined, and (b) provisions were made enabling him to stop the behavior.

2. Tim experiences an ego boost. He has helped another human, and thus his concept of self-worth is enhanced.

3. Other class members feel secure: DC's behavior did not take their teacher from them.

4. You enhance *your* self-concept by dealing constructively with a challenging situation.

Question: But DC had unmet needs! Shouldn't he have been allowed to work them out on the floor with the chalk? The pictures weren't hurting anything!

Answer: Nonsense. DC's behavior was destroying the learning climate in your classroom. Furthermore, if DC had been permitted to continue unchecked, he would have experienced progressive feelings of:

GUILT ("Teacher is mad at me. I'm bad.")

PANIC ("Help! I'm losing control!")

ANGER ("Why won't someone *stop* me?")

SITUATION NUMBER TWO: DC keeps interrupting a small discussion group. You feel the children's annoyance at him, and this intensifies your own impatience with his behavior.

You let the tone of your voice, as well as your words, communicate the group indignation. "DC, you're butting in and taking other people's turns. I don't like to have you take over while I'm talking! Now, I want you to get the card box so we can help you take turns. Okay?"

You know from experience that your students all enjoy this game. The card box referred to holds about 50 blank 3 x 2 cards. Each person receives the same agreed-upon number of cards, and every time a student speaks he must put one of his cards back in the box. When someone's cards are used up, he cannot talk until everyone else's cards are gone. (The students learn through trial-and-error how many times they are willing to permit DC to speak, and thus commit *themselves* to speaking.)

Comments:

1. DC is grateful that his unacceptable behavior was identified with honest directness. (A disturbed child cannot tolerate a honey-sweet, "Let's not do that anymore," ladled out through clenched teeth. It comes through to him as, "I'm pretending to like you, but only because I'm afraid of my real thoughts. I wish you'd drop dead.") The other students are also grateful because your acknowledgment of resentment allows them to feel comfortable with, instead of guilty about, *their* anger toward him.

2. Again you're given prompt assistance

with impulse control, involving other group members. By playing a game that structures "equal rights," the pupils have a pleasurable as well as constructive role in helping their classmate.

3. You feel better and better. As you involve everyone in helping DC, it becomes "our" class instead of "my" class. A family bond begins to evolve.

Question: But DC is getting extra attention. Is that fair?

Answer: Who said life is fair? An emotionally ill person is a dependent person and requires extra attention. Don't you, as an adult, pay extra taxes to provide for patients in prisons and mental hospitals?

SITUATION NUMBER THREE: DC refuses to do a written assignment at his desk.

Withdrawal behavior presents a special challenge. Your first response might well be to hypothesize *why* he is refusing:

Too short an attention span? Call on a dependable pupil: "Jill, here is my stopwatch. Would you see how long it takes DC to complete his worksheet? DC, see if you can finish it before ten minutes are up."

He just can't do the work? "DC, I want you to do at least the first sentence now. I'll sit here and help you with it."

He simply won't do the work? "DC, I'm sorry you aren't ready to write today. Maybe tomorrow you'll be able to." (Coaxing or pleading will only reinforce the behavior you wish would go away.)

Comment: Of course there's a chance that none of these approaches will work. If he shows total resistance, keep your cool and retreat for awhile.

Question: But doesn't that mean he wins?

Answer: Wins? Who declared war? This child is *not* attacking you; he is just protecting himself from real or imagined danger.

Question: Well, after I've retreated for awhile, should I try again to get him involved?

Answer: Of course. Does a doctor make out a single prescription, and then abandon his patient if it doesn't work?

In the above three incidents, you responded differently to different problems, but your approach each time included:

1. Stating clearly to the child what his inappropriate behavior consisted of

2. Identifying your own feelings about this behavior

3. Providing a supportive structure for a change of behavior

4. Using, whenever appropriate, the participation of other students in this supportive structure.

Incorporating these basic steps, you can deal with a variety of disruptive classroom situations. DC could be a girl instead of a boy, of course. (While statistically we have more disturbed boys than girls, how many giggly girls disrupt a lesson because they were brought up as "first a female" while they heard their brothers challenged to be "serious students" first of all?)

Or instead of being age 10, DC could be 4 or 14. (Although he may be emotionally ill, a high school student must have mastered a fair amount of impulse control to survive in that structure.) Also, DC's behavior could take the form of *repression* of hostile feelings rather than expression of them. (A silent resister can sometimes hold up group effort more effectively than the loud-mouthed extrovert.)

(One unholy situation which has not been discussed is what to do when a *number* of DC's are placed in your already overcrowded classroom. In my opinion, you'll have to give up. The only question is how you go about throwing in the sponge.)

In the foregoing discussion, our disturbed child was compartmentalized as though he were much different from his peers. In reality, no clear line can be drawn between "healthy" behavior and that which isn't so healthy. Each of our students moves up and down his own continuum of neurotic responses which he employs to master a particular environment at a particular time. But the disturbed child makes *compulsive responses* which occur *day after day* and which *interfere regularly* with classroom goals.

While there are constructive ways to cope with a DC, such as those suggested above, as long as a teacher is asked to contain sick psyches while he teaches subject matter, he will have cause for deep frustration. Happily, there is help on the horizon in addition to that which may be available to your school system from experts in special education. One form this help is taking is the study carrel, with CAI (computer assisted instruction). R. Louis

Bright of the U.S. Office of Education predicts that within another decade "almost the entire academic portion of instruction will be on an individualized basis in most schools."

If this forecast becomes fact — and if subject matter is fed into machines, to be reached for by each learner as he becomes ready to assimilate it — DC's behavior will no longer stop other pupils from gaining academic instruction.

No longer will you, the teacher, face the dilemma of "*his* needs or *theirs?*" Rather, with the help of educational technology, you will have added time for those caring relationships which every human hungers for and which bring to him a sense of self-worth. You will have more time, through small-group encounters, to help each of your students experience individual growth by making important contributions to the needs of others.

What Do You Do When Your Student Has A Gun?*

A teacher in a Philadelphia high school reprimanded one of his students during class. Later in the day, the student returned with a gun and shot and killed the teacher.

—A football coach in a northeastern Ohio high school narrowly escaped death when a student fired four shots at him and somehow missed his target.

—Last month, in a Stow High School chemistry class, an honor student, reportedly upset about some test grades, shot and seriously wounded his teacher.

Is there a way to spot troubled youngsters before they go over the brink? Are there patterns of behavior that might give the teacher some warning?

*Reprinted from *Ohio Schools*,© 1972 by Ohio Education Association. Used with permission.

—Dr. Jack A. Whieldon, a Columbus psychiatrist, past president of the Ohio Psychiatric Association and presently an associate clinical professor at Ohio State University's department of psychiatry, was asked by Ohio Schools to respond to these questions.

There are obviously no simple guidelines, nor hard and fast rules for teachers to follow, but Whieldon does believe there are some definite signs that would indicate something was going to happen. Following are his comments.

I think you are really talking about two things. First, the problem of anticipating. The second is what you do when you are actually confronted.

Almost always, a person who performs an act like this voices some threat — usually to other students, but not infrequently to the victim. I think a threat, anytime, should be taken seriously. There are threats and there are threats. Threats that are made in a rage usually would follow the teacher having disciplined the youngster.

The teacher should never walk away from disciplining a student. He should stick by him and if at all possible, spend some time with the student he has disciplined to try to work it out so the kid sees that it's not just a hostile act on the part of the teacher. The teacher should try to help him understand that he is helping the student learn some self control.

Masculinity Contest

The second thing is that a teacher should never demean a boy. Very frequently, this becomes a contest as to strength, masculinity, acceptability and all the rest. You should never run a boy into a corner or embarrass him in front of his peers.

If there is a change of personality in the boy — if the boy has grown sullen — this is a danger sign. This kind of person, a true schizophrenic paranoid, will usually give you some real indications that he is hostile. He will throw furtive glances at you that are unwarranted and have no basis in your personal relationship.

I would point out that usually these things happen to a person who has experienced some deep insult to his self-esteem. That's one of the most important things. Perhaps grades were an important thing to him, or he was excluded from the team, or he was made fun of.

In some cases, we have students who lose control and take some impulsive action.

Now the planned act, where the student brings a gun into the classroom, is different. There will be many, many indications of that kind of thing before it happens.

I would look for the brooding kind of a student who carries a grudge. Where a boy who has been performing at a very high level starts failing, that's an indication that something very drastic is happening. He would probably develop a schizophrenic reaction, you see. Some significant change in performance, particularly scholastic performance, is a very major indicator. It would be the actual change in performance — not an inability to perform — that is so important.

If the teacher becomes concerned about a student, there is usually a cohort of that student in the class — someone you could ask, "What's with so and so?" Not infrequently, some very important leads will be given. An expression of honest concern on the part of the teacher will usually bring back an honest answer from the student's friend.

Then the teacher could very well take a little time to spend with the student. It doesn't take long and it may very well pay off a tremendous dividend.

How should a teacher react if he suddenly finds himself faced by a student with a gun?

Fright Invites Aggression

Usually the teacher is frightened. And a fright reaction invites further aggression. The woman who is being beaten up by her husband, who cowers in the corner, just gets beaten more. It's a strange thing — the invitations to violence that we give people or that people give us. There are some kinds of things that activate violence and passivity is one . . . passivity or fear.

This may not seem relevant, but it is extremely relevant. In Holland, where they have a lot of canals, any student that learns to drive, must learn to handle himself if his car were to run into a canal and the pressure of the water was so heavy that he couldn't open the car door. They are only losing one out of ten drivers in this type of accident now. They used to lose all ten, because people panicked.

Being Prepared

And so, when a teacher finds himself in a crisis situation, if he has prepared himself ahead of time for that situation, he can anticipate it and meet it and hopefully not get hurt by it.

Let me give you an example. A young man who was going to be the chairman of the department of psychiatry at a large eastern university had treated the son of a fellow professor. The boy had a paranoiac-psychotic reaction and the doctor recommended hospitalization.

After about six months, the boy was released and he came to the doctor's home. As the doctor was coming down the stairs, he didn't recognize the boy until he got down to the first floor. The boy said, "You sent me away and now you don't recognize me." The doctor said, "Oh it's you," with disdain, and with that the kid pulled out a gun and shot and killed him.

Now the way that this might very well have been handled is if the doctor had said, "I'm sorry, I've forgotten your name, but I do remember you and I'm so glad to see you are better." This would have taken the boy off guard. You invite him in and ask your wife to get him some coffee.

Most people who act violently usually give the victim some time to react before he strikes. If the teacher can show a positive reaction of concern for the student, he will reduce the tendency toward violent action a person can have. "Gee, I didn't realize you felt this way. What have I done to make you feel this way? I apologize. I am truly sorry I have hurt you in some way."

Often, it becomes a contest of wills or strength. Men particularly are constantly caught up in this. It's infantile, it's childish, it's the Freudian position related to masculinity. This would be especially true in a male teacher-student relationship. You see this all the time with high school boys speeding with their cars. The car becomes an instrument to demonstrate their virility, their masculinity, their power.

The very last thing to do is to forcibly take the weapon away from the student because almost invariably someone gets hurt. It becomes a further contest. The boy thinks what a tremendous humiliation it would be if the teacher wrenches the gun away and he will fight simply because of the unconscious need to protect his masculine image — not to anybody else, but to himself.

The most important thing, then, is to try not to aggravate the confrontation, realizing that it is a mascculinity contest. You should become humble, but you must not grovel. Passivity invites aggression. Very few people recognize this.

And I want to emphasize the Holland analogy. The incidence of death due to drowning has been cut by 90 per cent because the drivers had prepared themselves.

A teacher can prepare himself for this kind of crisis. If you think, repeatedly, how you would react if a student confronts you, it may very well pay off.

Love Therapy*
Laura G. Johnson

I shall never forget the day that my principal implied that I had the worst discipline of any teacher at the school. He said, "Mrs. Johnson, I think that your classroom is responsible for all the noise at your end of the building." (There were two fifth-grade rooms, two sixth-grade rooms, and one fourth-grade room in that wing.) His words reverberated in my ears for days, and I was completely chagrined.

It was true that the atmosphere in my classroom was hardly tranquil, but there were reasons. One of the reasons was James — the belligerent one who lived with a perpetual black eye. Battle-scarred from head to toe, he had fought with almost every child in the class, not to speak of those on his block. He felt that he had to fight to keep up his "rep." Actually he was miserable because he knew deep down that one day he was going to come out on the losing end. I found out that his father was serving a prison sentence. The children had started teasing him about it and the teasing resulted in the fights.

Another reason was Hannah, who was from a family of no-goods. Hannah had heard so many people disparage her relatives and say, "You're going to be just like the rest of them," that she seemed determined to prove their words. She was boisterous, used profane language, picked on the other children, and "took over" whenever I was out of the room.

And there was Julian, the one who was always hungry. His mother was dead, and his father unreliable. I found out that Julian left home each morning without breakfast and remained at school all day without lunch. Because of his empty stomach, he couldn't concentrate on his lessons, and his hunger made him angry at the world. He would talk and laugh aloud at the slightest provocation. He would draw obscene pictures, tear up

*Reprinted from *NEA Journal*, February 1962. Used with permission.

paper, track mud into the room, and engage in all sorts of mischievous antics.

Then there was Freddie, an orphan being raised by an aged maiden aunt who had never really tried to understand why Freddie stole anything and everything — pencils, toys, chalk, erasers, string, paper. Even though he had absolutely no need or use for some articles, he took them just the same.

And last on my list was Isiah, the chronic absentee who was the only one in his family that had gone above third grade. Isiah was fifteen years old and in the sixth grade, but he could not do sixth-grade work or even the special work I gave him. He rarely came to school, but when he did appear, everybody knew he was there. He played ridiculous jokes on the children and kept them forever upset.

Incidentally, the morning that he walked into the room late and dropped a large green lizard on my desk was the morning that the principal happened to be in the room next to mine. I will leave to your imagination the chaos that took place in my classroom that instant.

The boy seemed to have the philosophy, "If I can't, then I'll see to it that nobody else does." Whenever he succeeded in getting the attention of the class directed solely on him, he seemed to receive some sort of perverse satisfaction.

After reviewing my problem cases, I determined to bring about some improvements. I changed my schedule. I made careful studies of each child and then grouped and regrouped my pupils according to special abilities, age level, sex, special needs, and friendships. I bought educational materials which I thought would interest them and keep them engaged in meaningful experiences.

I lectured, scolded, pleaded, and prayed, but although each step I took definitely helped for a period of time, finally all good effects would wear off. There were times when I was pushed to the point of exasperation and felt like giving up on this seemingly hopeless situation. But give up, I didn't. I ordered materials on discipline and read everything I could find on the subject from professional books and magazines. My nights were spent pondering my plight.

During my extensive reading I came across an article that told about how patients in a rehabilitation center had been miraculously helped when families "adopted" them and showered them with genuine love. I saw that in essence this was "love therapy."

I said, "Well, why not?" I had just about exhausted my resources, and after all, love is strongest of the three primary emotions. Hungry for love, a little child may irritate his mother or become naughty in an effort to win her attention. George W. Crane says, "Though the child gets punishment, he prefers his mother's hands upon him even in punishment than to be disregarded altogether." Similarly, pupils may deliberately provoke the teacher: They need attention and will go to almost any length to get it.

Following this train of thought, I decided to try a kind of love therapy as a new approach to the discipline problems in my classroom.

The next time I had to be out of the room, I made it a point to have Hannah come sit at my desk and "keep" the room. I had her visit me on week ends. We went grocery shopping together and to church on Sundays. I did everything I could to let her know that I loved her and had confidence in her. Gradually her behavior changed and she became a lovely girl.

Each morning I arose a little bit early in order to have time to fix Julian a couple of sandwiches. The other children caught on and began to save him a cookie or fruit from their lunches. He was deeply appreciative and changed his attitude of mischief to one of helpfulness. He became "Available Jones" who could always fix a broken pencil sharpener, adjust an uncomfortable desk, or open a window that was stuck.

Freddie grew to be my trusted friend. I let him take the lunch money to the office, and I would deliberately leave things like my watch or fountain pen on the desk and place him in situations of confidence, saying, "Freddie, watch my desk while I get a drink of water." I had a conference with his aunt who had long since branded him a kleptomaniac. I told her of my plans and she agreed to go along with me. Together we gave him the security of love which he had for so long been without.

As for Isiah, the chronic absentee — I made a home visit and got his parents' consent to send him to school just as soon as the crops were "laid by." When he arrived, he began his usual antics, but I was prepared by now and started his "treatment," being careful not to let the rest of the class realize that I was actually teaching him to read. I had collected enough interesting material on his level to keep him busy. That day after school I had an informal talk with Isiah. He said he thought that he acted up because he couldn't keep up with the class, and didn't know what to do with himself.

I said, "Isiah, you're a big boy who will very soon have to stop school altogether and help with the work at home. Then you won't have a teacher to love you and take an interest in your education and your future."

He replied, "Mrs. Johnson, I didn't know school teachers loved chi'ren."

"Isiah," I said, "you have the wrong idea of teachers. We are your friends who are interested in your success in life. Look, if I promise that I'll have you reading and writing, and working problems and experiments in no time at all, will you meet me half way?"

He grinned and answered. "Ye'm I sho' will do ma bes'." He thought for a moment and then added, "Well Mrs. Johnson, now I feel like you some kin t'me."

I said, "Yes, Isiah, that's the way you feel about someone you love." He smiled and I patted him on the shoulder as he left the room.

The atmosphere of love in the classroom must have touched James too, because he stopped getting into fights for a long time. Then finally one day when he lost control of his temper and was on the verge of fighting, I surprised the daylights out of him by putting my arm around him and kissing him on the cheek. After he came out of shock, he told me, "Mrs. Johnson, that's the first time anybody ever kissed me."

I said, "James, I kissed you because I love you very much and I want you to accept me as a friend who wants to help you in any way I can."

He replied, "No, nobody loves me; everybody hates me." I reassured him that yes, I did love him. We had a long talk which ended with James' promising to bring all of his problems to me. From that day on, I never had any more trouble from him; we were allies.

On many occasions I have found that "love therapy" really works. After all, the classroom is not designed as a battleground between teacher and pupils. The teacher should not try to assume the role of a stern and impersonal sentinel in the classroom but should strive instead to become the friend and trusted confidant that many lonely youngsters long for so deeply and need so desperately.

I do not speak from the psychologist's point of view, nor the consultant's. I am only one of the group of classroom teachers who is on the scene daily and who knows from firsthand experience that love, along with faith, understanding, and perseverance, can accomplish wonders.

Do Guidance and Discipline Mix?*
William Ratigan and Walter F. Johnson

The nature and pervasiveness of discipline make it a significant concern of all who help boys and girls achieve maturity. Good discipline must be undergirded by certain important guidance principles: emphasis on understanding causes of problem behavior rather than on responding to symptoms; emphasis on preventive factors rather than on corrective ones; emphasis on guidance of the individual to free him for learning rather than on demanding unquestioning obedience. Thus, it would be

difficult to argue that the school counselor should not be *involved* in school discipline. A strong case can be made, however, for defining and delimiting the nature of his involvement.

In perceiving his role, the skilled school counselor sometimes sees himself as attorney for the defense in some problem situations. Or, he may see himself in an explanatory or supporting role similar to that of a chaplain. In other cases, he may see himself as the diagnostician of an obscure disease which defies treatment until a plausible cause is established. But, he does

*Reprinted from *NEA Journal,* December 1961. Used with permission.

not see himself as a punitive disciplinarian.

Take the case of Joe, tenth grader in a Midwestern school of suburban population. He had a habit of throwing erasers in his English classroom. The teacher put him on detention, but this failed to have more than a temporary effect. Joe was reported to the principal, who exacted further disciplinary measures and finally made a referral to the school counselor.

After the counselor gained Joe's confidence by respecting his rights as an individual and by showing that there would be no judgments passed or sentences executed, the boy began to talk freely about himself. It developed that this misbehavior always occurred during the short study periods held each day in his English class. He realized that the lack of personal communication at these times made him so uneasy that he felt compelled to do something to get the group stirred up.

As the story came out, the counselor discovered that the boy's basic problem was loneliness. Going back into Joe's early childhood, the counselor found that the boy's father had worked a night shift and that his mother, being lonely herself, had taken Joe everywhere she went, even awakening him to accompany her to the grocery store or to pick up his father at work.

Counselor: Couldn't she have hired a babysitter?

Joe: (slowly and with real insight) Sure, I suppose so, for *me*, but then she wouldn't have had anybody with *her*.

The mother had transferred her loneliness to the child, and the result had appeared as overt misbehavior in a tenth-grade English study period. No amount of detention or stiffer discipline could have solved the basic maladjustment; but as Joe talked things out with the counselor as his sounding board, he began to see what had

been bothering him and started groping toward self-discipline.

The above case study illustrates a fundamental guideline in counseling. *The school counselor is concerned with cause rather than effect.* His aim is to get at the roots of maladjustment rather than to deal with the obvious symptoms. Within the accepting, non-punitive climate of the counseling office, the individual pupil begins to strive toward self-improvement and self-discipline.

The trained school counselor, of course, recognizes his own limitations. Faced with problems that seem beyond his capacities, he makes immediate and necessary referrals to other specialists. He does not attempt to be manipulative nor does he have the mistaken impression that he can solve all the troubles of the universe in a ten-minute interview. In short, he is very different from the efficiency-expert, disciplinary-minded counselor described by a high-school girl in this rather bitter comment:

At our school, the counselor spends most of his time arranging our lives for us and brushing us out of the office so he can arrange all the rest of the lives in school. He manipulates us as if we were a set of checkers, and he was playing a game with God. If President Kennedy called on him for help, he'd solve the international situation: Put the whole world on detention, double the homework assignment, and get everything under his thumb. What young people like me are afraid of is that it's going to be an old thumb like his that pushes the panic button and turns us all radioactive.

Perhaps the counselor portrayed above was so bogged down in administrative details, such as attendance enforcement and other disciplinary functions alien to the counseling program, that circumstances forced him to become authoritarian and mechanical in his contacts with students. At any rate, it seems apparent that the girl saw no benefit in counseling that pontificated and used discipline as a club.

At this point, it should be indicated once again that the effective school counselor does *not* disassociate himself from discipline; he has a role and function to carry out both before and after corrective discipline has been imposed upon an individual.

Briefly, the school counselor's function before disciplinary action is largely of a preventive nature. He tries to communicate to the pupils his faith that youngsters will operate in positive directions if given a fair opportunity. He expresses his belief, not in the infection of badness as expressed in the analogy of the bad apple spoiling the rest of the barrel, but in the affection of goodness. He shows respect for the pupil's dignity and separate identity.

The other step in counseling prior to punitive discipline is to explain alternatives to the pupil in much the same way that they are pointed out in occupational and educational matters. Just as the pupil must be told that unless he takes certain subjects and makes certain grades he won't have much chance to get into certain jobs or schools of higher learning, so must he be told the consequences of disobeying rules.

The school counselor must also be ready to accept the possibility that even when the consequences have been pointed out, the pupil may decide to disobey the rules anyway. Should this result, the counselor becomes neither judge nor executioner.

Irrespective of innermost feelings, he adheres strictly to professional ethics and to school policy. When rules are flouted, the general welfare of the student body must be safeguarded. Neither an informer

(except in extreme situations involving great danger to self or others) nor an apprentice principal (except when he confuses his role), he recognizes that it is the administrator's duty to carry out punishment and enforce discipline.

The counselor's responsibility is to give the administrator all available information about the individual to provide the basis for making a fair judgment for a course of action. Should the administrator refer a student for counseling, the counselor's appropriate role is to attempt to help the student achieve greater self-understanding, accept the consequences of his behavior, and profit from experience.

A statement from the textbook, *Pupil Personnel and Guidance Services* (1961. McGraw. $6.50), coauthored by one of the writers of this article, sums up why it is inadvisable for counselors to have punitive responsibilities:

The relationship of discipline and attendance enforcement to the function of the secondary-school counselor is a subject of considerable controversy. For the most part, professional counselor educators believe that assigning the counselor responsibility for these two activities interferes with his counseling work. Nevertheless, many school administrators continue to assign this action with the premise that students who are in trouble because of infractions of the rules regarding behavior or attendance are in need of counseling.

The usual counterargument is that the enforcement of rules is an administrative rather than a counseling function; therefore, the counselor should be assigned to work with these students only after the administrator has decided upon and enforced whatever disciplinary action is thought suitable. If this method is used, the counselor is then free to explore with the student in a nonjudicial and nonpunitive fashion the reasons for his maladaptive behavior and the possibilities for changes in attitudes. In any event, the extent to which a person attempting to serve as counselor represents an authoritarian threat to his counselee will have a profound influence on what the counselee will be willing to share with him.

At the present time, many schools assign their discipline and attendance functions to a dean or subadministrator, thereby leaving the counselor free to perform the functions for which he has special training.

Chapter VIII

Discussionette

1. What can teachers do to minimize and best treat conflicting factors in group behavior and discipline?

2. Since many discipline problems develop spontaneously, can teachers have ready made solutions to problems?

3. What can be done to minimize inadvertent conflicts between teachers and students?

4. What can teachers do so as not to accidently behave in a manner which would offend students?

5. Have you ever observed where "love therapy" has worked?

6. What is the basis behind "love therapy"?

7. In what ways do school counselors act as "attorneys for the defense," "chaplains," and "diagnosticians"?

8. Do you agree with the statement, "the school counselor is concerned with the cause rather than the effect"?

9. How can counselors help guide students in self-discipline?

10. Can the "card-box" be used in a normal classroom situation with ordinary students?

11. What are most school districts and county systems doing to help the disturbed child?

Discussionette Words and Concepts

alienation	normal	anxiety
depersonalization	readiness	maturation
conflict factors	disturbed child	predelinquent
physical factors	forecasting	fright

Try to use these words.

Try to explain these words.

Try to relate these words and their concepts to current or emerging educational patterns regarding therapeutic discipline.

CHAPTER IX

PSYCHOLOGICAL APPROACHES

Introduction

WITHIN THE PAST TWENTY YEARS or so tremendous studies have been taken to understand and deal with the psychology of the individual. Considerable research has been conducted to better understand why individuals act the way they do.

Teachers who have a strong foundation in psychology can usually relate to and work better with students, parents, administrators and other teachers. By understanding child psychology and the newer psychological techniques of student control, teachers can reduce their disciplinary problems.

Such individuals as Freud, Jung, Skinner, Malcolm, Rogers and others have provided considerable research in understanding the individual which can be invaluable to teachers in working with children. The relevance of this material can not be overemphasized in today's complex society and should be required reading for today's teachers to better understand group and individual behavior.

This chapter offers several readings which will provide the teacher with psychological approaches to disciplinary problems.

Discipline Isn't Dated*

Ruth Strang

Three-year-old Tommy was a fighter. More than that, he was a perpetual fighter, always hitting — or trying to hit — the other children in the nursery school.

It was the consistency of Tommy's aggressiveness that worried his teacher. All preschool children are aggressive from time to time, but usually not for very long. If they hit a playmate one minute, chances are they'll be hugging him the next.

"I just don't know what to do with

Tommy," the teacher told the school psychologist. "Whenever I catch him lighting into another child, I stop him. But the moment I turn my back, there he is — hitting somebody again."

The psychologist smiled sympathetically, then replied: "Would you mind trying an experiment with Tommy, Miss Mathews? Instead of paying attention to him when he's hitting another child, give him your attention *only* when he makes a friendly gesture."

"That's pretty hard to do," Miss Mathews

*Reprinted from *The PTA Magazine*, November 1966. Used with permission.

said. "It's impossible if another child's being hurt."

"Yes, of course, but most of the time the other children will protect themselves, won't they?"

"That's true. They often solve their own discipline problems. Well, I'm willing to try anything with Tommy if there's a chance it will work."

Using the new approach, Miss Mathews watched for any signs of friendly behavior on Tommy's part. Whenever she noted one, she promptly gave him a smile of approval, a reassuring nod or pat, or a comment that called attention to his friendly act. But whenever he stopped being friendly and lapsed into his familiar behavior, she immediately turned to other children or other duties. She followed this plan continuously and consistently.

To her surprise Tommy quickly began to show more friendliness toward his playmates. By the second day his friendly actions slightly outnumbered his aggressive ones. By the ninth day, more than two-thirds of the time he was moving *toward* the other children rather than *against* them.

From then on Miss Mathews expressed her approval less frequently. She took Tommy's friendly behavior for granted and called attention to it only when it was exceptional in some way. Then she gave it specific recognition: "How nicely you helped Beth get her rubbers on!" or "I'm so glad you let Arthur play awhile with your truck."

Since Tommy's aggressiveness had been within the normal range of behavior for a child of his age he responded well to the theory of social learning that the psychologist had suggested. Many other discipline problems can be solved in the same way. Discipline originally meant the treatment necessary for a "disciple," or

learner. We learn discipline just as we learn games or mathematics.

In any Head Start program there are always many problems of discipline at first. Disadvantaged children have learned to grab whatever they want as fast as they can. Experience has taught them that if they don't grab it someone else will. Here too it is sound practice to pay attention to good behavior.

If the teacher says, "How nice of Mary to let Billy use her crayons!" other children will want to win her approval and attention by behaving the same way. If the teacher says, "I see seven children who are standing in line without touching anyone else," then those who are pushing others may want similar recognition. When children see a teacher engaged in a pleasurable activity with one child, they will all want to do it, too. For preschoolers seem to choose the activities that bring them the largest amount of adult attention and approval.

The Pleasure of Praise

Children's interests develop in the same way. Once established, any interest or type of behavior tends to continue. Praise and encouragement thus have a long-range influence as well as immediate effects.

This theory has an important implication. If parents and teachers reserve their greatest enthusiasm for the most desirable aspects of their child's behavior and the best developed of his skills, he will tend to improve without specific instruction. Note that the adult produces the desired result by the systematic giving and withholding of his attention, not by the amount of his attention.

It is still true that a child's present behavior is affected by the consequences of his previous behavior. However, the old idea of discipline was to punish the child for acts that we do not want him to repeat: "A burnt child dreads the fire." Today's discipline emphasizes "do" rather than "don't." It seeks to forestall discipline problems by rewarding the child for good behavior. "Make lovable to her everything I would wish her to love." Monsieur Bonnard, an old scholar in a novel by Anatole France, summed up in these words the philosophy he applied in educating his young ward. This is exactly what modern psychology is saying.

The method worked in the case of Tommy. It has worked in many Head Start programs. But how would it apply to two-and-a-half-year-old Jerry? Jerry was never still. He was always into everything. He would dart into a room, head straight for a table, grab anything detachable, drop it, and probably break it. To prevent such catastrophies his mother would race him to get to the object before he did. This was all highly exciting to Jerry. Even the slap or the spanking that followed did not make him forget the thrilling race to the table. Since the end result of every such incident was satisfaction, it tended to be repeated. Punishment failed.

In this case there was a physical factor to be considered — the fact that Jerry's tense muscles needed relief in active play, which life in a small apartment did not provide. His mother therefore cleared the apartment of breakable objects. Then she calmly ignored his dash to the table and paid no attention to him when he threw an unbreakable object on the floor. But she did give him her attention and approval whenever he bounced his ball, climbed his little steps, or engaged in some other lively but non-destructive activity. This approach did not completely solve the problem, but it helped.

With a child like Jerry, who is hyperactive and impulsive, we do not withhold approval until he has done the right thing. Instead we reward *any* move in the right direction. If he merely looks toward a ball, we nod approvingly. If he starts in the direction of the little steps that he can climb up and down on, we show that we are pleased with him. Children of this kind need immediate reassurance.

Older preschool children can be guided step by step into more acceptable behavior by a series of tokens that add up to some special privilege or by receiving a coveted toy. The tokens may be stars or even check marks on a chart, slips of colored paper, or pennies to put in a bank. They can be given for any of a number of acts that combine to form a pattern of more cooperative behavior. Sammy's chart was checked every time he hung up his coat when he came in, instead of letting it drop on the floor where he took it off. Sally was given a "receipt" whenever she played pleasantly with her little sister instead of teasing her. David put a penny in his bank whenever he shared one of his toys with a friend.

You may well ask, Doesn't this procedure represent the giving of "extrinsic rewards" — the practice educators have frowned on for many years? Haven't parents and teachers been told repeatedly not to give stars but to attach satisfaction to the act itself? True, but some children need objective, immediate rewards as a step toward establishing the desired interest. There is of course some danger that children and adults may get bogged down at the token-giving stage. But it is hoped that this is only a stage. The interest itself should soon become the goal.

The Seeds of Action

What is the principle we must keep clearly in mind in administering discipline? That the consequences of an act tend to determine the child's subsequent behavior. If he does not relate a present act to previous experiences and their consequences, the act becomes in a sense purely impulsive. The child must learn to look ahead, to reflect on the probable consequences of the act.

If a mother habitually lets a child do the wrong thing and then punishes him for it, she is encouraging impulsive behavior. If, on the other hand, she anticipates the wrong behavior, warns the child that he will have to make a decision, and gives him clues that will guide him in the right direction and help him to avoid mistakes, she is fostering reflective behavior. Such a mother encourages her child to anticipate the consequences of his action and be guided by his previous experience. Whenever he does the right thing, it pleases both child and mother and thus further reinforces the desirable behavior. If the child not only gets satisfaction from doing the right thing but also associates the satisfaction with the action, many disciplinary problems will be avoided.

Being allowed to make a decision for himself is tremendously satisfying to the child who is going through a period of wanting to assert his independence. One father was concerned about his son's reluctance to eat a good breakfast, go to bed at a reasonable hour, and abide by other routine regulations — so concerned that he consulted a child psychiatrist. The psychiatrist suggested that the parents give the boy more choices. For example, instead of saying, "Eat your cereal," give him a choice: "Would you rather have oatmeal or cornflakes?" or even "Would you rather have sliced banana or cereal?" (both nutritious). This procedure worked so well that one day, when father and son were passing a toy shop, the boy said, "Daddy, would you rather buy me a cowboy suit or a truck?"

This psychological principle of systematically rewarding desirable behavior and ignoring undesirable acts whenever possible is not an infallible method of preventing discipline problems. Children's behavior is far too complex for that. However, certain tendencies are established very early and are likely to influence the child's behavior at any subsequent moment.

Data on Discipline

Previous isues of *The PTA Magazine*, as well as the books and pamphlets listed in the guide for study and discussion of this topic, contain many sound suggestions for dealing with discipline problems. Among these are the following:

—Watch your own behavior as well as the child's; it is possible that *you* are wrong, not the child.

—Look at a situation from the child's point of view. Try to see how it looks to him, what were *his* reasons, *his* motivations for acting a certain way?

—Examine the conditions under which discipline problems occur. Are there times when you may be making it difficult for the child to mind?

—Examine the act itself. Is it willful disobedience, or does it represent the child's attempt to take a forward step in his development as a more competent and independent person? Be knowledgeable about what to expect at each stage of his development.

—Give your child examples of kindness and consideration. Children tend to imitate the people they see and know.

—Help your child to acquire the skills he needs. Many discipline problems arise from frustration—from inability to accomplish appropriate tasks.

—Watch for clues that the child himself

gives. Learn to read "the language of behavior," so that your expectations will fit the child's abilities.

—Set positive limits on your child's actions, and be sure he clearly understands them. Then hold to these limits firmly without vacillating.

—If punishment is necessary, administer it with reference to the future, not to the past; with reference to the child's intent and developmental needs rather than to the punishable act itself; and always with affection for the child as a person.

Discipline is a complex affair, but its very complexity is a challenge. To avoid being overwhelmed by too many things to bear in mind, focus on two central ideas: (1) Discipline should be synonymous with learning, and (2) future behavior is changed by the consequences of present behavior. What is desirable should be consistently rewarded, what is undesirable should be consistently ignored unless punishment becomes absolutely necessary. It is far more desirable to forestall discipline problems than try to correct them after they appear.

A Positive Approach to Elementary School Discipline*
Frances Holliday

One of the most challenging and often one of the most baffling problems parents and teachers have to face is that of channeling the ceaseless activities of children into an organized pattern of self-controlled behavior.

When is discipline good? Is it a question of domination by a teacher, of obedience to orders, of complete self-direction? All of these philosophies have been followed, but is any one of them enough to accomplish our purpose? How do we know when we have attained the ultimate in behavior?

Domination probably plays a part in growth: If self-control breaks down, the responsible adult must be ready to control the situation. Certainly, obedience is a part: A child who cannot obey cannot learn to control himself. Also self-direction, with the aid of expert guidance is essential to growth.

No one approach can stand alone, however, for as we analyze the goal toward which we are striving, we are convinced that the only good discipline is that which

*Reprinted from *NEA Journal*, April 1961. Used with permission.

is evidenced by a growing self-control. Good teaching, well planned by the teacher and leading to co-operative teacher-pupil planning, is essential.

No "class" in self-control can accomplish the task. On the other hand, when children live together and take part in carefully chosen experiences in which they have a voice, they may be on the way to standards of behavior which are acceptable in a democratic society.

But a philosophy alone is not enough. Teachers need to incorporate this philosophy into the lives of children. Many opportunities for doing this arise in the normal activities of the classroom. Here are a few concepts and suggestions which may be helpful in making good use of these opportunities.

—Co-operative making of rules as the need arises may gain the interest of children while teacher-imposed rules may create resistance.

—Discussion of behavior problems as they appear will probably develop attitudes and a social consciousness that may guide the children in future decisions.

—A day filled with stimulating activities will allow little opportunity for idleness and mischief.

—Helping each child both to lead and to follow a leader may help him attain higher standards of group behavior.

—Having a clear understanding of the acceptable limits of behavior can give children a feeling of security and hence lead to better behavior.

—"Please do this" tends to foster co-operation. Always make a positive approach.

—Well-established routine minimizes behavior problems.

—Creative participation in classroom activities strengthens a feeling of worth and reflects itself in self-control.

—Group and individual tasks that give the child added responsibility for his own actions aid in development of independence in attaining good behavior.

—Varying activities will give a wholesome change of pace. Interest is sustained when we alternate tasks that require high concentration with those that permit greater freedom of movement.

—Every child needs a feeling of success in some activity.

—Expecting one type of behavior today and another tomorrow leads only to confusion and discouragement. Be consistent.

—Health and comfort should be furthered in the physical aspects of the environment. When a child is comfortable, it is easier for him to be well-behaved.

—Plan for a quieting five minutes at the start of the day, after recess, and after lunch periods.

—Work at being the kind of teacher that children like and trust. Strive for firmness with fairness, sincerity with tact, sympathy without sentimentality, humor without sarcasm. Remember the importance of a pleasant voice and good enunciation.

—Keep in mind that misbehavior is valuable energy directed into the wrong channels. The remedy for misbehavior lies in redirection rather than in suppression.

—Separate children who seem to have a bad effect on each other.

—Do not humiliate a child or make him the center of attention by public reprimand. A private conference is more effective and allows the child to save face.

—When a child's misbehavior disrupts the group, isolate him by having him sit apart from his classmates until he has a chance to cool off.

—Handle the normal range of misbehavior yourself, but don't hesitate to seek help for occasional problems that call for the skill of a psychologist or other specialist.

These are only a few of the manifold opportunities that present themselves to the alert teacher.

As we analyze desirable behavior in a democratic society, we realize that the essential ingredient is consideration of the rights and feelings of others. Evaluation of growth day after day and taking a step at a time in the difficult task of attaining self-control should help children to attain that final goal — living harmoniously and purposefully together.

Children Look at Their Own Behavior*

Ronald Lippitt, Peggy Lippitt, Robert Fox

Children today are avid consumers of technology. Chances are that the small boy in the third row, fourth seat knows more about the second-to-second prepara-

*Reprinted from *NEA Journal*, September 1964. Used with permission.

tions for a space shot than he does about the day-to-day work of his father at the office or plant.

Youthful enthusiasm for technology need not be limited to the race for the moon, however. It can also provide motivation for learning about matters much closer to the child's everyday world. In Michigan, for example, children are learning about the ways people behave toward each other in much the same way the children might learn about the behavior of a space ship in orbit.

In the Michigan Social Science Education Project, elementary school teachers, assisted by curriculum specialists and behavioral scientists from the University of Michigan, are introducing their pupils to some of the scientifically accepted methods for studying human behavior, particularly everyday behavior experienced by the pupils in their classroom life. Begun two years ago, the Project involves several first through sixth graders in the university town of Ann Arbor and in industrial Willow Run, as well as the pupils at the University of Michigan Laboratory School.

The methods and techniques by which the children study human behavior are, of course, simplified to fit their various levels of comprehension. Nonetheless, the children are able to acquire useful information about themselves, about their own reactions to situations, about interpersonal relationships in the classroom and about scientific method.

"Friendly and Unfriendly Feelings" is the title of one of the units introduced in the curriculums of the three participating school systems. In this unit, the children are encouraged to look objectively at their own human relations. Although the children acquire a surprising amount of knowledge about what behavioral scientists have learned about emotional behavior, the em-

phasis in "Friendly and Unfriendly Feelings" is on methodology — the children learn to use the scientific method as an inquiry procedure, as a way of asking and answering questions.

The learning techniques presented during this and all the units depend on the pupils' grade level and, to some extent, on the teacher's ability to work with a particular method. So far, the teachers have succeeded with learning procedures that incorporate role playing, unfinished stories, simplified interviewing and observation techniques, pupil-made graphs and charts, and group projects. The lecture-by-teacher method is rare; participation by the children is stressed.

Before the children begin the unit, they are given an orientation to what "behavior" is as an object of study and to ways of exercising their scientific curiosity.

How objectively the children are able to observe behavior is perhaps best illustrated by the experience one mother had with her little girl who was in the third grade last year. The girl was having trouble getting to sleep one night and she asked her mother's advice.

"Think about something interesting," said the mother.

"I'll think about behavior," said the child.

The mother, concerned, asked her daughter if she were having trouble at school. "Oh, no!" was the reply. "Don't you know that all actions *are* behavior?"

The purpose of the orientation is to build children's ability to differentiate between scientific observation and a value judgment. In the long run, this ability helps them to articulate and share more intelligently the many different values they have. The atmosphere of tolerance and trust in which the children learn encourages them to develop some new and more positive attitudes toward their classmates, teachers, and families.

After the orientation period, the children undertake specific study projects. A third grade teacher, for example, may present his children with the problem of what makes people become angry. He may choose to begin with one of the laboratory exercises described in a special guide designed by some of the experienced teachers and scientists involved in developing the "Friendly and Unfriendly Feelings" unit.

Each exercise is designed to present a specimen of behavior which the children can examine and from which they can draw tentative hypotheses. For example, one exercise involves a standardized role-playing scene in which conflict develops over children taking turns.

In this case, Jim refused to let Jack have the bat in a game of rounders. Jim says that he is not finished batting. When Jack tries to grab the bat from Jim, Jim pulls it away. Jack then hits Jim in the face.

The children observe the role-playing scene as members of observation teams. One team is given the task of collecting data on the different feelings exhibited by the actors. Afterward they tabulate the data on a chart showing how often feelings of friendliness or unfriendliness were revealed in the scene. Another team is assigned the task of observing one actor. Afterward they will be asked to make a team report on how that person reacted.

The teacher assigns the observation tasks on the basis of what the unit builders think the children should learn from the experience. The guides also include criteria for evaluating the experiences.

In the case of the children observing Jim's reaction to relinquishing his turn, they might study the accuracy of their report by comparing their independent observations. The scientists call this reliability of observation.

As the children become more adept at observing simple interactions between people, they are able to draw some conclusions from the sequences of behavior they see. For example, they may be asked to interpret "Why did Jack hit Jim?"

At this point, the children's answers involve no assigning of right and wrong in the situation, only *why* the action happened. Once they can describe and explain the action, they can seek ways of resolving conflicts with more desirable results.

In the final part of the unit, the children learn to draw parallels between the kinds of forces influencing the behavior witnessed in the laboratory exercises and the forces operating in their own minds. This ability helps them to evaluate their own behavior and to find ways for making it more rational and more effective.

Thus far, the children have shown a surprising ability to understand basic principles of human relations and to use intelligently the methods and techniques of the behavioral scientists. Boys and girls from the third grade up have learned to read and construct data charts. The children also read with understanding summaries of some experiments mentioned prominently in professional journals.

In the sixth grade last year, pupils developed skill with interview techniques. The subjects for their interviews were first graders; the purpose was to compile an inventory of attitudes toward older children. The thoroughness and objectivity represented in some of the final reports show a real grasp of the scientific approach.

Perhaps the greatest difficulty in the Project has been to orient classroom teachers to the subject matter and the teaching techniques involved. The Project staff discovered that some teachers had little college preparation in the behavioral sciences and thus had trouble in differentiating between a value judgment and a scientific analysis.

Some teachers were also unable to restrain themselves from exercising an undue amount of control over their classes. In order for the children to study human behavior, they needed the opportunity to engage in social interaction themselves. This could occur only when the teacher was willing to permit a good deal of pupil participation and interaction.

To remedy these difficulties, visiting teams composed of experienced classroom teachers, college educators, and behavioral scientists meet with the teachers early in the school year to explain the methods and assumptions underlying the Project. The visiting teams also conduct weekly, voluntarily attended seminars during the school year. In addition, tape recordings of classes conducted by teachers with backgrounds in the behavioral sciences are available to less experienced teachers.

A basic assumption underlying the Project is that having the children study human behavior rationally will make a significant difference in their attitudes toward their teachers and other adult authorities, in their concepts of such ideas as cooperation and competition, in their understanding of themselves, and in their appreciation of differences in others.

Since the Project began, several teachers have noted a marked decrease in traditional anti-teacher feelings, particularly among disadvantaged pupils. They have also noted positive changes in their pupils' concept of cooperation. Prior to the Project, many of the children regarded cooperation as nothing more than helping each other to cheat on tests — to "beat the system" so to speak.

The children's enthusiasm for the Project, as evidenced by the high degree of participation and skill they exhibited at all elementary school levels, has strengthened the staff's belief in its feasibility and appropriateness. Furthermore, the children are discovering that there is no subject more exciting to study than the behavior of themselves and others.

Aversive Control of Behavior*

Daniel C. Neale

A widespread belief in psychology and education is that the use of aversive measures—e.g., physical punishment, sarcasm, ridicule, detention, writing "I will be good" 100 times—is to be avoided. Instead, teachers and parents are advised to rely upon positive reinforcement—to give approval, support, and encouragement and to develop friendly, warm relationships.

Some of the bases for this belief and advice have recently been challenged, and

aversive methods for the control of behavior are receiving new attention.

A Legend

Recommendations to "accentuate the positive, eliminate the negative" in the education of children have a long history. Such names as Rousseau, Pestalozzi, and Froebel come easily to mind. John Dewey, and those he inspired, waged an incessant war against teachers who tried to force students to undertake unpleasant and meaningless tasks with threats of punishment.

*Reprinted from *Phi Delta Kappan,* February 1969. Used with permission.

More recently, those in a variety of helping professions, e.g., social work and clinical psychology, have been impressed by the power of support, acceptance, understanding, and love to catalyze significant personal growth in those who are troubled. Often such troubles are ascribed to an early history of rejection, failure, and punishment.

Experimental psychologists, too, have believed that "positive reinforcement" procedures were to be preferred to the use of aversive measures in the training of a variety of animals, including man.

Most prominent among such experimental psychologists has been B. F. Skinner, a man whose ideas have recently had a strong influence upon educators. His criticism of the use of "aversive stimuli" in education is in two parts. First, he argues that the use of such aversive stimuli is inefficient. Basing his conclusions upon certain animal experiments performed in the 1930's, Skinner has argued that the effects of punishing undesirable behavior are only temporary, that once the punishment is no longer administered the undesirable behavior returns in full strength. Skinner has also argued that, when one wishes to encourage some desirable behavior, punishing "errors" help little because it fails to give the organism information about what is desired. Instead, one should rely on giving positive reinforcements for successive approximations to the correct response.

A second criticism of aversive control by Skinner and others is that it often has undesirable side effects. In extreme cases debilitating anxiety or neurotic behaviors may result. Otherwise, learners may develop such an aversion for the training situation or the learning task that they avoid it. Thus children who experience unpleasantness in connection with school tasks may develop an aversion for teachers, schools, and learning. They then develop a variety of behaviors to avoid learning and even school itself.

Another experimental psychologist, R. L. Solomon,[1] has termed the prevailing beliefs about aversive control "a legend," challenging their scientific basis. After a survey of recent experimentation, chiefly with infrahumans, he has suggested that aversive methods may under some circumstances be effective and that undesirable side effects need not necessarily occur. Another psychologist, Ivar Lovaas,[2] has reported remarkable success in treating childhood schizophrenics, using, in part, aversive stimulation.

The challenge to existing legends needs our careful consideration.

Three Procedures

Experimental psychologists distinguish three ways in which average stimuli may be used to influence behavior.

1. *Escape training.* In this case an aversive stimulus is presented and the organism must make some specified response to end the aversive stimulus. For example, in the laboratory a dog may be placed in a cage whose floor is electrified. A shock is administered and the dog may end the unpleasantness by jumping over a barrier into another cage where there is no shock. A similar procedure has been used by Lovaas with schizophrenic children. A child who would never come to adults when called stood barefoot on an electric grid. Shock was administered and the experimenter said, "Come here." When

[1]Richard L. Solomon, "Punishment," *American Psychologist,* April, 1964, pp. 239-53.

[2]Bradley Bucher and O. Ivar Lovaas, "Use of Aversive Stimulation in Behavior Modification," in M. R. Jones (ed.), *Miami Symposium on the Prediction of Behavior, 1967*: Aversive Stimulation. Miami, Fla.: University of Miami Press, 1968, pp. 77-145.

the child moved toward the experimenter, the shock was turned off.

2. *Active avoidance.* Sometimes labeled merely "avoidance," this second procedure is similar to escape training, except that if a specified response is made the aversive stimulation will never occur. Thus the dog in his electrified cage might be given a signal, e.g., a light, and 10 seconds later a shock. If he jumps before the 10 seconds have elapsed, he avoids the shock. Such avoidance training begins as escape training because at first the dog does not "know" the shock is coming and jumps only after the shock comes on. However, within a short period of time the dog learns to jump before the shock comes on.

Similarly, in Lovaas's work the experimenter may say, "Come here," and if the child moves toward the experimenter no shock is given. The child avoids the shock by moving toward the adult.

3. *Passive avoidance.* Another name often given is "punishment procedure." Here some specified behavior already exists and the purpose of the procedure is to eliminate it. When the behavior occurs, an adverse stimulus is administered. In the laboratory a rat has learned to press a bar. Then, when he presses the bar he receives a shock. As training proceeds, the rate at which he presses the bar decreases and he may cease pressing altogether. By "not responding" he avoids the aversive stimulation. Lovaas has used such a procedure to reduce "self-stimulatory" behavior, the aimless rocking and waving that sometimes occupies three-fourths of a schizophrenic child's time. Lovaas administered one-second shocks each time such behavior occurred. In situations where this was done, self-stimulation quickly disappeared.

Some Phenomena

The main basis for labeling current be-

liefs about aversive control "a legend" is not so much what *is* known as it is what is *not* known. The truth is that the effects of aversive stimulation have not been extensively and carefully studied, especially with children. One reason for this is ethical, because our society has deep reservations about cruelty to animals in general and people in particular. Therefore our knowledge about aversive control is limited. We do not know if our current beliefs are true; they are like a legend.

In recent years studies of aversive methods have been started, however, mostly with animals and in some cases with disturbed people. The results of such studies do not give us a complete understanding of aversive control, but they do raise significant questions about our legends. The following phenomena illustrate the kinds of questions that are being raised.

Escape and Active Avoidance

Research with rats who learn to press a bar in order to turn off a shock has been reported by James A. Dinsmoor[3] to show that such escape training is quite efficient, perhaps even more rapid than similar training with positive reinforcement. He finds that in such escape training the effects of different schedules of reinforcement are similar to those observed under positive reinforcement. Rats can easily learn discriminations and chains with such procedures. Nowhere in Dinsmoor's research, in which moderate degrees of shock are used, is there evidence that the shock leads to neurotic behaviors or inhibits learning severely.

Some fascinating results have come from research by R. L. Solomon and his colleagues,[4] who studied "traumatic" avoid-

[3]James A. Dinsmoor, "Escape from shock as a Conditioning Technique," in Jones, *op. cit.,* pp. 33-76.

ance learning in dogs. As described above, dogs were first given a signal and 10 seconds later a very strong shock. After a period of intense panic, the dogs would *escape* the shock and signal by jumping over a barrier. Within five trials the dogs learned to jump before the 10 seconds and thereby avoided the shock altogether. With continuing trials, several important phenomena were observed.

1. The latency (time after the signal) of the dogs' jumps grew shorter until it stabilized around an average of 1.6 seconds. This is puzzling, because any jump within 10 seconds would avoid the shock and because during this period the animal received no further shocks.

2. The dogs would continue to jump for hundreds of trials with no sign that the tendency to respond was growing weaker, even though during that time the dogs never received a shock. One of the remarkable (and most difficult to explain) characteristics of traumatic avoidance behavior is its extreme persistence.

3. After the avoidance behavior was well developed (when the latency had become short), the dogs behaved in a perfectly "cool" manner with no signs of anxiety. If, however, the dog was prevented from executing his avoidance response, say, by a barrier, an intense anxiety reaction occurred.

In Lovaas's work with schizophrenic children, mentioned above, a similar avoidance procedure with moderate shock levels or slaps on the thigh has proved extremely effective in producing a variety of desirable behaviors with no evidence of undesirable side effects. These results have been obtained with children who had been psychoanalyzed and "loved" for years with no noticeable improvement in their behavior.

Of course, laboratory experiments with dogs and rats and schizophrenic children do not tell us directly what to do in elementary or high schools about aversive control. However, they do provide a basis for questioning a legend that says aversive control procedures are ineffective and have disastrous side effects. In fact, they suggest the possibility that desired behaviors may in some cases be established more quickly, and, when aversive stimulation is intense, such behaviors may be more resistant to extinction than when positive reinforcement is used.

Passive Avoidance

Similar questions about the legend are raised by experiments which explore the power of aversive stimuli to eliminate undesirable responses.

First, the early experiments showing that aversive stimuli delivered after a rat's bar press produced only a temporary suppression of the response have been shown to be limited in their generality. If the punishment is made more intense or if an alternative response gets the rat his food pellets, punishment is extremely effective and its effects are almost permanent.

Second, the effects of punishment on behavior have been shown to be an extremely complicated affair, depending on the species, the kind of response that is punished, the age of the subject, the timing of the punishment, and other factors. Inspecting a review of available research by Solomon,[5] one is led to hypothesize that punishment is extremely effective in eliminating undesirable behavior when: 1) the aversive stimulus is strong and delivered immediately after the undesired behavior begins; 2) the punished response is not extremely

[4]Richard L. Solomon and L. C. Wynne, "Traumatic Avoidance learning: The Principles of Anxiety Conservation and Partial Irreversibility," *Psychological Review*, Vol. 61, 1954, pp. 353-84.

[5]*Ibid.*

strong; 3) the aversive stimulus is not one that has been used frequently before; 4) an alternative response, incompatible with the undesired one, is rewarded.

That these hypotheses may be true is also suggested by Lovaas's work, described above, where a one-second shock administered after self-stimulatory behavior reduced such behavior from 70-80 percent to zero almost immediately. After three days of training no further shocks were administered for 11 months. Self-stimulatory behavior did not occur in the situation during that period. Significantly, incompatible behaviors were being reinforced at the same time.

Punishment procedures have also been shown to be effective in eliminating unwanted behavior in classrooms. Professor Ogden Lindsley of the University of Kansas has shown teachers how they can eliminate unwanted, talking in elementary school children by having children put on a surgical mask for a period of time when they talk out of turn. Often just by announcing such a contingency the unwanted behavior is stopped. The procedure has been applied by numerous parents and teachers to a variety of behaviors and a variety of punishing events with considerable success.

As with escape and avoidance learning, enough research on punishment procedures has been conducted to raise serious questions about any legend that says that aversive methods of control are ineffective or necessarily lead to seriously undesirable side effects.

Some Cautions

Although enough is known to question certain legends about aversive stimulation, one should not therefore support programs of police or teacher brutality nor discount the effectiveness of positive reinforcement procedures.

First, one can argue against aversive control on ethical grounds. The pain and discomfort inflicted must always be carefully weighed against the good accomplished and cannot be defended if alternative methods will serve as well.

Second, although undesirable side effects may not *necessarily* occur, such side effects *may* occur. For example, it is still possible to argue that aversive stimuli used in training may make the entire training situation aversive. Also, increases in anxiety and aggressive behavior have been noted.[6]

Third, the characteristics of behavior developed by certain aversive procedures may be undesirable. For example, in traumatic avoidance, the response may be an inflexible, stereotyped response. In many situations this is the opposite from what we wish to develop, that is, behavior that is adaptable. Parallels have been drawn between traumatic avoidance behavior and the rigid, self-defeating behavior of neurotics.

Fourth, the experimental results that present a challenge to existing legends come from a few situations and may be specific to such situations. For example, Lovaas has hypothesized that schizophrenic children may lack the anxieties that normal children possess. Aversive methods may be especially effective with schizophrenics because they build such anxieties. Or, Dinsmoor's research showing escape training to be efficient may apply only to the kind of laboratory situation where an animal has no alternative way to terminate unpleasantness. In "natural" settings organisms may find undesirable alternative ways to escape aversive stimuli.

[6] N. H. Arzin and W. C. Holtz, "Punishment," in W. H. Honig (ed.), *Operant Behavior: Areas of Research and Application.* New York: Appleton-Century-Crofts, 1966, pp. 380-447.

Thus, until our knowledge about methods of aversive control is broadened to include situations like those faced by teachers, caution is in order.

Some Theory

In the face of ignorance how does one proceed? The conduct of educational institutions cannot wait until we have perfect knowledge.

My own view is that we take as a basis for action the best-supported theories that we can find and use them to help us think about situations we face. Without accepting the conclusions we reach as gospel, we can judge the relative consequences of alternative actions on the basis of our theory.

With respect to methods of aversive control, the best theory available to handle existing data is the two-process conditioning theory.

The theory suggests that when aversive stimuli are presented, the resulting pain or fear reactions become conditioned to aspects of the situation. Subsequently, the same or similar situations elicit portions of the original pain or fear response (a conditioned response sometimes labeled "anxiety").

Instrumental responses are strengthened or weakened as a function of whether or not they are followed by either the original pain-producing stimuli or the conditioned stimuli that elicit "anxiety."

According to our best present knowledge, escape and active avoidance procedures may be expected to work in obtaining desired behavior, providing that the behavior is well specified, clear to the learner, and easier for him to make than other alternative responses that also escape or avoid. However, one should beware the possibility that an association may develop between the situation and the aversive stimulus. Aspects of the situation may themselves become aversive, and this side

effect may lead to the development of other undesirable responses. For example, such procedures in school may develop in students a general aversion to school and reinforce behaviors, physical or mental, that represent escape from school.

The use of intense ("traumatic") shock appears to require special theoretical treatment. The 1.6 second latency found by Solomon, for example, has been interpreted as the maximum delay that would prevent the autonomic nervous system's "anxiety impulses" to be registered in the central nervous system. Thus in traumatic avoidance the animal does not experience the anxiety associated with the signal. This would help to account for the fact that such responses are extremely difficult to extinguish (a response must be made to be extinguished; because the anxiety does not occur, it cannot be extinguished). In addition, Solomon has hypothesized that extreme fear or pain may produce permanent changes in the nervous system. Thus such anxiety responses could never be eliminated. The moral to this theoretical story is, "Watch it." If your aversive stimuli produce extreme pain or fear, what you do may be hard to undo.

In eliminating undesirable behavior, punishments probably will be effective, especially if they are strong, promptly delivered, infrequently used, and if some behavior incompatible with that which is undesirable is rewarded. Punishments may not be effective on very strongly established behavior and may make aspects of the situation in which punishments are administered aversive.

Finally, this brief treatment hardly does justice to the growing experimental literature on aversive control or to the usefulness of two-process theory in accounting for a wide variety of phenomena. Its main purpose has been to illustrate an exciting area of research that questions some existing dogmas and provides a way to think about the effects of aversive stimuli on behavior.

Bibliography

Arizin, N. H. and Holtz, W. C.: Punishment, in W. H. Honig (ed.), *Operant Behavior: Areas of Research and Application*. New York, Appleton-Century-Crofts, 1966, pp. 380-447.

Bucher, B. and Lovass, Ivar O.: Use of aversive stimulation in behavior modification, in M.R. Jones (ed.), *Miami Symposium on the Predic-tion of Behavior, 1967: Aversive Stimulation.* Miami, University of Miami Press, 1968, pp. 77-145.

Dinsmoor, James, A.: Escape from shock as a conditioning technique, in Jones, Miami Symposium on the Prediction of Behavior, 1967; Aversive Stimulation. Miami, University of Miami Press, 1968, 33-76.

Solomon, Richard, L.: Punishment, *Am Psychologist*, April, 1964, 239-253.

_____ and Wynne, L. C.: Traumatic avoidance learning: The principles of anxiety conservation and partial irreversibility, *Psychol Rev*, 61:353-384, 1954.

The Newer Control Techniques

Leslie J. Chamberlin

Concepts Not New

Within recent years, the field of education has been bombarded by a variety of techniques and approaches to student control and school discipline. The diversity is so great that it has led to some confusion and misinterpretation. However, when we look at the basic learning theory research and other psychologically based research that underlies these approaches, we find that the basic concepts involved are not new. They are concerned with understanding how to effectively motivate and relate to people. They are attempts to apply psychology to the new life and work of the teacher and pupil. In short, they are tried and true principles that have always been used successfully by good teachers.

A Rose By Any Other Name

Unfortunately, these concepts are presented in whole or in part under many different titles, names, or phrases. This, of course, leads to additional confusion for the practitioners attempting to use the methods, for they are led to believe that each approach is new and completely different. However, in most cases, there is great similarity between the techniques. Also, the underlying principles are closely related. Some of the titles, names, and phrases used to denote the current approaches to improving behavior and school discipline are: Behavior Therapy, Behavioral Counselling, Reinforcement Therapy, Behavior Modification, Contingency Management, Operant Procedures, Token Economies, Modeling, Social Modeling, Shaping, Behavioral Approach, Contingency Contracting, and others.

Benefits

The real benefit to these approaches is that they direct the teachers' attention to the majority of students who normally try to behave, please, and succeed. These approaches require that the teacher alter his perceptual field, that is, to notice the kind of behavior he approves of rather than what he doesn't approve. The teacher is asked to take a positive approach and to emphasize the growth, development, and success of his students, rather than the occasional errors, or poor judgment of his students. The concept that is basic to these approaches is that an activity is more likely to be repeated if it's followed by a positive response than if followed by a negative response. Therefore, the teacher is told to respond positively to only the kinds of behavior of which he approves. It must be emphasized that much more than a change of attitude is involved in successfully implementing these psychologically-based approaches to improving student behavior.

Another benefit is that the thinking and planning necessary to prepare for such a program gives the teacher a "psychic-readiness" to act. These approaches use direct rather than indirect means to changing behavior and require that the teacher be prepared to exhibit certain behaviors himself, if the program is to be successful. Also, the teacher is directed to deal with the individual student and must tailor-make techniques and procedures to suit the individual's needs. The approach involves a particular view of behavior and a set of procedures that are intended to change the student's behavior directly.

General Reinforcement

The teacher who hopes to apply reinforcement practices to improving student behavior and school discipline as a general technique, should:

I. *Specify the Desired Behavior.*
   A. Demonstrate the desired behavior.
   B. Make rules clear, explicit, few in number.
   C. Repeat often.
II. *Ignore Disruptive Behavior.*
   A. Attend to positive behavior (except for physical danger, destruction of property, or when the unwanted behavior is very intense and/or frequent).
III. *Praise for Improvement.*
   A. Catch the students being good.
   B. Specify behavior that is appre-

ciated.
   C. Reward appropriate behavior promptly.

Probably one of the most difficult things to understand about the principles upon which these approaches to improving student behavior are based is that they go on working all the time, whether the teacher pays any attention to them or not. The laws do not work only during certain classes or only during school hours. They are in operation at all times. Reinforcement that follows any behavior will strengthen that behavior regardless of where it occurs. As one becomes familiar with this fact, the importance of observing the reinforcement involved in a particular situation becomes obvious. Once the teacher understands the activity-reward sequence, the use of it seems far more sensible and desirable.

Specific Reinforcement Application

At times, a teacher may wish to apply reinforcement to a particular situation on either an individual or group basis in addition to the general use of reinforcement theory. This can be accomplished with or without a written "contract" being involved. However, the procedure will be described in terms of a written contract for purposes of clarity. Careful attention should be given to the following six points:

1. The contract reward should be immediate.
2. Beginning contracts should reward small approximations.
3. Reward frequently.
4. The contract should reward accomplishment not obedience.
5. Reward follows performance.
6. The contract must be fair, clear, honest, and positive in nature.

Once contracting has been established as a procedure, it should be maintained and care should be taken not to reward undesirable acts. The best way to eliminate unwanted behavior is to make certain that it is never reinforced in any way; rather, some other desirable behavior must be reinforced.

When teachers first attempt to institute such a positive action approach, they have a little difficulty in determining exactly what can be used as reinforcers. The following is a list of some of the privileges which have been used by teachers as reinforcers:

- Attention to making the child feel praised.
- Make him feel competent.
- Make him feel appreciated.
- Positive physical contact, eg., "pat on back."
- Friendly verbal interaction.
- Smiling at him.
- "Good citizen" sign is placed on his desk for a few hours.
- Access to a quiet play, art, or science exploration area.
- Being a monitor for a period of time.
- Working on a bulletin board.
- Being in charge of a particular activity.
- Many tasks, such as erasing the chalkboard, sweeping floors, washing desks, cleaning aquarium, cleaning erasers, etc.
- Coming in early in the morning to "help."
- Being messenger for a day or two.
- Answering the door, taking messages, answering the phone.
- Passing out papers, etc.
- Being line leader.
- Leading the morning pledge to the flag, song, or other ritual.
- Choosing the story to be read to the class.
- Being captain of a team in some room activity or in gym.
- Giving the spelling words.
- Choosing a new seat in the room.
- Helping school secretary.
- Visiting in another classroom.
- Getting to go to lunch or recess or home.
- Being allowed to move on to another activity.
- Extra long recess.
- A "free choice" activity period in the room.
- Having the teacher read a story.
- Working on a project such as a skit, special display, redecorating the room.
- Being allowed to do independent work assignments in any order desired by the individual.

Misuses of Reinforcement Theory

The wonderful thing about reinforcement theory is that it works. However, some teachers use it to simply restrict children even more so than they have been in the past. Too much emphasis is placed on solving the teacher's problems and not enough on helping the student to enjoy school more and benefit even more from it. The good teacher relates his use of reinforcement theory to worthy educational goals and not to the trivia of running a classroom. Remember, no tool or technique can be better than the person using it.

Chapter   IX

Discussionette

1. What is the difference between scientific observation and a value judgement?

2. Is it *really* desirable for children to study human behavior?

3. Discuss the procedures in which aversive behavior may be used to influence behavior in several school situations.

4. How do you think parents would respond to teacher used "amateur psychology" on their children?

5. How well does reverse psychology work with different age groups?

6. Is reverse psychology apt to turn on its user and provide more problems?

7. Which suggestions for dealing with discipline problems do you feel will work best? Why?

8. Which suggestions are easiest to follow?

9. When *is* discipline good?

10. Which suggestions are the most helpful? Why?

Discussionette Words and Concepts

affective learning	psychological	conflict
defense mechanism	behavior modification	compulsion
transactional analysis	reality therapy	role playing
positive approach	contingency management	aversive control

Try to use these words.

Try to explain these words.

Try to relate these words and their concepts to current or emerging educational patterns regarding psychological approaches.

CHAPTER X

∬ LEGAL APPROACHES ∬

INTRODUCTION

Litigation of all kinds appear to be on the increase and school litigation is no exception. Teachers are as vulnerable to the law in the classroom as out. He should face this fact honestly and realistically and prepare for student confrontations that could erupt into heated legal involvements.

A number of well-meaning, but unsuspecting teachers have suddenly found themselves being sued. Traditionally the courts have been somewhat protective of teachers; however, the paternalistic attitudes of the courts has ended. Because of this, teachers and school officials should take definite steps and establish specific procedures to acquaint themselves and their staffs with the legal implications of working with children.

Under teacher liability, the courts hold teachers responsible for the foreseeable consequences of voluntary acts, even though the teacher meant no harm. Negligence and being reasonable and prudent with average foresight and providing adequate supervision must be faced by today's teachers.

Teachers must be knowledgeable of school laws to protect themselves and their students. There are far too many teachers facing litigation simply because they did not understand the law nor did they provide what could be defined as a legally sound classroom environment.

Discipline—The Teacher and the Law*

Leslie J. Chamberlin and James L. Niday

Teachers are as vulnerable to the law in the classroom as out. He should face this fact honestly and realistically, and prepare for student confrontations that could erupt into heated legal involvements. A number of well-meaning but unsuspecting teachers have suddenly found themselves being served with subpoenas. Litigation of all kinds appear to be on the increase and school litigation is no exception. Traditionally the courts have been somewhat protective of teachers; however, the paternalistic attitude of the courts has ended. Because of this and the "sueitis mania" that permeates our society, teachers and school officials should take definite steps and establish specific procedures to thwart student confrontations and the consequential law suits.

*Reprinted from *Education*, November, December 1969. Used with permission.

Student-teacher confrontations can and do lead to civil law suits for damages. The wise teacher prepares for disruptive influences in order to prevent such confrontations especially in light of today's demonstrations and protests. It is usually the unforeseen encounter by a teacher who is untrained in legal rights and "due process of law" that leads to legal involvements with students. A law suit may arise from highly charged words or actions, or from silence and inaction under certain circumstances. In most cases it is the thoughtless word or action in an unexpected situation that causes trouble.

There is a pressing need to minimize disruptive influences which lead to student-teacher confrontations. Today's teacher should first analyze himself as to what the students would refer to as his own "hang-ups." Secondly, a comprehensive understanding of social dynamics could help eliminate or minimize such confrontations. The student of today brings problems and tensions to school which in many cases are beyond the teacher's control. "It is estimated that there are more than half a million mentally ill children in the United States classified as psychotic or border-line cases. Most of these children are suffering from the psychiatric disorder known as childhood schizophrenia" (1). Since only a very small percentage of the total are receiving any kind of psychiatric treatment, the classroom teacher should know his own capabilities, limitations, and legal rights. Today's teacher should make it a point to learn the legal rights of students especially in light of the implications of the recent decision of the United States Supreme Court relating to the Gault case. Synoptically the Gault case decision held:

1. The juvenile has a right to notice of charges.
2. The juvenile has a right to counsel.
3. The juvenile has a right to confrontation and cross examination of witnesses.
4. The juvenile has the privilege against self incrimination.

Teachers and school officials in some instances create situations and problems which ultimately lead to confrontations which could easily result in personal damage suits. Battle lines are easily and quickly drawn over such things as codes of dress and hair styles as in the complaint in the Civil Case, Cordova vs. Pierson, et al. which was filed in the United States District Court, Northern District of Ohio. Fourteen-year-old Corlin Cordova brought suit against the officials of the Perrysburg Exempted Village Board of Education for compensatory and punitive damages of $35,000.00. Allegedly this suit was brought because of the violation of the student's constitutional rights of (1) privacy, (2) free speech and expression, (3) due process of law, and (4) privileges and immunities of a United States citizen; as well as punitive damages for his suspensions and harassments which caused him mental anguish. A similar case occurred in the Cincinnati area when John Fremont, 16, named officials of the Princeton School District in the suit, claiming his constitutional rights were violated when he was suspended from Princeton High School because his hair was not in compliance with the school dress code. There are always students willing to "pick up the gauntlet" even when the teacher doesn't realize one has been dropped.

Some court cases arise from a teacher over reacting in an emotional and tense moment. At times violence is inside everyone and the outburst seems to be almost impulsive. Highly charged words are exchanged and an explosive situation is born. The resulting imprudent action on the part of a teacher acting emotionally may lead to a law suit for damages. Recently a thirteen-year-old New York girl was awarded over $40,000.00 in damages which was upheld upon appeal to the State Supreme Court. This suit resulted from a teacher striking a girl while pushing her from her classroom desk. Thus hasty or spur of the moment disciplinary measures with a ruler or pointer can turn an apparent harmless push into a cause for litigation. Even a well-meant, but not quite ethical publicized comment which is meant to encourage slow or obstinate students can result in a damage suit. Thus a thoughtless or idle comment made in front of a class could create trouble for the teacher and embarrassment for the entire teaching profession.

What makes well-meaning, well educated, professional educators allow serious situations to develop, and to become so deeply and emotionally involved? The first impulse is try to place the blame on either the teacher or the student; forgetting the problem and the circumstances which caused it. However, the problem needs to be analyzed and all possible causes carefully examined in order to understand and work with the present situation and similar problems of the future. Disruptive influences causing student-teacher confrontations need to be studied and identified.

Disruptive Influences

Knowing what to expect from students is very important in detering disruptions. Many teachers would find difficulty in handling student protest, the militancy of the SDS and other such groups, and some of the commonplace problems of the disadvantaged student. The unique set of social problems facing educators today need thoughtful, positive, and creative so-

lutions. Before a teacher can understand and work with an individual or within a problem community, he should be able to identify certain socio-cultural and psychological aspects of students. One important factor in understanding disruptive influences is to understand the situational influence relevant to the behavior of the lower-class child and his continual adjustment that must be made between the lower and middle class subcultures.

The attitudes, mannerisms, skills and prejudices that each child brings to school, the physical condition of each child, the very room in which the teacher must teach, the neighborhood in which the school is located, the beliefs, attitudes, behavior, economic and social standing of the children's parents, and untold other factors contribute from time to time to classroom management problems. The very composition of the class may be a causitive factor in breach of discipline. Large city school systems that are changing from the neighborhood school organization and are going to the open enrollment plan are experiencing this problem. Students brought to a school from a different social, economic and cultural level of society create a totally new school environment. In many cases the adjustment takes place by children separating into their own groups, thus keeping to themselves with only fringe interaction. Within the classroom where each child is forced to interact with the total group, problems often come to the surface.

Some students help to create a calm, quiet and creative atmosphere. A few students provide leadership; some creatively and some disruptively. Most children seem to be primarily reactors to the environment. When the lesson is well organized and things are going well, the students are more likely to be well behaved. When one of the more disruptive students is vying for attention in his own way, the normally well behaved students react in sympathy with the disruptive student and become contributors to the classroom confusion. Every child makes his particular contribution to the group climate that exists in the classroom. Teachers need to be very conscious and give considerable attention to the minor disturbances which often produce discipline problems.

Teacher Reaction

In more cases than not, the initial impulse of a teacher when responding to a disciplinary situation within his own classroom is one of anger, resentment, and often personal indignation. This emotional reaction only defeats the teacher's efforts to maintain a good learning situation and feeds the fires of discontent. In most cases there is nothing personal in the child's act and even in a few cases where there is an attempt on the part of the student to hurt the teacher, the situation is only worsened by responding with a personal reaction. Discipline problems should be dealt with objectively and firmly, but without rejecting the misbehaving child as a person. The teacher needs to look at the whole situation and try to locate the cause of the trouble, and not just react to the symptom.

All teachers have discipline problems. Some have many while others have relatively few. A teacher can expect problems; some of which will persist so tenaciously that he may feel that he is sure to lose his temper or do something desperate. The record shows that many teachers do over-react and find themselves facing court action. Therefore, techniques are needed to safeguard the teacher and to prevent confrontations. Every teacher needs to think through the possibility of a serious problem developing, and to have one or more plans of action. The plan of action selected should provide a safeguard for the teacher by giving temporary and immediate relief to the situation; that will give the student and all those involved time to consider the consequences (a cooling off period); and provide for the intervention of a disinterested person (preferably an adult; however, a child of ten or older is presumed to be competent as a witness). Some teachers, by their own characteristics and idiosyncrasies, have a propensity to become involved with students which greatly increases the possibility of their being involved in a law suit. It is not uncommon today for a teacher to be charged in a civil suit for assault and battery, or some other tortious case.

Teacher Liability

A tort is usually defined as a "violation of a right not arising out of a contract." In addition to the existence of a right and the violation of that right, two other conditions must be present for an act to constitute a legal tort: (1) THE WRONG-DOER MUST HAVE ACTED INTENTIONALLY OR BEHAVED NEGLIGENTLY. (2) THE WRONGDOER'S ACT OR BEHAVIOR MUST BE THE *APPROXIMATE CAUSE* OF THE INJURY. Generally speaking then, tort liability is a legal wrong for which the law will give a particular redress. The courts hold a person responsible for the foreseeable consequences of his voluntary act, even though the actor meant no harm. For example, if a teacher should cause a child to be injured in the process of correcting or punishing him, that teacher could be held guilty of negligence. Negligence is considered to exist if harm befalls as the result of an action which could have been foreseen by a "reasonable and prudent" person, using ordinary care, in an effort to avoid trouble. Various court decisions have emphasized that the teacher must exercise "reasonable" caution, an "average amount of foresight," and provide "adequate supervision."

Teachers should request in-service programs to learn more about tort liability and the civil charges that can be brought against them. For example, "The teacher 'must' be charged in law with a knowledge of the unlawful character of his act. As a joint tort feasor with the school board he is liable, not withstanding their direction in the premises. "There can be no innocent agency in the commission of an act upon its face unlawful and tortious". A teacher can be held liable for an injury or negligent act while transporting a student, or for the negligence of someone else who has borrowed his car. An exceptionally high degree of vulnerability for liability occurs in out-of-class activities such as field trips, hazing, and horseplay. *Nonfeasance* (failing to act) in the performance of the duties of teaching, training, and controlling students under certain conditions can be just as actionable in a court of law as *malfeasance* (an illegal act). Thus the classroom teacher needs to know what is legally required of him. In-service programs, conferences, and seminars are only a few ways of providing this knowledge to the entire school staff.

Bibliography

1. The National Association of Mental Health, *Facts About Mental Illness*, 1963 Fact Sheet, New York, New York.

Smoking in the Public Schools*

Smoking is an increasingly serious problem which plagues a vast majority of secondary school administrators. In seeking advice and counsel from recognized authorities on the subject, NASSP's Executive Secretary contacted Dr. Jesse L. Steinfeld, Surgeon General of the United States. He replied:

There is no question medically and scientifically that cigarette smoking is this nation's number one health problem. Implicit encouragement of this pernicious habit by school authorities through officially condoned smoking areas is not in the best interests of our children or of our citizens. It seems to me that school authorities have a responsibility to set an example to the students for whose instruction they are responsible. Presumably there are parents who condone smoking by their children, but I hope that members of our school boards, who obviously are concerned about the health and welfare of the students,

*Reprinted by permission of the National Association of Secondary School Principals, from a March 1972 bulletin.

will do nothing to encourage this dangerous habit. Your interest in combating this serious health hazard is very much appreciated.

Most communities and school systems have ordinances and regulations relating to health and safety that include no-smoking laws. The enforcement of these laws, however, has become progressively more difficult. In public schools, the smoking problem has become a serious administrative and legal problem. This memorandum illustrates current law on the matter, both statutory and judicial; provides, for purposes of information, two representative programs now in operation; and suggests some guidelines that school administrators can follow as preventive measures.

State Statutes and Local Ordinances

State laws generally regulate smoking only indirectly through laws relating to licensing, taxation, and distribution of tobacco products. In some states, however, smoking is regulated directly through laws which forbid it in areas where food and beverage are prepared and stored. Most states, too, explicitly prohibit the sale or giving of tobacco to minors. Twelve states make it illegal for a minor to smoke. Local fire safety ordinances, on the other hand, nearly always regulate smoking directly by prohibiting it in certain public and private places, e.g., industrial sites, forest or wilderness areas, hospitals, and public buildings and vehicles.

Although several states have laws relating to smoking and minors, few statutes expressly prohibit minors from smoking on school property. This behavior is commonly controlled by local school district regulations. In Massachusetts, nevertheless, the school code specifies that students be taught the ill effects of smoking and alcohol; and, in Iowa, the advertising of tobacco is forbidden within a certain distance of public schools.

Case Law

Court decisions ruling directly on the validity of school antismoking regulations are also few. The following cases, however, are representative of current judicial attitude on the subject.

"*Davis v. Ann Arbor Public Schools,*" 313 F. Supp. 1217 (1970), examined the no-smoking regulations in Michigan public schools. In this case, a junior high school student who was suspended for smoking charged that the school district violated his right to due process and sought reinstatement. Although the student had a history of "incorrigible conduct," and his smoking in violation of school rules was simply the last of a long series of rule infractions, it was the proximate cause of his suspension. The court *did not* rule directly on the reasonableness of the regulation,

but it did rule that the student had received all reasonable consideration, and that the requisites of due process (i.e., knowledge, notice, reasons for suspension, and informal hearing) had been satisfied. Therefore, the court by implication upheld the school antismoking regulation as reasonable, stating:

Public school authorities may formulate rules and regulations thought necessary or desirable for maintenance of orderly programs of classroom learning, and in doing so they have wide latitude of discretion, subject only to restriction of reasonableness.

In another recent and important case, "*Anderson v. Independent School District*" No. 281, 176 N.W. 2d 640 (1970), a Minnesota high school student was suspended for violating the school antismoking regulations. The student, at the time of his first infraction of the regulation, was reminded that he could be expelled for repeated violations of the school's no-smoking rule. After a second violation of the regulation, the student was expelled. School authorities had duly promulgated school policies which were communicated to all students in an official handbook. The rule governing smoking read:

Tobacco: Smoking is a serious and costly habit. Minnesota State Law states that a student cannot smoke until he is 18 years old. Smoking on school property (in the buildings, on school grounds and in cars on school grounds) or at any school function, dance, or athletic event will be met with severe disciplinary action. A student found with cigarettes in his possession shall be subject to suspension until the parents return for conference. A student who is smoking on school property, or at a school-sponsored function, shall be suspended for three days and must be reinstated by a panel. The second offense in any one year will be met with a referral to a court or a recommendation to the school board for expulsion from school for the remainder of the school year. Smoking offenses shall be recorded.

The lower court ruled:

Defendants are ordered to admit Steven to the regular educational program of the school from which he was suspended, or make provision for a comparable education elsewhere, subject to such reasonable counselling, educational, or disciplinary measures as the Defendants may deem appropriate for Steven's rehabilitation and the preservation of their governance.

The School Board appealed to the lower court injunction against the suspension, but before a decision could be reached, the case was dismissed as moot because the student voluntarily withdrew from school. The lower court ruling, however, in the words of the appellate court, apparently did not preclude the school board from hearing and ruling on the basic question of expulsion for violation of the no-smoking regulation.

In Scottsdale, Ariz., a high school student in *Burnkrant v. Saggau*, 470 p. 2d 115 (1970), called on the court to enjoin the school district from suspending him for the rest of the semester because of a second infraction of the school rule prohibiting smoking on school grounds. The lower court ruled for the student because school officials had failed to follow the established procedures for suspending students.

Although the Arizona Court of Appeals did not rule directly on the issue of the validity of the smoking prohibitions, it affirmed the lower court's decision and by implication upheld the school's no-smoking regulations.

The position of the school board was:

Arizona laws gave the superintendent the authority to suspend pupils for good cause; that smoking has been proven harmful to health; that minors are prohibited from possessing tobacco; and that, accordingly, possession of tobacco by a minor constitutes good cause for suspension.

The law recognizes this need for school officials to have the right to discipline pupils in many ways, including suspension or expulsion from school. Rather, the law is that 'The enjoyment of the right of attending the public schools is necessarily conditional on compliance by pupils with the reasonable rules, regulations, and requirements of the school authorities, breaches of which may be punished by suspension or expulsion.

The Appellate Court found that:

While courts do possess a limited species of ultimate power to review the reasonableness of school disciplinary regulations and actions taken thereunder, they are not "super school boards"; the government of the schools has been vested by the legislature in boards of trustees and boards of education and if there exists a reasonable basis for rules made and actions taken, the same must be upheld. We note, in this connection, that the trial judge's remarks on the subject in his ruling from the bench failed to include a reference to the fact that is a misdemeanor in Arizona for a minor to have cigarettes or smoking tobacco in his possession.

Concurring in the decision of the Appellate Court, one member of the court in a separate statement commented: "The [school smoking] rule being in conformity with the announced public policy of the state certainly cannot be said to be either unreasonable or unnecessary for the education of our youth."

School Codes

Every school system must confront the issue of smoking in light of local conditions and requirements. The examples below illustrate how two school systems are currently handling the problem.

School Regulation Prohibiting Smoking

Fairfax County, Va., School Board Policy, Section 3 Smoking:

A. Smoking is considered a hazard to health by medical authorities and the School Board.
B. Students shall not smoke on school buses or in school buildings at any time or on school grounds at any time during the school day. (The school day begins with the arrival of the first bus in the morning and ends with the departure of the last bus in the afternoon.)

C. Reappraisal of this policy and its enforcement will be undertaken by the end of the first semester of the 1971-72 school year. [Remains in effect]

School Regulation Allowing Smoking

The Montgomery County, Md., Public School system resolved after finding that "all attempts to enforce the present Montgomery County Public Schools Regulation 540-1, which prohibits student use of tobacco on school premises, have brought increased control problems to the secondary schools," [and finding] "parental support of the prohibition not sufficiently supportive," to repeal their antismoking regulations and enacted the following:

The decision regarding establishment of areas on school grounds where students in each senior or junior-senior high school may use tobacco will be made by the school principal based on discussions involving students, parents, and school staff. If the decision is to establish such areas, the following guidelines shall apply:

1. No Smoking will be allowed within the school building.
2. If the decision favors the establishment of student smoking areas, the specifics as to when and where outside the school building student smoking will be permitted should be developed jointly by representatives of the student body, the school staff, and the parents.
3. It is anticipated that regulations will vary somewhat from school to school because of such local factors as grade organization, schedules, physical layout of the school plant and grounds, and neighborhood setting.
4. Regulations regarding the use of student smoking areas must be carefully delineated, and broad communication of these regulations must be provided by the school administration and the student government.
5. Students must share the responsibility for the proper use and upkeep of the student smoking areas.
6. Penalties for infractions of student smoking regulations must be forceful and must be conscientiously and consistently administered.
7. A forceful, meaningful program of education highlighting the hazardous effects of smoking has been implemented in the upper elementary grades and must continue through the senior high school. Senior high school students should accept a share in this educational responsibility as their influence, particularly upon younger students, has great possibilities.

Conclusion

As evidenced by the statutory material, court decisions, and school codes, the solution to the issue of smoking in the public schools is far from clear. Certain conclusions, nevertheless, can be drawn.

There is a general agreement that it is one thing to assume moral positions and another thing to implement those positions. Also, it is difficult to impose adult views on students and have significant behavioral changes in a practice like smoking. The 26th Amendment of the U.S. Constitution adds the further dimension of assigning legal adult status to 18-year-olds. However, it is also clear that principals and all educators are faced today with a question to which they must react.

Whatever the case in the past, there is now undisputed knowledge that smoking is a causal factor in many injurious, debilitating, and often fatal diseases. Given this awareness, the question becomes whether to condone smoking on school premises (allow is not the proper term as very often it is not within the practical power of the school principal to prevent).

NASSP suggests that student smoking lounges may well implicitly promote smoking in the public schools. Therefore, in lieu of establishing them, NASSP suggests that intensive educational programs to inhibit and/or finally terminate smoking be instituted. NASSP also recognizes the imperative need to involve students, faculty, parents, and the community at large in deliberations on this sensitive subject.

The following position statement from

the American Association for Health, Physical Education, and Recreation (AAHPER) is cited as a representative statement from an association vitally concerned with this issue.

[All school guidelines should provide the following:]

1. Assuming responsibility for curriculum experiences in smoking education which are timely and stimulating and provide accurate content, as an integral part of the ongoing, unified health instruction program, kindergarten through the twelfth grade.
2. Providing appropriate in-service training opportunities for school personnel, classroom instructional resources, and supervision and consultative services to teachers.
3. Maintaining a physical and emotional school atmosphere that positively reinforces the ob-

jectives of the ongoing health instructional program.

4. Encouraging staff and adult visitors to the school to realize the exemplar role they play and the importance of compliance with smoking rules and regulations.
5. Recognizing that parent example, pupil-peer relationships, and other community influences are important in the development of desirable health behavior.
6. Utilizing classroom situations as well as learning experiences in other curricular and extracurricular activities to reinforce the educational process.
7. Emphasizing the exemplar role of all school faculty and staff in relation to smoking on the school property.
8. Adopting "no smoking policies" for all groups utilizing school facilities.
9. Abolishing student and faculty smoking facilities.

Student Rights—Locker Searches*
Eric Olson

Every school administrator is by now aware that minors are entitled to the protection and rights guaranteed by the United States Constitution and that this applies in particular to students in their relationships with the public schools.[1] Among the provisions of the Constitution are those of the Fourth Amendment relating to searches and seizures:

The right of the people to be secure in their persons, houses, papers, and effects, against unreasonable searches and seizures, shall not be violated, and no warrants shall issue, but upon probable cause, supported by oath or affirmation, and particularly describing the place to be searched, and the persons or things to be seized.[2]

This article will deal with searches of student lockers.[3] To say that school authorities must be cognizant and respectful of a student's Fourth Amendment rights hardly answers any concrete question, however. What is prohibited is not searches and seizures but "unreasonable" searches and seizures; reasonableness must be determined in terms of the school context, which involves considerations and factors not necessarily present in other search and seizure situations (as of a car or house).

The school administrator is justly concerned with knowing and should know the nature of the students' Fourth Amend-

*Reprinted from *NASSP Bulletin*, February 1971. Used with permission.

[1] *Tinker v. Des Moines Independent Community School District*, 39S US 503 21 L.Ed. 2d 731, 89 S. ct. 733 (1969) (the "black armband" case). *Cf In re Gault*, 387 US 1, 18 L.Ed. 2d 527, 87 S Ct. 1428 (1967) (constitutional protections in juvenile proceedings).

[2] That individuals are entitled to Fourth Amendment protections from acts of the state. See *Mapp v. Ohio*,

367 US 643, 6 L.Ed. 2d 1081, 81 S Ct. 1684, 84 ALR 933 (1961).

[3] Outside the scope of this article are the closely related questions of search of a student's person, clothes, or handbag, of a student's car at school in or out of a school parking lot, medical examination of a student with symptoms suggesting that he may be under the influence of drugs or alcohol, and similar questions. The answers to some of these may not be the same as on locker searches.

ment rights for at least the following reasons:

1. A public servant is presumably desirous of performing his official public acts in accordance with the laws defining his obligations and not in violating another's legal rights. The courts have frequently, as in the *Tinker, Mapp,* and *Gault* cases, commented that the government generally and the schools in particular have an obligation to set an example of obedience to the law by respecting others' rights even when they could get away with violations.

"2." A violation of the law may well lead to civil liability for himself and/or his school district.[4]

"3." If evidence of a crime or evidence indicating grounds for juvenile proceedings is uncovered in a manner violating the Fourth Amendment, that evidence will not be admissible in criminal or juvenile proceedings and may as a practical matter render any such proceeding impossible.[5]

"4." If evidence indicating grounds for

[4] 42 U.S. Code §1983 ("Civil Rights Act") as well as under various state laws. After these, California Superintendent of Public Instruction Max Rafferty, in October 1969, sent his famous letter urging that school districts make systematic locker searches in conjunction with the police, the ACLU publicly announced that it would seek to enjoin the action if they knew of it in advance, and would sue for damages in other cases. This author was and is of the opinion that the ACLU would likely be successful as to such broad-ranging searches. In discussing the proposal with school administrators at the time, I found that they had already rejected the idea regardless of its legal merits. Their feelings are probably fairly generally summarized in the idea that it did not constitute "fair dealing" with the students regarding the implicit understandings relating to their receipt of the lockers (no matter what might appear on paper) and in general would constitute undue invasions of the students' privacy. Many of these are administrators the author considers "hardheaded" and who were fully as concerned about the problems of drugs as anyone else. These general non-legal beliefs may be probative of and reflective of what is "reasonable."

[5] See *Mapp,* note 2 supra and cases in note 7, intra.

school discipline is uncovered in a manner violating the Fourth Amendment, that evidence *may* not be admissible as a basis for discipline; this question has never been answered in any reported case known to me and must be considered quite unclear.[6]

The Decided Cases

My research has revealed reported cases on locker searches from only three states, California, New York, and Kansas, and one case involving a state university dormitory room search from a U.S. District Court in Alabama.[7] In all the cases the searches were found reasonable and lawful.

Briefly, the facts of the cases are as follows:

"1. *Donaldson*" (California). A student reported to the vice principal that "speed" could be bought from Donaldson and another. He later reported buying some and gave the pills to the vice-principal, who then searched Donaldson's locker for more pills and found some marijuana cigarettes and a bag of marijuana.

[6] See annotation at 5 ALR 3d 678. The question was raised in *Moore v. Student Affairs Committee of Troy State University,* 234 F. Supp. 725 (1968 M.D. Ala.) but not answered when the search was found lawful. The question is briefly and inconclusively discussed in "School Expansions and Due Process" at note VI in 1 Indiana Legal Forum 413 (Spring 1968) reprinted in "Current School Problems" (Practicing Law Institute 1968) pp. 20-21.

[7] *In re Donaldson,* 269 CA 2d 506, 75 Cal. Rptr. 220 (1969) (Calif. Ct. of Appeals Petition to Calif. Supreme Court denied).

Overton v. New York, 25 NY 2d 522, 349 NE 2d 366 (1969) (prior proceedings 393 US 35, 21 L.Ed. 2d 218, 89 S. Ct. 252; rch. den. 395 US 992, 21 L.Ed.2d 457, 89 3 Ct. 441; 20 NY 2d 360, 263 2d 22, 229 NE 2d 596; 51 Misc. 2d 140, 273 NYS 2d 143.

See also *Overton v. Rieger,* 311 F. Supp. 1035 (1970).

State v. Stein, 265 Kan. 638, 456 P 2d 1 (1939) Cert. den. 397 US 947.

Moore v. Student Affairs Committee of Troy State

University, 284 F. Supp. 725 (1968 M.D. Ala.).
For future cases see West Key numbers "Schools and
School Districts" 169 and "Search and Seizure" 7
(27) and annotations numbered 120, 121 and 207b
in USCA Constitution Amendment IV.
The author of "School Expulsions and Due Process"
note 6 supra) indicates that he was unable to find
any cases as of the publication of his article.

2. *Overton* (New York). Police came to
the vice-principal with a search warrant
(later found to be technically deficent)
to search Overton's locker for drugs, which
were found.

3. *Stein* (Kansas). The day after a burg-
lary in town, police came to school to
question Stein about it and to ask Stein
if they might look in his locker. Stein, in
the presence of the principal, did not
admit the crime but consented to their
looking in his locker; later he asserted that
his consent was ineffective as unlawfully
obtained, since he hadn't been given his
"rights" (you have the right to remain
silent, etc.) prior to being asked for consent. In Stein's school locker was found
the key to a public locker where the stolen
money was found.

4. *Moore* (Alabama). Police informed a
responsible college administrator that they
believed that drugs could be found in
Moore's (and certain others') dormitory
room. The students were beginning to
leave the campus at the end of the semester
and it was feared Moore would leave,
taking the evidence. The administrator
took them to Moore's room, where the
drugs were found.

Reasonable Grounds

Basing my opinion on the decided cases
(and always subject to more recent cases,
particularly by a court in your own jurisdiction—state or federal—or the U.S. Supreme Court), it is safe to say that a
search by a responsible school officer of
a student's locker is lawful (and the duty

of the school) if the following four circumstances exist:

"1." The search is based on reasonable
grounds for believing that something contrary to school rules or significantly detrimental to the school and its students will
be found in that locker.

"2." The information leading to the
search and the seizure are independent of
the police.

"3." The primary purpose of the search
is to secure evidence of student misconduct for school disciplinary purposes, although it may be contemplated that in
appropriate circumstances the evidence
would also be made available to the police.
If evidence of a crime or grounds for a
juvenile proceeding is lawfully obtained by
school personnel, it may be turned over to
the police and used by them.

4. The school has keys or combinations
to the lockers and the students are on
some form of prior notice that the school
reserves the right to search the lockers.

No exact definition of "reasonable
grounds" (my phrase, not a term of law)
can be given, although it was stated in the
opinion in *Moore* (see note 6) that less is
required than is indicated by the constitutional phrase "probable cause" to obtain
a search warrant. Perhaps it is simply information from an apparently reasonably
reliable source or based on sufficient
facts to indicate a reasonable likelihood of finding something improper
in the locker. It probably means something more than that the student has been
generally a "bad actor" in the past, although that fact added to more specific
information might be among the circumstances indicating reasonable grounds. The
facts of the cases recited above at least
show four situations believed by the courts
to show such reasonable grounds. It may
be noted that in three of the cases the in-

formation throwing suspicion on the student came from the police. Perhaps the police may be considered a highly reliable source of information, without inquiring into the basis for their belief (see below regarding police generally); in dealing with an informant of less certain reliability, it would be wise to ask the source of his belief so that it may be evaluated.

The mention of prior notice, at least implicit, that the school reserves the right to inspect the contents of the locker is of importance. (Prior notice as used here indicates notice before the situation arises, not the notice to the student just before his locker is opened.) The question of the reasonableness of a search is in part related to the degree of privacy the student might originally have been led to expect. In addition, if he was on prior notice of potential search it may be fairly asserted that he consented to search when he accepted or continued to use the locker. The fact that the school supplies the lock and combination or key (or requires that it be given by the student) may be sufficient to indicate to the student that the school can and probably does plan to inspect it in appropriate circumstances. It is, however, probably fairer all around, and legally more secure, to have in writing that the school reserves the right to inspect the contents of the locker and to remove anything contrary to school rules or detrimental to the school. Perhaps this could be printed on the card given to the student when the locker is issued, as well as being noted in the student handbook.

The Police

If evidence is lawfully obtained by a search and turned over to the police, it may thereafter be lawfully used by the police in a criminal proceeding.

The impact of the presence of the police prior to discovery of the evidence is un-

clear, particularly where the police are to proceed if the evidence found is what was sought. As noted earlier, the fact that the police think there is something in the locker is probably sufficient reasonable grounds for the school administrator. In the California case (*Donaldson*), the court made quite a point of the fact that the police were not involved and indicated that if there were a "joint operation" between the school and police a warrant might well have been required.[8] If some of the other cases are saying that as a general proposition the police, rather than getting a warrant, can simply tip off the school administrators, who will search and if they find anything will probably turn it over to the police, serious question can be raised as to their correctness. In view of the condemnation of the "silver platter" situation in *Mapp* (note 2) and other cases, and the solicitude of the Supreme Court for the protection of the rights of juveniles in *Gault* (note 1), it is hard to believe that a broad proposition is acceptable. On the other hand, all of these cases involve somewhat unusual situations and it may well be that they cannot be read for such a broad proposition. Prudence strongly suggests that if the police show an interest in searching a locker, at least an attempt should be made to see if the student's consent to a warrant can be obtained. There is no reason why the locker cannot be put under surveillance or sealed for the time necessary to get a warrant.

[8]*Stapleton* v. *Superior Court,* 70 C 2d 97, 73 Cal.Rptr. 575, 447 P.2d 967 cited in *Donaldson* discusses situations hard to distinguish from those in the other three cases. See also *U.S.* v. *Blok* (D.C. Cir. 1951) 186 F.2d 1019 holding that a search of an employee's desk in a government office at the request of the police was in violation of the Fourth Amendment even though it might have otherwise been lawful.

It has recently been reported in the press[9] that in at least one major city dogs specially trained to sniff out marijuana are used by the police. The dogs are occasionally taken to the high schools, where they are walked along the lockers. Assuming that the dogs were to act as if they had found something at a particular locker, it would appear that the prudent action would be to get the student's consent to open it or to keep the locker under surveillance and secure a warrant. A recent California case has indicated specifically that the police could not make a warrantless search under these circumstances but that probable cause for a warrant is indicated.[10] While the actions of the dog probably provide "reasonable grounds," it would appear that the loaning of the dogs by the police may well make it a "joint operation," thus subjecting any search to the more rigorous rules applicable to the police.

Indiscriminate Searches

The discussion under "Reasonable Grounds" above relates to the search of a particular locker. Nothing in any of the cases suggests that an indiscriminate search would be permissible even though it could be anticipated with a fair degree of confidence that on almost any campus an indiscriminate search would uncover a certain number of things which shouldn't be there; the discussion in Moore indicates that such a search would be "impermissible."[11]

Emergencies

An emergency, particularly of a grave nature, will justify actions, including searches, which would not otherwise be justified.[12]

Non-Punitive Searches

All of the above discussion relates to

searches with a punitive object. Discussions with school administrators indicate that in the schools informally surveyed it has been the practice occasionally during the school year to have a general cleaning of lockers to avoid a buildup of trash which may be a fire hazard or garbage which may become a health or "nose pollution" or vermin problem. Although there are no cases on this, perhaps understandably, it is the consensus of school district legal advisers with whom I have spoken that this is perfectly acceptable (assuming prior notice) and that evidence uncovered has been lawfully obtained, all subject to two caveats: It may not be used as a ruse for indiscriminate punitive searches, and it must be carried out in a manner consistent with its purpose (e.g., no searching for elephants in matchboxes or trash paper in jacket pockets).[13]

Conclusion

Locker searches are yet another of those areas where school administrators are caught between their general responsibilities for the welfare of the students as a whole and their obligation to give *reasonable* respect to reasonable private interests of individual students. From the reported cases it appears that the courts will give them reasonably broad discretion and further that they have generally exercised that discretion appropriately. (Note that the issue has only been raised in criminal or

[9]*Pasadena Star News,* November 15, 1970. *Parade* magazine; p. 6.
[10]*People* v. *Marshall,* 69 C.2d 51, 59, 69 Cal. Reptr. 585, 442 P.2d 665 (1968).
[11]284 F. Supp. at 730.
[12]*People* v. *Roberts,* 47 C. 2d 374, 977, 303 P.2d 721 (1956).
People v. *Marshall,* 69 C.2d 51, 57 fn. 2, 69 Cal. Rptr. 585. 442 P.2d 665 (1968).
[13]See, e.g., *People* v. *Roberts,* 47 C. 2d 374, 378-9, 303 P.2d 721 (1958).

juvenile proceedings, which are involuntary proceedings where the student's counsel should raise every possible question in defense; so far no one has felt sufficiently aggrieved to sue directly to redress a felt wrong.) So long as the administrator keeps both of these interests in mind in dealings with potential search situations he will probably act appropriately.

Expulsion Laws Confront Due Process in Federal Courts*

Stephen J. Voelz

It is becoming increasingly apparent that due process of law requires that public school students facing possible expulsion or long-term suspension be given notice of the charges against them and some opportunity for a hearing on those charges prior to their dismissal from school.

Recent judicial decisions have emphasized the critical importance of formal education to success in modern society. They have held, therefore, that students may not be deprived of school attendance, be it deemed a right or a privilege, for any significant length of time without first having the benefit of reasonable notice and some opportunity for a fair "hearing," however informal, on the possible reasons for such deprivation.

Because most state statutes make no explicit provision for notice and hearings prior to dismissals from the public schools, an emerging constitutional standard requiring such safeguards can be found in the decisions of the federal courts during the past decade. Beginning with the ground-breaking *Dixon*[1] decision in 1961, which established basic procedural requirements for notice and hearings on the nation's college campuses prior to lengthy dismissals, the case for increased procedural sophistication has been pressed in the secondary school. The supporting rationale is that legal proceedings considered vital on the college campus become all the more crucial in the high school, since high school completion is a necessary prerequisite for college entrance.

As the courts become more definitive in their application of due process to public school dismissal procedures, the resulting constitutional standards will act to supersede existing state laws on the subject—a phenomenon which occurred a few years ago in reference to formal prayers and Bible-reading in the nation's public schools. No state may now enact a valid statute requiring either practice in its schools; such actions have been declared unconstitutional by the federal courts.

The Problem: Increased Fairness Through Litigation

The problem for the school administrator thus becomes, not one of resisting constitutional standards, but of avoiding involvement in those local controversies which result in the eventual court action which has been instrumental in redefining procedural due process in the schools. The lack of applicable statutes in most states places the responsibility on the local board of education to formulate policies guaranteeing fair treatment of student offenders. In the absence of such policies, the building principal may be faced with deciding which procedures to afford the student accused of violating a school regulation.

The concern of the enlightened school

*Reprinted from *NASSP Bulletin*, February 1971. Used with permission.

[1] *Dixon* v. *Alabama State Board of Education.* 294 F.2d 150 (5th Cir. 1961).

administrator should, then, be twofold: "(1)" his sense of fairness, together with the highest aspirations of the school community, should prompt him to provide the accused student the fullest opportunity to present his side of any situation involving the serious infraction of school regulations —any situation exposing the student to serious punishment or loss of possible rights. In the absence of state laws or school board policies in this area, recent court decisions are beginning to define constitutional standards which guarantee a basic minimum of fairness to the accused student in the form of adequate notice and some opportunity for a hearing prior to dismissal. "(2)" Subordinate to the need for fairness, mere job efficiency should require the school administrator to take all precautions necessary to avoid the involvement of his district and its personnel in controversy and litigation which may prove embarrassing, expensive, and possibly self-defeating. It is self-defeating if the student's case is confirmed as correct in court; the student has not only written new law in that jurisdiction but has also won his way back into the school system which expelled him and whose efforts to defend questionable procedures he has met and overcome.

Such involvement can be avoided by the prior installation of clear-cut procedural policies, at either the district or local building level, which spell out the current constitutional stance assumed by the courts.

"State Laws and Due Process"

The litigation which has produced the court opinions applying the Due Process Clause of the Fourteenth Amendment to student dismissal procedures has emanated from both the vacuum and the vagueness of school board policies and state statutes

in this area. Board policies on a nationwide scale vary greatly in their extension of specific procedural rights to students accused of rule violations; a small sampling of district superintendents across the country by this writer disclosed that more districts purport to afford procedures exceeding merely notice and some opportunity for a hearing than do not.

However, a parallel study of pupil suspension and expulsion statutes in each of the 50 states[2] revealed that the laws in the majority of the states are vague and incomplete in specifying or describing even the constitutional minimums of notice and hearing for the student liable to dismissal from school. Moreover, state court cases, opinions of attorneys general, and state department of education guidelines in this area disagree as to the number and type of procedural safeguards necessary to afford the accused student the constitutional standard of "fundamental fairness."

The statutory and case law of only 19 states makes mention of notice in regard to the dismissal of students from the public schools. Of these, only six require notice to the pupil, the statutes of Connecticut and Kansas requiring it in written form. Sixteen states require notice to parents or guardians of students dismissed from school, and 12 of these stipulate that it be written. Nine states demand that such notice contain reasons for the dismissal.

The statutes of Kansas and Wyoming provide for written notice to parents of students dismissed within 24 hours of such actions, while Connecticut stipulates that written notice must be given the student and his parents at least five days prior to a hearing on the dismissal. The laws of

[2]Voelz. *The Legal Status of Pupil Suspension and Expulsion and Due Process,* Unpublished Doctoral Dissertation (The University of Iowa, 1970).

New York and Montana provide for "reasonable notice."

The statutory and case law of 14 states affords dismissed students a hearing below the state level of appeal, while the law of an additional six seems sufficiently vague to be construed as possibly requiring a hearing also. Except for the Kansas and Wyoming statutes, which list specific requirements, the laws of the other dozen states mentioning hearings remain general enough to sanction almost any type of school board and student dialogue; they do, however, afford an aggrieved student some opportunity for a "hearing" of sorts before either his local board or some type of decision-making authority. The law of 36 states neglects to require even this degree of communication at the local level of school government.

State Laws and Specific Procedures

Some states have exceeded the basic requirements of notice and hearing and have included specific elements of due process such as assistance of counsel, cross-examination of witnesses, and appeal of a decision to a higher authority in their laws concerning the treatment of students liable to expulsion or long-term suspension. The statutes of five states, for example, permit the presence and assistance of counsel to varying degrees at disciplinary hearings. No state denies the presence of counsel or the presence of the student or his parents at such a proceeding.

Local school boards in Kentucky and Wyoming may invoke compulsory process at board hearings, while state department regulations in Georgia permit the swearing of witnesses before local boards. There seems to be no form of compulsory process required or authorized in regard to pupil dismissal proceedings before local boards in the law of any other state. Wyoming seems to be the only state which has made its administrative procedure act applicable to student dismissal proceedings at the local level by statute.

No statute requires that hearings occur before anyone other than decision-making authority and, although the existence of a hearing usually *implies* permission to present evidence in one's own behalf, the laws of 11 states explicitly require that such evidence be heard and received.

Although hearings in other states undoubtedly include the practice, only the new Kansas statute declares that the accused student may hear or read a full report of testimony of witnesses against him. The statute does not mention the right to cross-examine opposing witnesses, however, the only statutes requiring this feature being those of New York and Wyoming. The Kansas statute is the only one mandating a hearing which is to result in a "fair and impartial decision," while the Supreme Judicial Court of Massachusetts has termed an impartial tribunal a "minimum requirement."[3] The Kansas and Wyoming statutes are also the only laws demanding that a record of the proceedings be maintained at the local board level; however, records of disciplinary hearings are very likely kept in those jurisdictions experiencing appeals to reviewing bodies.

In order to initiate a hearing or some form of appellate review of a dismissal decision made by either a teacher or administrator, or perhaps by the board itself, pupils in eight states are permitted by statute to petition their local school boards for a reconsideration of their cases.

Students in 22 states, pursuant to statutes governing either disciplinary appeals or all types of appeals from decisions of

[3]*Leonard* v. *School Committee of Attleboro,* 349 Mass. 704, 212 N.E. 2d 468, 473, 14 A.L.R.3d 1192 (1965).

local boards of education, may petition for review of adverse decisions of their local boards to administrative bodies such as their county superintendents or county boards of education, their state superintendents or state boards of education, or, as in South Dakota, directly into court by statute, receiving a *de novo* original consideration of their cases. Such statutory appeals are sometimes *de novo* and sometimes not, often requiring a copy of the record of the local board hearing certified by the district superintendent or the secretary of the school board.

Students in the remaining 20 states desiring to appeal adverse decisions of local boards of education seem to be thrown back on an appeal directly into court on theories of either mandamus for reinstatement in school, injunctive relief, or tort in an action for damages. In the absence of a statute permitting them to hear the case on the merits of all issues, however, the courts are allowed to decide only the reasonableness of the school board's decision, being authorized to overturn it only if the board exceeded its authority or acted arbitrarily or capriciously in its initial decision.

That many statutes concerning student rights prior to dismissal from the public schools stand in need of clarification should be apparent. Some statutes have undergone recent change, and other states have new statutes pending. Experience has demonstrated that where legislatures and/or state departments of education do not act, resultant controversies will force courts and offices of attorneys general to do so, often in a temporary or piecemeal manner still leaving many questions unanswered and future controversies unresolved.

Elements of a Fair Hearing

Although a few courts and many commentators have listed specific procedural elements which define adequate "notice" and describe what combination of features comprises a fair "hearing," such descriptions vary from situation to situation. Moreover, judges and writers seem to agree that the number of elements providing "due process" or procedural fairness in one situation will probably differ from the requirements of another.

In a recent Michigan case involving a student expelled from school without notice and a hearing for alleged possession of obscene literature on school premises, a federal judge ordered the school board to grant the student a hearing to be held on notice of not less than five days and stipulated further that a hearing was to be conducted in accordance with the guidelines laid down in the *Dixon* case. The court then reviewed those elements of due process included in the guidelines:

These guidelines include notice containing "a statement of the specific charges and grounds which, if proven, would justify expulsion under the regulations of the Board of Education"; a hearing affording "an opportunity to hear both sides in considerable detail" preserving the rudiments of an adversary proceeding; names of witnesses against the student; and the "opportunity to present to the Board . . . his own defense."[4]

The court severely reprimanded the school board for not "providing plaintiff with the opportunity to offer his explanation of the circumstances *prior* to the actual expulsion action by the Board." (Emphasis is the court's.)

Professor William G. Buss of the University of Iowa, in an article which thoroughly examines the structure of the school disciplinary hearing in light of the Due Process Clause, makes a strong case for the inclusion of four basic procedural requirements in all school hearings involving pos-

[4]*Vought v. Van Buren Public Schools.* 386 F. Supp. 1966, 1968 (1969).

sible expulsion or long-term suspension. He recommends: (1) the participation of legal counsel; (2) cross-examination of witnesses; (3) the hearing before an impartial decision-making body; and (4) the right to appeal decisions of this body.[5]

Suspension Hearings v. Expulsion Hearings

Since the term *suspension* usually describes a relatively brief interruption of school privileges and attendance, while the terms *expulsion, dismissal,* and *exclusion* imply absences of longer duration, the resulting loss to the student should determine, to a degree, the relative formality of the "hearing" preceding his departure, that is, the type and combination of elements of procedural due process required to accord him "fundamental fairness" in this instance. Most state laws permitting any form of "conference" in connection with a suspension do not deem it a hearing in the student-rights sense of the term, such a proceeding usually being reserved for the greater penalty of expulsion or extended suspension.

Because the time lengths of long-term suspensions in some school districts exceed those of expulsions in others, it would seem reasonable that the type of hearing afforded the accused student would be somewhat dependent on the length of time absent from school, rather than on the terminology used to describe such absences. The formality of the hearing, or the number and type of elements of procedural due process incorporated into it, ought to be commensurate with the gravity of the alleged offense and the amount and quality of education which would be

denied the student if found guilty. Although the "amount" of schooling might be determined by counting school days, the value of the education about to be withdrawn from the student should be considered also; expulsion during days preceding crucial examinations might work a greater hardship on a student than deprivation of those school days at the beginning of a semester.

Whereas "emergency" suspensions, used to isolate the offending student from the school environment immediately, may require little or no investigation of guilt, the typical three-day suspension would be more justifiable if a conference were held just prior to it during which the accused student would be encouraged to render a complete account of his side of the story to the school principal or other official having authority to suspend. The three-day suspension may also offer sufficient time to allow for adequate notice and preparation for a hearing to determine whether or not the suspension should be extended.

Recommendations

In the absence of specific statutes outlining the procedures to be employed prior to student dismissals from school, local boards of education and school administrators might be well advised to develop policies which set forth a step-by-step procedure to be followed pending the dismissal for disciplinary reasons of students under their control.

Students facing serious disciplinary action might be permitted access to those elements of procedural due process which transform a mere interrogation into a truly complete and fair proceeding. All the features of a criminal court trial need not be written into such a policy, but the inclusion of any or all of the following practices would increase the fairness of any hearing:

[5]Buss. *Procedural Due Process for School Discipline: Probing the Constitutional Outline,* U. Pa. L. Rev. (December, 1970).

1. Presence of accused, parents, counsel, and possibly accusers.
2. Opportunity to answer the refute charges and present evidence and witnesses.
3. Opportunity to view evidence and to confront and cross-examine accusers.
4. A hearing before an impartial tribunal with decision-making powers.
5. A record of the proceedings (transcript or tape recording).
6. Some opportunity for an appeal to a higher authority.
7. Possible consideration (in larger districts) of the employment of an "ombudsman" available to students.

Student Rights and Responsibilities*

This article is drawn from *Code of Student Rights and Responsibilities*, a new NEA publication. The Code, which was developed by the NEA Task Force on Student Involvement in accordance with NEA Resolution 69-12, deals with applications of rights and responsibilities of students at the secondary and post secondary levels. It is divided into three sections as follows:

I. The Institution's Relation to the Student
  A. The Right of Access to Education
  B. The Right to Affect Organized Learning Activities
  C. The Right to Confidentiality of Information
II. Student Affairs
  A. The Right to Freedom of Association
  B. The Right To Participate in institutional Government
  C. The Right to Freedom of Inquiry and Expression
III. Law, Discipline, and Grievance
  A. The Right To Establish Standards for Discipline and Grievance
  B. The Right to Just Enforcement of Standards

The last topic, The Right to Just Enforcement of Standards, is quoted almost in its entirety in this article, although extensive footnotes have been omitted. As in other parts of the Code, *must* in the affirmative and *must* or *may* in the negative express absolute necessity. *Should* expresses recommendation, and *may* in the affirmative expresses permissibility.

The Task Force realizes there is little likelihood that most institutions will meet all the proposed standards in the near future. Its members include: George Gumeson, community college professor and member of the NEA Executive Committee, chairman; Taylor Brelsford, high school student; Marilyn Godfrey, elementary teacher; Charles Gonzales, college student; William Barney Heath, high school student; James Melton, college student; Norman Najimy, secondary teacher; Janet Portolan, college student; and Charles Wad, dean.

*Reprinted from *Today's Education*, January, 1972. Used with permission.

A revolution in rights has begun throughout our society during the last de-cade. Those who claim rights are being required to recognize the rights of others. A man's rights to control other men is being challenged; a man's right to make his own decisions and act on them is being recognized and exercised. The shift from external to internal control is difficult, because for every new right a person gains over himself, somebody else has to yield up the authority to tell him what he must or must not do. Out of the struggle a more balanced concept of rights is emerging; the line where one man's rights end and another's begin is being drawn more nearly half-way between them instead of far to one side.

The newly won rights imply corresponding responsibilities. A person is responsible for the way he exercises his rights: He must accept the consequences of his actions imposed by the operation of natural or man-made law. He is also responsible for accepting the boundaries of his rights, because each exercise of an individual's rights must demonstrate respect for the rights of others. Secondary and postsecondary students are pointing out that they are actively engaged in the practice of living and that therefore they have the right to assume responsibilities other people bear.

The idea that the student's right is the right to choose for himself only those things adults would choose for him is being rejected as a basis of relationships between adults and young people. It has become evident that young people have contributions to make to the society and the schools—in viewpoints, in ways of dealing with problems, in ideas—that adults cannot make and may not willingly accept, but that are valuable nevertheless. Furthermore, as Margaret Mead has pointed out, the young people of today have had experiences that no adult has had at the same age, so they have a unique perspective. If their ideas and experiences are to

benefit rather than divide our society, students must exercise the right to make choices that will make a difference, not just "pretend" decisions.

A person must grow into responsibility for the actions he chooses through examination of other people's experiences, followed by his own experiences, evaluation of the consequences, and adjustment of assumptions.

The rights of students are of two kinds. As citizens, they have a right to fair treatment, in the school as in the society. The educational institution must not discriminate against them because of their age, their race, or any other reason, but must grant them the same legal rights accorded other citizens. The schools must act toward every student with equal respect and without prejudice, regardless of his identity, resources, or affiliations, in every matter from admissions to disciplinary procedures. The educational institution must grant students the rights guaranteed by the Bill of Rights and legal precedent. For example students of all ages have a right, in disciplinary cases, to be presumed innocent until found guilty and to benefit from the use of fair procedures for determining facts and imposing penalties. Some of the other rights all students derive from their status as citizens are the right to privacy; the right to form groups to pursue their interests; and the right to express themselves through such activities as planning and presenting programs or reproducing and distributing their writings and other communications.

Other rights of students derive from the status as clients of an institution. Like other clients, they have the right to influence the effects the institution has on them. As other institutions exist to serve their clients, schools at all levels exist so that people attending them can learn.

More than most institutions, schools influence the course of their clients present and future lives. Students therefore have the right to substantial influence over the educational program, including the goals they pursue, the topics they study, the learning materials and learning processes they use, and the criteria for evaluating accomplishment.

The Right to Just Enforcement of Standards

Students have the same rights of privacy as any other citizens and surrender none of those rights by becoming members of the educational community. No institution may use any medium of communication to monitor discussion without the permission of the participants or to photograph students inside or outside of regular learning activities without their permission. No institution may maintain agents to secure information about student activities or deputize staff members to report on or search students. Such practices prevent students from exercising without fear such rights as freedom of speech, of inquiry, and of association. They create distrust among students and between students and staff members. They cannot therefore be condoned in an educational institution or in a free society.

The rights of privacy extend to residence hall living. Nothing in the institutional relationship or residence hall contract may expressly or impliedly give the institution or residence hall officials authority to consent to a search of a student's room or property by police or other government officials. Premises occupied by students, and the desks, lockers, or personal possessions of students must not be searched unless the ordinary requirements for lawful search have been complied with. If necessary to prevent injury to persons, exception may be made on institutional property after showing of probable cause and particular description of the things to be seized. Probable cause exists where the institution has substantial proof that a serious offense has been or is being committed. In every case, whenever it is possible the student's consent must be obtained and he must be present.

Law enforcement officers may be summoned to the institution for the purpose of restoring or maintaining order only when their presence is demonstrably necessary to prevent injury to persons. They may be summoned only with the consent of a standing committee elected by and from the faculty and student body in equal numbers and including an administrator. The committee should not be too large to assemble rapidly. It may consider requests from students, faculty, or administrators, but may not grant any request from any party outside the school.

Any law enforcement officer liable to be dispatched to an educational institution must meet high standards of professionalism, maturity, and ability to conduct human relations.

Any administration of discipline by the teacher within the learning situation must be demonstrably necessary to maintain the continuity of learning. No disciplinary action may injure the human dignity of the student by humiliation or any other means. Discipline should be designed not only to maintain the learn-in process of the group, but to weaken the factors that motivate the behavior in question.

In cases in which discipline is not administered within the learning situation, the body designated to receive complaints may make a preliminary investigation to determine whether a charge can be disposed of informally by mutual consent of the complainant and the accused. The preliminary investigation may concern the fact of guilt or innocence of the accused person, the disposition of a case in which the facts are undisputed or both.

Pending final action on any charges against him, the status of a student must not be altered, nor his rights to continue learning activities suspended, except when his continued presence on campus poses clear and present danger to his physical or emotional safety; to the safety of student, faculty, or institutional property; or to the continuation of the learning process. Any such interim action must be subsequent to a preliminary hearing as to its necessity unless it is demonstrably impossible or unreasonably difficult to accord such a hearing. In this case, the student must within 24 hours be given a written statement explaining why a hearing was not accorded, and a hearing must be held as soon as practicably possible.

The following procedures will provide fair treatment and incorporate the elements of procedural due process in situations involving severe sanctions, that is, suspension for more than one day or expulsion.

1. A person who allegedly fails to meet the established standards of conduct must be notified in writing of the regulations he is accused of infringing and of his rights of due process. If he does not choose to dispute the facts presented, the regulation cited, or that the facts constitute a violation of the regulation, he must be offered the opportunity to amend his behavior or make reparation rather than enter into a disciplinary proceeding.

2. The accused person entering into a disciplinary proceeding must be informed, in writing, of charges against him, with sufficient particularity and in sufficient time to assure him opportunity to prepare an adequate defense.

Drugs: Legal Controls and Restrictions*
Federal

1914 *Harrison Act* — Regulates and controls the importation, production, sale, purchase and distribution of the opiate drugs.

1922 *Narcotic Drugs Import and Export Act* — Intended to completely eliminate the illegal use of narcotics in the United States.

1942 *Opium Poppy Control Act* — Prohibits the growing of opium poppies, except for legitimate purposes.

1951 *Boggs Act* — Provides for stern, mandatory penalties for convictions

*Reprinted by permission of Frank Dick, superintendent, Toledo Public Schools, 1971. Adapted from *Drug Abuse*, prepared in collaboration with the inter professional Toledo Area Program on Drug Abuse and the Family Life Education Center of the Toledo Public Schools.

on narcotics violations.

1956 *Narcotics Control Act* — Provides for harsh penalties for convictions on narcotics or marijuana violations.

1965 *Drug Abuse Control Amendments* — Provides for tight control and regulation over LSD, depressants, stimulants and other commonly abused drugs, with provisions to add new substances to the list as they are required.

State of Ohio (Ohio Revised Code #3719)

Depressants and Stimulants

Sales — 1st offense — up to 5 years in prison and up to $1,000 fine.

Using — 1st offense — up to one year in jail.

Glue

Sales — 1st offense — up to one year in prison and up to $1,000.00 fine.

Using — 1st offense — up to one year in prison and up to $500.00 fine.

Hard Narcotics (including Marijuana)

Sales — 1st offense — not less than ten years nor less than twenty years in prison.

Possession — 1st offense — not less than two years nor more than fifteen years in prison and up to $10,000.00 fine.

Hallucinogens (LSD, mescaline, etc.)

Possession — 1st offense — up to one year in prison and up to $10,000.00 fine.

Laws to Assist School Officials

Our lawmakers and our courts have recognized that schools cannot do an effective job unless they are operated in an orderly manner. Under state law a board of education may adopt rules regulating the behavior of pupils in school and also during the period when they are on their way to and from school. Also, Boards of Education, through its *Administrative Code,* can make each principal responsible for the order and discipline of pupils. Every teacher has the responsibility for enforcing the rules and regulations of the school. Laws have been made to assist in the maintenance of order and the enforcement of school rules. Some of these are:

DELINQUENT CHILD — *Section 2151.02 Ohio Revised Code* defines a delinquent child as follows, in part: ". . . . includes any child:

1 Who does not subject himself to the reasonable control of his parents, teachers, guardian or custodian, by reason of being wayward or habitually disobedient;

2 Who is an habitual truant from home or school;

3 Who so deports himself as to injure or endanger the morals or health of himself or others; . . . . . ."

CORPORAL PUNISHMENT — *Section 3319.41* of the *Ohio Revised Code* gives teachers and principals the right to use corporal punishment when it is necessary to preserve discipline and order.

"A person employed or engaged as a teacher, principal, or administrator in a school, whether public or private, may inflict or cause to be inflicted, reasonable corporal punishment upon a pupil attending such school whenever such punishment is reasonably necessary in order to pre-serve discipline while such pupil is subject to school authority. Such person may also, within the scope of employment, use and apply such amount of force as is reasonable and necessary to quell a disturbance threatening physical injury to others; to obtain possession of weapons or other dangerous objects upon the person or within the control of the pupil, for the purpose of self-defense, or for the protection of persons or property."

LIABILITY OF PARENTS — *Section 3109.09* of the *Ohio Revised Code,* a recent act of the state legislature, has made parents liable for acts of destruction committed by their children. This law reads:

"Any owner of property is entitled to maintain an action to recover actual damages in a civil action in an amount not to exceed eight hundred dollars and costs of suit in a court of competent jurisdiction from the parents, having the custody and control of a minor under the age of eighteen years of age, who willfully damages property belonging to such owner. A finding of willful destruction of property is not dependent upon a prior finding of delinquency of such minor."

COMPULSORY ATTENDANCE — *Section*

3321.01 Ohio Revised Code states that prompt and regular attendance is mandatory, and when necessary a written explanation must be submitted to justify absences and tardiness.

1 "A child between six and eighteen years of age is of compulsory school age.

2 Every parent or guardian, or other person having charge of any child of compulsory school age, who is not employed under an age and schooling certificate and, who has not been determined to be incapable of profiting substantially by further instruction, must send such child to a school, which conforms to the standards prescribed by the state Board of Education, for the full time the school is in session."

SUSPENSION AND EXPULSION — *Section 3313.66* of the *Ohio Revised Code* says that the principal may suspend and the superintendent may expel a pupil for acts of a serious nature. Some acts for which suspension and expulsion may be considered are:

1 Open or persistent defiance of authority and/or school rules and regulations

2 Threatening, striking, or assaulting of any school employees

3 Unprovoked attack upon another pupil

4 Threat of physical assault on another pupil to obtain money or other materials of value

5 Damaging of school property

6 Habitual profanity

7 Immorality

8 Theft

9 Failure to abide by corrective measures such as detention for previous acts of misconduct

10 Possession of a weapon

11 Use, sale or possession of narcotics, intoxicating liquors, glue, etc.

12 Smoking contrary to Public Schools regulations

CREATING A NEW SECTION 17-1-6 AND 17-1-7 OR THE TOLEDO MUNICIPAL CODE: AND DECLARING AN EMERGENCY.

WHEREAS, assaults, threats, menaces and obscene language have become prevalent in the schools and toward pupils on the way to and from schools, NOW, THEREFORE, BE IT ORDAINED BY THE COUNCIL OF THE CITY OF TOLEDO:

SECTION 1. That a new Section 17-1-6 of the Toledo Municipal Code be enacted to read as follows:

Section 17-1-6. *Assault Upon a Teacher, Disrupting A Class or School Activity.*

Whoever unlawfully assaults, strikes, threatens, menaces, or uses improper, indecent, or obscene language toward a teacher, instructor, professor, person in charge of a class of students, or employee of any school, college or university while in the performance of their duties, or who disrupts, disturbs, or interferes with the teaching of any class of students, or who disrupts, disturbs, or interferes with any activity conducted in a school, college or university building, or upon the campus or grounds thereof or in any public place, shall, upon conviction, be fined not more than One Thousand Dollars ($1,000.00), or imprisoned not more than one (1) year, or both.

SECTION 2. That a new Section 17-1-7 of the Toledo Municipal Code be enacted to read as follows:

Section 17-1-7. *Assault Upon a Student or Other Person Going To or From School or Upon School Grounds.*

Whoever improperly and unlawfully assaults, strikes, threatens, menaces, follows, pursues, lays hands upon, or uses profane, indecent, or obscene language toward a student or other person in a school, college or university building, or upon the campus or grounds thereof, or upon the way to or from any school, college or university, or on the way to or from any school, college or university sponsored activity, shall, upon conviction, be fined not more than One Thousand Dollars ($1,000.00) or imprisoned not more than one (1) year, or both.

Section 3. That this ordinance is hereby declared to be an emergency measure and shall take effect and be in force from and after its passage. The reason for the emergency lies in the fact that this ordinance is necessary for the immediate preservation of the public safety and welfare.

Chapter X

Discussionette

1. What are some possible circumstances which may develop into legal suits?

2. Where can teachers go for assistance in legal matters?

3. Discuss each of the ten suggestions given by the author for maintaining effective discipline.

4. Which do you accept or reject?

5. Do police belong in our schools?

6. Should teachers and administrators have to rely on uniformed and armed guards to resolve problems?

7. Should teachers and administrators handle their own problems?

Discussionette Words and Concepts

liability	delinquent	incorrigibility
in loco parentis	corporal punishment	negligence
self incrimination	due process	counsel
expulsion	litigation	reasonable and prudent

Try to use these words.

Try to explain these words.

Try to relate these words and their concepts to current or emerging educational patterns regulating legal approaches.